Happy Birthday you

!!! FUCKTARD !!!

Your friend always,

El Waynedawgola.

ASHES TO ASHES

Gideon Haigh has been a journalist for more than thirty years, contributed to more than a hundred newspapers and magazines, written thirty books and edited seven others. His book *On Warne* won the British Sports Book Awards Best Cricket Book of the Year Award, the Cricket Society and MCC Book of the Year Award, the Jack Pollard Trophy, and the Waverley Library Nib Award; it was also shortlisted for the Australian Book Industry Awards Biography of the Year, the Victorian Premier's Literary Awards, and the Adelaide Festival Awards for Literature. *The Office* won the NSW Premier's Literary Awards Douglas Stewart Prize for Non-fiction. Other recent titles include *Uncertain Corridors: Writings on Modern Cricket*, *End of the Road?* on Australia's automotive industry, and *The Deserted Newsroom*, about media in a digital age.

ALSO BY GIDEON HAIGH

GIDEON HAIGH

ASHES TO ASHES

How Australia Came Back and England Came Unstuck, 2013–14

**SIMON &
SCHUSTER**

London · New York · Sydney · Toronto · New Delhi

A CBS COMPANY

First published in Great Britain by Simon & Schuster UK Ltd, 2014
A CBS COMPANY

1 3 5 7 9 10 8 6 4 2

Simon & Schuster UK Ltd
1st Floor
222 Gray's Inn Road
London WC1X 8HB

www.simonandschuster.co.uk

Simon & Schuster Australia, Sydney
Simon & Schuster India, New Delhi

A CIP catalogue record for this book is available from the British Library

ISBN: 978-1-47113-173-8
ebook ISBN: 978-1-47113-174-5

The author and publishers have made all reasonable efforts
to contact copyright-holders for permission, and apologise
for any omissions or errors in the form of credits given.
Corrections may be made to future printings.

Text design and typeset by Samantha Jayaweera

Printed and bound by CPI Group (UK) Ltd, Croydon, CR0 4YY

Contents

INTRODUCTION

Between July 2013 and January 2014, Test cricket's original rivals, England and Australia, played out their ultimate showdown: ten Test matches, five on each side of the world. I attended each day, watching as Australia steadily undid a four-year English ascendancy in the Ashes, the hinge point being essentially Australia's taking of six English wickets for 9 in a frantic half-hour at the Gabba on 22 November. The decisive factor was Mitchell Johnson, an international cricketer of uniquely discrepant highs and lows, just commencing a summer-long high. In years to come, it will be a proud boast that I was there.

But, of course, I wasn't present merely for fun. I was trying to make sense of this sporting epic for readers. Cricket writing begins to date the instant it is written, particularly in this day and age when there is just so damn much cricket, when fluctuations of form are so marked and quality of play is so uneven. Nothing, I suspect, stands up more poorly than daily reportage, vulnerable as it is to instant irrelevance. I tender *Ashes to Ashes*, a collection of my contemporaneous writings, in that spirit: it contains the daily reports as I filed them at stumps for *The Times* and *The Australian*, and match reports I bashed out the day after each game. They're not history – only first drafts, faithfully recording what I was thinking at the time, including the false dawns and red herrings. Looking back, for example, I can see I was persuaded that Phil Hughes' innings at Trent Bridge would lead on to better: it didn't. I saw something I liked in Jonny Bairstow's innings at Lord's: wrong again. Between the two series, I thought Johnson's ODI form was significant: points for that. I thought the same about George Bailey's: oh well . . .

Somehow, though, this seems a fairer way to account for things. If everything unfolded in sport the way we predicted, where would be the pleasure in watching? I did at least always see the rivals as pretty evenly matched, despite England's good recent performances in India and Australia's sharp reversals there: I didn't see either team as sufficiently excellent to dominate from start to finish, and I sensed that the longer-term trends were of English plateauing and Australian improvement. But I imagined as I set down in England in July that the hosts would win 3–1 at home, and do just enough to share the series Down Under – even if that was with all things being equal and, of course, they never are.

The timespan covered by my last book, *Uncertain Corridors*, finished at the nadir of Australia's fortunes, their 0–4 defeat on the subcontinent; *Ashes to Ashes* begins with the perhaps inevitable reckoning, the sacking of coach Mickey Arthur barely a fortnight before the First Test. In years to come, people may forget the astonishing chaos that then enveloped the Australian team, which had not won a game in the Champions Trophy, whose captain seemed permanently in the hands of medicos, whose players were being suspended left and right for disciplinary infractions, to the perplexity of their high-performance overlords. Little did we know that the more significant tour matches were those played at Bristol, Belfast and Edinburgh by Australia A, led by Brad Haddin and coached by Darren Lehmann. Because they meant that when Arthur was laid off, Lehmann was on hand to take over, after not so much as an Egon Zehnder worldwide talent search. It looked like panic, and it was – Michael Clarke's account on pages 22–26 of *The Ashes Diary* evoke his own dismay and disorientation. But it can be a good thing to take over a team in a trough – it lowers expectation and buys time, and Lehmann used both to advantage, in ways that would probably not have been open to Arthur. In Ryan Harris, available after a year recovering from injury, Lehmann also had the services of the best bowler on either side. Harris's effect on the Lord's Test was immediate, even if it was drowned out at the time by the clatter of Australian wickets.

At Old Trafford, Riverside and the Oval were then seen the first signs of English insipidity under pressure, although they rallied each time, and might even have taken the series 4–0 but for fading light. The Fifth Test was actually Clarke's worst captaincy moment in six months: not since Hansie Cronje has a captain made such a self-mortifying declaration, and Clarke wasn't even getting a leather jacket out of it. He barely escaped the consequences. On his very next day of Ashes cricket, three months later in Brisbane, Clarke gloved a lifter into short leg's hands, and not in his decade as an international cricketer had he seemed so insecure.

Over the next two days, first his captaincy then his batting were stunningly revalidated, and England simply blasted off the park, confirming those weaknesses previously glimpsed. I suspect that what we saw thereafter was the difference between a team for which winning was the main thing and for which winning was the only thing – but this, of course, is something we can hardly ever know for sure.

One of the joys of Ashes cricket is the huge and ready supply of comparison at the disposal of the historically minded writer. Proceedings in the press box in England had been enlivened, for example, by the daily readings from '1948-o-meter' of my esteemed colleague Malcolm Knox: how close were we to reliving the Invincibles with the countries reversed. One evening in Durham, the *Times* obituary editor Richard Whitehead and I amused ourselves by projecting a Down Under rerun of the 1958–59 Ashes, which caused me on returning home to reread the tour books of that series by Fingleton, Moyes, Peebles, Bedser, et al.: the notes I took led to the piece in *Ashes to*

Ashes on pages 214-16. In the end, I gravitated towards a childhood memory. The first Ashes series I watched was 1974–75. This is the closest I can recall to that dynamic of a pace triumvirate, with a single finger spinner in reserve, laying multiple, overlapping sieges: for Lillee-Thomson-Walker-Mallett, read Harris-Johnson-Siddle-Lyon. By the final Test, Cook's team were even more broken than Mike Denness's had been – winless, hapless and wracked by disagreement. The Ashes of 2013–14, then, were a little breath of personal past, a reminder of how sport fuses with our own lives.

The six months these Ashes took out of my own life were made more pleasant by excellent workplace company, especially Mike Atherton, Simon Barnes and Richard Hobson from *The Times*, and Peter Lalor, Wayne Smith and Andrew Faulkner from *The Australian*. To Mike, whose family again hosted mine in the UK, I owe a particular debt of gratitude. My daughter now lives in the country holding the Ashes for the first time in her life. She doesn't know who Mitchell Johnson is. But I dare say I'll tell her about him one day.

Gideon Haigh
January 2014

Part I

England, July–August 2013

PREAMBLE

THE GREAT TRADITION

Mark Taylor remembers it well, a luncheon hosted in the most pucka English traditions for the 1989 Australian team ahead of their Ashes campaign. 'Gentlemen,' boomed the special guest in a rousing finale, 'let us hope that at the end of this forthcoming series that it's not Australia or England who are winners . . . but that cricket is the winner.'

Applause reverberated. 'Hear-hears' were intoned. Glasses were raised and cigars puffed approvingly. Just then, Taylor felt a tap on his shoulder, from none other than septuagenarian Denis Compton, the beau ideal of English sport. 'What a load of #$%^&* crap!' he said.

Quite – and you would disagree at your peril. When authorities minted a medal in 2005 to be presented to the outstanding player in each Ashes series, they named it for Compton and his old Australian mucka Keith Miller, as an expression of the pair's long friendship. But in doing so, they also tapped into a proper and prideful impatience with too many niceties, too much rhetoric, too much #$%^&* crap. Australia and England play cricket against each other to win. Far from inhibiting them, their tight, rich and ancient cultural links license the two countries to play one another with extra vehemence, vigour, and even vulgarity. What Sir Robert Menzies wrote fifty years ago has hardly been truer: 'We know each other so well that, thank Heaven, we don't have to be too tactful with each other.'

It's been ever thus. Everyone knows the story of Fred Spofforth bowling Australia to victory in the 1882 Oval Test, after which the fabled spoof death notice for English cricket was published, announcing that 'the ashes would be taken to Australia'; fewer are aware of Spofforth's role in the sequel six months later, as an indirect result of which these sporting cinders were given their famous physical form.

Spofforth's expertise was bowling from one end in boots with long steel spikes, then coming on at the other to bowl into the muddy footmarks he had left. He did this in the Sydney Test, taking 7 for 44, although to no ultimate avail: England won the game narrowly, and thus the series.

England's decorous amateur captain Ivo Bligh kept his own counsel in public, but raged in letters home about Spofforth having 'cut up the wicket more disgracefully than I have ever seen done before', reporting that the game's aftermath came 'rather near to fisticuffs' between the players. Coded allusions in the contemporary press suggest that a blow or two may even have landed. With no ICC referee round to invoke the Code of Conduct, things were smoothed over, and Bligh politely accepted a funerary 'Ashes' urn in token of his team's victory. But the spirit of the Ashes might be said to be 100 per cent proof – for strong heads only.

It was fifty years after those events that heads needed to be hardest, when another English amateur captain, Douglas Jardine, stretched bounds of propriety tautest of all by harrying Australia with an explosive pace attack, led by Harold Larwood. The Bodyline series left a lasting scar on Anglo-Australian relations, as well as becoming the exception to prove the rule that historically it has been Australians who have been prepared to pursue ends that little more intensely, push for victory that little bit harder; Jardine became a pariah, and played no more Ashes cricket.

Yet Bodyline was a perverse sort of tribute to its chief target, Donald Bradman, who played cricket as relentlessly as anyone – operating on bowlers, as his teammate Jack Fingleton put it, 'like a butcher at the abattoirs, wading deep in their agony and frustration'. And it was in the main Bradman's influence that turned Ashes cricket from a sporting rivalry to a quest for outright dominance, expressed best in the scale of Ashes cricket's two greatest annihilations.

When Bradman was injured in the last Test before World War II, England kept Australia in the field for eight sessions and won by an innings and 579 runs. When Bradman returned for the resumption of Test cricket after the war, Australia took advantage of a storm so torrential it washed the covers and stumps away, to inflict defeat on England by an innings and 332 runs. Two of Bradman's first three Ashes hundreds coincided with defeats, then none of the next sixteen: the Bradman Line was closer to impenetrable than the Brisbane Line could ever have been.

Bradman played cricket in only Australia and England, of course – the Ashes was the axis of his world. And at times over the last twenty years, the Ashes has been denigrated as a monocultural, monarchical anachronism, old-fashioned and footling because it neither confers the status of world champion, as in theory does a World Cup, nor incarnates more modern global relations, like the Frank Worrell or Border-Gavaskar Trophies.

One thing the Ashes has kept, however, is the form of the epic, if not always its substance, being decided still over the course of five full-scale Test matches. But nobody would shorten it, even in a culture naturally inclined to compression, whether it's fame to fifteen minutes, thoughts to 140 characters, or innings to 20 overs. Fans want to savour the Ashes gradually, coolly, at their leisure; finance men relish letting them, as the cash continues to roll in.

Ten Tests in six months is a mighty undertaking, and quite possibly too much of a good thing. But timeless Tests before World War II stretched some series out like *Lord of the Rings:* the five Tests of 1907–08 spanned twenty-eight sprawling days. Later attritional tactics produced such monuments of self-denial as Tom Veivers' 95.1-36-155-3 at Old Trafford in July 1964, and Bob Cowper's 307 in 727 minutes at the MCG twenty months later – an innings so long that his country began it using pounds and pennies and finished it using dollars and cents.

What has helped sustain fan interest in Australia and England is also a quite remarkable parity in results. Despite some protracted periods of Australian invincibility – nearly twenty years from 1933 and sixteen from 1989 – sixty-six Ashes series over thirteen decades have been split almost as evenly as imaginable: 31 to Australia, 30 to England, five drawn.

Where many spend lifetimes supporting sporting clubs to little avail, the Ashes has actually bestowed generous rations of happy memories on followers in both countries. Long gaps between some successes have been conducive to sweeter victories. Consider the similarity of scenes at the Oval in 1953 and 2005 following long-awaited Ashes triumphs: much had changed in England between times, but not, apparently, the intensity of thanksgiving at getting the better of Australia. A joy very nearly as great was the knowledge that anyone saying otherwise was talking #$%^&* crap.

The Fall of Mickey Arthur
DROPPING THE PILOT

It has become a bit of a conversational theme in cricket circles that Australia is now to be described in all the ways that one used apply to England: brittle, panicky, backward-glancing, inward-looking.

But not even England ever sacked its coach two weeks before an Ashes series. England used to go through the rigmarole of garment-rending committees, reviews and reports . . . then do what was always intended. Australia? Never. We were always committed gradualists who hastened slowly, coolly and rationally. Just before the Ashes series of 2010–11, for example, Cricket Australia reappointed coach Tim Neilsen for three years. Smooth, confident – everything was under control.

Then it wasn't. Neilsen ended up serving a year before being 'restructured' out. Now his successor, Mickey Arthur, has been 'restructured' with extreme prejudice. Arthur survived five years as coach in politically tempestuous South Africa. He has not even lasted two in wealthy, secure, self-involved Australia. That tells you something – and not just about Arthur.

What did Arthur do wrong? Up to the tour of India four months ago, not much, at least on the scoreboard. Australia under his coaching had at that stage won ten Tests and lost two, and won 18 and lost 13 ODIs. But for James Pattinson playing an Adelaide Test he probably shouldn't have, Australia would at least have shared a series with the world's number one team.

Then came the retirements in short order of Ricky Ponting and Mike Hussey. Their presences would not have changed the ultimate custodian of the Border-Gavaskar Trophy, but it is difficult to imagine that communications between team and management would have broken down as abjectly as they did in India.

The mantle of disciplinarian did not settle readily on Arthur, an affable and sympathetic man. Although his zeal was pardonable, the suspensions of Pattinson, Shane Watson, Usman Khawaja and Mitchell Johnson highlighted problems without really resolving them, and the 'line in the sand' lasted as long as the next tide. The initially desultory then suddenly decisive response to David Warner going walkabout suggested a house divided against itself.

It's been officially denied that Shane Watson complained about the discrepant punishments handed out in what has become known as Homeworkgate and what has surprisingly not become known as Warnergate – which *does* call to mind Claude Cockburn's injunction not to believe anything until it is officially denied. But, frankly, Watson would have been well within his rights to feel exactly the way that he . . . er . . . officially didn't.

Did this, though, merit Arthur's defenestration? After all, it's not Arthur's fault that there were half as many centuries scored in the

2012-13 Sheffield Shield as there were twenty years earlier. Nor is it Arthur's doing that Australian cricket's rewards system sets greater store by scoring 20 off 10 balls than 150 in six hours.

At the moment, Australian cricket is full of people walking round clutching their foreheads and complaining about 'the culture' with all the comprehension of someone looking at a photocopier that has suddenly stopped working. In actuality, the Australian cricket team has exactly the culture Cricket Australia deserves. How could the outcome have been otherwise?

Because CA is an organisation whose chief interest is management rather than cricket, they imagined that one report and a tweaking of the executive diagram would fix everything. But read the Argus Review again – I like to occasionally, just for laughs – and see if you can make out exactly how many of the deficiencies which it identified have been remedied.

There have certainly been management changes. For the last eighteen months, for instance, CA has had an 'executive general manager, people and culture', one of whose roles is to 'coach [the] National Men's team in Leadership and Team Values for high performance'. Wonder how her last performance review went? But what else has happened? If anything, the commercial is even more in the ascendant at CA, the new television rights deal being received as confirmation that everything is 'tracking well'.

At least Arthur's successor, Darren Lehmann, is on a hiding to nothing. Forty-eight hours ago, nobody expected much from the Australian team in these Ashes Tests; now they will expect even less. Lehmann can only benefit. He was a shrewd cricketer, is a more analytical coach than he appears, and has always been an infectious enthusiast. He will have a honeymoon period, and the opportunity to take advantage of it.

Having started his working life on the assembly line at Holden in Elizabeth, South Australia, he draws on different influences than his young charges. This can only do the players good. And having grown up in simpler times, he is also inclined to speak his mind – indeed, CA actually reprimanded him for the habit last season. This can only do the administrators good.

In the short-term, the individual most awkwardly placed is Michael Clarke, who stood shoulder to shoulder with his coach in India, but who has lain face to physio's table most of the time since, belatedly turning up after Warner's suspension to look suitably cross. With whom has he sided in this 'restructure'? How accountable is he for the dressing room's drift into anomie? He has at last relinquished the selection responsibilities he should never have had in the first place, but uneasy lies the head that wears the crown, not to mention the back supporting that head.

In the medium-term, a figure whose future bears closer examination is James Sutherland. In July he will have been chief executive of CA for twelve years, and also turn forty-eight, having come to authority as a young man. Sutherland came out swinging, as it were, in the aftermath of the Warner's late-night brain fade. He spoke well, and feelingly, about the responsibilities shared by team and management to set and enforce standards of behaviour. But when Shane Warne lost his temper pyrotechnically during the 2012–13 Big Bash League, Sutherland declined to condemn him, and even praised Melbourne's biggest Star as 'phenomenal' – of which there is no doubt, but there are times and places for such affirmations.

Sutherland has also signed off on a memorandum of understanding and a television deal that, for all the Argus Review's talk of pay for 'absolute performance', will make this particular generation of Australian cricketers far wealthier, more or less irrespective of how well they do. One wonders how that will impact 'the culture'. And once a buck starts rolling, who knows where it will stop?

Watson's Progress
COME IN NUMBER ONE

On the office wall of Tory cabinet minister Norman Tebbit used to hang a framed list of 'The 6 phases of an election': enthusiasm,

disillusionment, panic, search for the guilty, punishment of the inno-
cent, and praise and honour for the non-participants. In dealing with
the coaching of the national team, Cricket Australia might be thought
to following it perfectly.

Don't get me wrong. Many reasons exist to think well of Darren
Lehmann, a shrewd head and a buoyant spirit when this team has
need of both. But misgivings must remain about aspects of the change,
and there will be consequences which Lehmann will need to deal with.

In any sport, the sacking of a coach is a de facto validation for
the players, to a degree exonerating them of blame for poor performance by conveying the idea that they are superior to their previous
level of achievements and will blossom under new management. But
was this *actually* the message to be taken from Australia's calamitious
tour of India? Were the players *really* only the blameless victims of
poor coaching by Mickey Arthur? We are left to draw that inference
because while Arthur has been peremptorily sacked, every one of those
players has represented or will represent Australian teams in the 2013
English summer, and only Moisés Henriques, Glenn Maxwell and
Xavier Doherty have been trimmed from the Ashes squad. Their status as the best paid and most lavishly accoutred group of cricketers in
Australian history has been not just ratified but reinforced.

Giving his best 'Blue Steel', Shane Watson now stares down from
billboards advertising Foxtel's forthcoming coverage of the Ashes series.
Not bad for a player who 'acts in the best interests of the team sometimes', as he was not long ago publicly described, by CA's executive
general manager high performance Pat Howard. That comment, by the
way, was unkind, unwise and unfair. But it's far from the only remark of
the last five months made to look decidedly odd by recent events.

Cast your mind back to the February 2013 presentation to CA's
board by Howard, and selectors John Inverarity and Rod Marsh. CA's
chairman Wally Edwards emerged from this conclave to state 'une-
quivocal' support for every aspect of their approach. The team, he
said, had done 'extremely well'. Public mistrust of 'informed player

management' was simply a case of misunderstanding. 'I'm confident we're on the right track,' Edwards averred.

CA then bore with Howard, Arthur, captain Michael Clarke and manager Gavin Dovey in March as they tried enforcing accountability on their team in India by suspending Watson, James Pattinson, Usman Khawaja and Mitchell Johnson for . . . well, you know what, and I can hardly bear writing it again. Edwards issued a statement on behalf of his directors: 'The board is completely supportive of the actions taken by team management.' Even two months afterwards, CA's chief executive James Sutherland was pronouncing himself 'a really firm believer in the fact that those decisions will ultimately stand us in good stead as we build to sustained performance at the highest level'.

In this, he echoed the public emanations from the Australian camp, including from an impressively sincere Pattinson: 'The easy thing for me was to make excuses and say it's a harsh punishment. But the reality is it's not – it's part of playing cricket for Australia. You've got to do everything right.'

Want to guess who did the easy thing? 'I think it is very harsh,' said Watson. 'At this point in time I'm at a stage where I'm sort of weighing up my future and what I want to do with my cricket in general, to be honest.' Except that in his case it was hardly harsh at all, for he missed a Test he was scheduled to skip anyway, and resumed in the next match as locum captain for the injured Clarke. And guess who, after one hazy punch from David Warner, has now been confirmed in their original view? Not Pattinson but Watson. Turns out that you don't need to 'do everything right' when you play for Australia. You can not only be pardoned but rewarded.

Because the first player anointed by the new regime is the one who most effectively undermined the previous regime by nearly two years' erratic availability and spasmodic performance. And at last week's press conference, where he responded to being confirmed by Lehmann in his favoured role as opener, Watson positively glowed with vindication.

The move itself has something to recommend it. Watson seems to have convinced himself that he needed to bat first in order to succeed, to the degree that his ambition has grown off-putting, even potentially divisive. If you eliminate his grounds for grievance, you might at last be on the way to harnessing his abundant talents, and world cricket contains few better sights than Watson playing in the V to fast bowling.

But after fifty-one innings without a first-class hundred, has Watson earned the indulgence of selection well in advance of the rest of the team, and dibs on the spot he covets? Hasn't Lehmann articulated his philosophy as 'if you're performing, you're in the side'? Australia has another four opening batsmen on tour. Now only one of them can bat in his preferred position, all so Watson can find his happy place again. One half-hearted swish of the stick, it seems, and Watson has been whisked back to Carrotland.

The other casualty of regime change, of course, is 'informed player management', which not so long ago was the way, the truth and the light, and now lies as apparently discredited as phrenology and Maoism. All logic was for the rotation policy, all sentiment against it. It made complete sense in a modern sporting environment, rather less in a game to which the cohesion and interpersonal dynamics of a dressing room are so fundamental.

Ironically, it is being discarded at the moment it has borne fruit: on the eve of the Ashes, Australia is equipped with its best six fast bowlers, fighting fit and ready for action. In this sense, it has arguably made a more positive contribution to Australian cricket over the last six months than Shane Watson. Watson now has it in his power to change that. But should he fail, it's not beyond imagining the further applicability of Tebbit's list.

Australia's Fast Bowlers
2013, A PACE ODYSSEY

They made it. All six of them. Watching Australia's selectors handle their pace attack over the last year has been a bit like following a waiter with a tray full of glasses working his way across a crowded room of clumsy guests. One misstep, one unexpected lunge, and the whole speed strategy would be set at nought. But now they're in England for the Ashes, the objective all along, and the relief is palpable.

Of the six, only James Faulkner has remained injury free; each of Peter Siddle, Ryan Harris, James Pattinson, Jackson Bird, and Mitchell Starc has been *hors de combat* at some time. Ben Hilfenhaus, Pat Cummins, Moisés Henriques, Mitchell Johnson, Josh Hazlewood, Ben Cutting and John Hastings, all of whom have represented Australia in the past year, have in the end been left behind. The path here has been controversial, even divisive, involving a contentious 'rotation policy', too tinged with sports science for traditionalists. Nonetheless, Australia has its optimal combination – a richer, deeper and better talent lode than in either of the previous two Ashes series.

Siddle is the only returnee from the 2009 Ashes, when he bowled with the unflagging spirit since become familiar. The rest have only thirty-four Tests between them, partly because they are young, partly because there has been an anxiety about wearing them out before their time. What Australia would do for a James Anderson, who always wants to play, usually does, and seldom fails. The strength of the six in depth, by the same token, might be felt greater than England's. Anderson's blessed run with injuries surely cannot continue indefinitely.

Were Ryan Harris a racehorse, the course stewards would long ago have fetched the screens. Thirty-three years old, fit enough only for a dozen Tests since his debut in 2010, he has not been a player around whom long-term plans have been possible. Yet when he forms part of the attack, he invariably looks the most impressive member: slick, skiddy, persistent, crafty. Not by luck has he come by 47 Test wickets at 23.6. With the Ashes at the back of every mind, he has not been risked in a Test for more than a year. If he plays as many as three Tests this summer, Australia will feel lucky.

The tall, strapping, 23-year-old Victorian Pattinson has long looked head and shoulders above his generation of pace bowlers – including, it happens, his own older brother Darren, who played a solitary ill-starred Test for England five years ago. Pattinson the younger was blessed from the first with the attributes of a delectable outswinger and a mean bouncer. Injured between times, he raked India's high-class batting order during Australia's series win eighteen months ago, and pinned their successors down as well as anyone during Australia's recent defeat in India. English conditions challenged him in the 2012 NatWest Series; he will need to have learned from the experience.

Mitchell Starc had a glimpse of English conditions in 2012 with Yorkshire, and liked what he saw, collecting 36 wickets at 15.3 overall. He has since advanced as far as any member of the Australian attack, capable of spells of head-turning pace and eye-catching reverse swing, including a yorker honed by already ample T20 experience. Few Australian bowlers have looked more imminently lethal than Starc in closing out the Hobart Test in December 2012 with four for 13 from 34 deliveries at the end of a long and wearying day.

Although his name sounds better suited to a GOP presidential candidate, Jackson Munro Bird from Tasmania has looked a shoo-in for this Ashes tour since he showed a full length and away curve reminiscent of Terry Alderman on his Boxing Day Test debut. His 11 wickets against Sri Lanka cost 16.2 each before he was cautiously invalided home from India with back pain. Rather more surprisingly, he missed out around the same time on a Cricket Australia contract.

James Faulkner shares with Bird the good fortune of playing half his first-class games on a pitch in Hobart that doesn't so much give bowlers assistance as provide them with artificial respiration and heart massage. He looked a couple of years ago to have grown overly infatuated with T20, at the expense of his first-class consistency, but inclusion in Australia's one-day international team revealed a knack of taking timely wickets and a contagious pleasure in the contest.

Nor is this the longest tail Australia has brought on tour. Siddle has just achieved his maiden first-class century against Scotland; Faulkner has made eight first-class half centuries in 50 games; Starc, who started his career as a junior opening batsman before a growth spurt encouraged him to tackle bowling, fell a single short of a maiden Test century in Mohali in April; Harris hits the ball hard with a minimal backlift; the compact fluency of Pattinson's cover drives recalls no less than Mike Hussey. They have taken the long way here. Now is the time to make the most of it.

Preview
A MATCH OF UNEQUALS?

A sporting contest commencing between a team that has won or drawn its last nine matches and a team comprehensively defeated at its last four starts would not normally portend a classic contest. It says something for cricket's intricacies and vagaries that the Ashes of 2013 remains an intriguing prospect, pitting a known English quantity against a pick'n'mix Australian contingent of dubious reliability if considerable raw talent.

England we know. Seldom can a home team have had such a low-key prelude to a series, the limelight diffused by the roaring Lions down under and the flying Scotsman at SW19. Its last internal dramas are almost a year behind it, when Kevin Pietersen's differences with his teammates appeared momentarily irreconcilable.

Those fences give the appearance now of thorough mending, belying some of the moment's more baleful predictions, including that of Australia's then-coach, Mickey Arthur, who opined that the rift might take 'years to heal'.

It was Arthur, of course, who ended up being on the wrong side of a more recent rift, in his case twofold – with players who objected to his strictness, and administrators who cavilled at his latitude. There was also a dawning sense that Arthur, a good coach and good man, might not be the right match for *this* team. His success had come with a group of experienced, knowledgeable, mentally strong South Africans; once he lost the services of first Brad Haddin, then Ricky Ponting, then Mike Hussey, he had a complement of some pretty brittle individuals, used to getting their own way.

All the same, it's unlikely Arthur would have been displaced had Darren Lehmann not been in situ, coach of Australia A on a parallel tour of England, and in favour, going back more than two decades with Cricket Australia's chief executive James Sutherland: when Lehmann relocated to Victoria in the early '90s, he played for Carlton, which shared a social club with the football team where Sutherland was CFO.

And while his is not a 'job for the boys', Lehmann's appointment *has* been a kind of reversion to convention, most akin in its way to the appointment of Bob Simpson as Australian coach twenty-seven years ago: a recall of the old stager, in order to reconnect with fraying traditions. There's an irony here, in that little love was ever lost between stern Simpson and laissez-faire Lehmann, oil and water as player and coach. But it stands Lehmann in good stead as he arrives at his own system that he knows what it is like to chafe against one. The appointment has also had the incidental benefit of subduing the outsized chorus of Australia's 'not-in-my-day' ex-players, never entirely comfortable with a foreign coach, and noticeably quick to endorse their old buddy in his new job.

The contrast in perceptions between Australia's vagrant Champions Trophy team, coached by Arthur, and its refreshed Ashes squad, under Lehmann's management, could now hardly be more acute. But it is probably more a case of where we're looking. Remember Julio Iglesias, the Spanish crooner who insisted that only his right profile be photographed? Were Australia able to make a similar stipulation, their combination would exude strength in depth. In bouncy Pattinson, ballsy Siddle, skiddy Harris and swingy Starc and Bird, they pack a lot of heat – the most, in fact, since Australia's last Ashes series win, at home in 2006–07. This may not have counted so much in a three-Test series, but it will certainly be material over a five-Test course forming half of a ten-Test cycle.

Some Australian problems, moreover, remain for the present irreducible. The tour's two opening games have proved somewhere between nothing and not much. International batsmen should plunder runs from Division 2 county attacks. Phil Hughes did so in 2009 when he smashed 574 runs in five first-class innings for Middlesex, only to fall by the wayside after the Lord's Test. The step up that awaits Australia's top six is of the magnitude of a Fosbury flop.

One dilemma of their own making is proving particularly stubborn. Since 2009, Australia has sustained more run outs than any other international team – a third more, for example, than England. Consecutive run outs befell Michael Clarke and Ed Cowan at Worcester. Such self-inflicted wounds can leave powder burns on Test matches.

Technique may be an issue; so might the sheer variety of runners in the Australian team, some skittish, some lumbering, some aggressive, some unambitious. Whatever the case, Australia has so far declined to take the first step to addressing a problem, which is, of course, admitting you have one. Arthur never made headway on the issue; given his predisposition to accentuating the positive, Lehmann may not find it easy either.

If Lehmann and Clarke do not appear to be singing from the same songsheet quite yet, Australia is at least making affirmative noises. So are Australians more generally. The uptick in optimism is welcome. The English team in 2010–11 were struck by the sheer public negativity around their hosts. 'Until I witnessed it,' writes Anderson in his recent autobiography, 'I would have thought it was inconceivable that the Australian public and the country's media, could be so negative towards their own team.'

This lead-in to the series has felt rather more like it, the glad embrace of Lehmann by Aussie cricket fans crystallising dissatisfaction with the regime of wellness forms, rotation policies, chaotic scheduling and constipating managerialism. Personally, I'm not convinced that these have been problems so much as symptoms of malaise: England is a better team for being supremely well-organised, and still accommodates players of flair and spontaneity. If not so much has changed that these do not remain England's Ashes to lose, this has been a happy last fortnight. We need our quotient of pommie-bashing and Aussie-baiting, otherwise what's an Ashes for?

THE FIRST TEST: Trent Bridge

GHOSTS OF ASHES PAST

In 1961 the photographer Henry Cartier-Bresson asked England's debonair Ted Dexter to be the subject of a pictorial essay about the life of a professional cricketer. When Dexter said yes, the Frenchman came to Sussex for a few days, snapping images around the dressing room and nets evocative of cricket and of the sporting life generally. Two charming and civilised men enjoyed the collaboration.

Dexter's next stop, however, was the First Test of an Ashes series at Edgbaston, and Cartier-Bresson asked to tag along for the drive down the M1. To his increasing bemusement, the gracious English conversationalist of the preceding days was gradually replaced by a brooding, taciturn, almost sullen man, given to shorter and shorter answers, and faster and faster driving speeds. By the morning of the match, Dexter's words had dried up completely: he confessed later to feeling both confoundedly rude and entirely incapable of doing anything about it, because such was the effect of the prospect of playing against Australians.

Modern cricket captains do not enjoy the same latitude, always being expected to say something, even if it is nothing: Alastair Cook and Michael Clarke were today exemplary in this regard, conscientiously talking without speaking. Otherwise, there was a pleasing sense of mouth-muting, sphincter-tightening tension around Trent Bridge as it basked in warm sunshine and warmer local self-approbation. Andy Murray and the Lions were freely mentioned during the media preliminaries; nobody invoked the Royal reproduction, though perhaps that is to come.

Nottingham advertises its cricket antiquity with the unassuming annotation to its brand: 'Trent Bridge, Est 1836'. The playing field sits between the Trent Bridge Inn, whose first publican was the ground's founder, William Clarke, and the Larwood & Voce Pub Kitchen, named for the county's foremost cricket pairing. There was a hint of them about today too, or at least of their controversial captain Douglas Jardine, as the captains declined to specify their starting XIs. It was Jardine who famously rebuked Australian journalists for seeking similar information from him during the Bodyline series of 1932–33: 'I'm here to win the Ashes, not provide scoops for your ruddy newspapers.'

That left the commentariat to cast runes, which they did willingly. Interestingly, the unfancied Australians will be as happy to begin this series here as anywhere. Cook has not made a half-century in eleven Nottingham Tests, and none of his top six colleagues average 40 at the ground; the last Englishman to make a hundred here, Andrew Strauss, is now comfortably ensconced among the aforesaid commentariat. Cook's slow-bowling trump card Graeme Swann also pays 65 runs per wicket at Trent Bridge, despite this having been his county home since 2005.

By the same token, only Clarke among the Australians can call on Test experience here, and it is nothing special. Arguably the best prepared of the visitors for the venue is Ed Cowan, with four first-class matches for Nottinghamshire behind him, but containing nothing special either.

The leading indicator of the Test is likeliest to be the fortunes of James Anderson, for whom this is a hunting ground happy to the point of euphoria: thirty-three wickets in five Tests. If his away curve achieves its usual voluptuous shape, England will be red-hot favourites; if it for some reason does not, Australia will feel a liberating relief.

The pitch, which spent most of today shrouded beneath a space-age hothouse-cum-hovercraft to preserve its dwindling moisture, will most probably be revealed as parched and abrasive, conducive to reverse swing, affording an edge at the selection table to specialist practitioners Mitchell Starc and Tim Bresnan in the composition of final XIs – Bresnan took eight for 141 and scored an unbeaten 39 here against West Indies last year. It will also almost certainly turn, and later play up and down, which may provide an opportunity for Steve Smith to slot in on the basis of his leg-breaks, even if the selectors seem to rate these more highly than the player himself.

Trent Bridge is the ground on which Australia secured the Ashes in 1989, 1997 and 2001, where England secured their series-winning lead in 2005. It will not, this time, be a location of such destiny, but may shape a rubber a long time in the offing, and a cycle set to be a long time in the unfolding. For whatever the outcome, a result is foretold, both by the cloudless skies and by the eleven years that have elapsed since the last draw here. One of Cartier-Bresson's mots about photography was his encouragement to capture everything and leave no holes, because 'afterwards it will be too late'. It's an exhortation that one fancies will apply quite well to this Test match.

Summary
THE YOUNG AND THE RESTLESS

In Graeme Swann's autobiography, he relates a story of meeting Stephen Fry in the museum at Lord's just before the Ashes of 2009. As the pair gazed on the urn, Fry took Swann into his confidence. 'I don't want to put any pressure on you,' confided the ubiquitous comic, 'but everyone wants you to win these Ashes back and my entire happiness and well-being depends on it.' So, no pressure. Watching the Trent Bridge Test of 2013, it was as though both teams had been privy to such a personal confidence, as though the players were as

fingernail-gnawing as their own audience, including Stephen Fry. It
was the player with least experience and fewest inhibitions who soared
highest; otherwise, the game had to make up for in spirit what it lacked
in quality, and did not so much fluctuate as veer, almost somersaulting England at the last. Something similar applied to the umpiring,
whose inconsistences were exacerbated by a technology meant to remedy them, and which had the final word on a breathless finish.

Australia sprang the first surprise, when Glenn McGrath appeared
in their pre-match huddle to settle a baggy green on the head of the
nineteen-year-old left-arm intern Ashton Agar, the work-experience
kid promoted to executive. Days earlier he had been pencilled in for
Australia A's series of internationals against Zimbabwe and South
Africa A, set to commence in a week's time. Now he was to become
Australia's 434th Test cricketer and alphabetically their first, even if this
was hard lines for Nathan Lyon, who of all Australia's bowlers advanced
most in India, losing little by comparison with local spinners by the
Fourth Test at Delhi. England also zagged with the taller, faster Steve
Finn when they had seemed likelier to zig with the more reliable Tim
Bresnan, although they ignored the overcast conditions and stuck with
a plan to bat on a pitch looking a browner shade of green after going
more than a week without watering.

At first, the toss did not seem so bad a one for Clarke to have lost,
for it was England who looked disarmingly tense and anxious to assert
themselves, being bowled out in 59 overs, while scoring no less than 83
per cent of their runs in the form of boundaries. Their highest scorer,
Jonathan Trott, looked nothing like the stoic stay-put Australians had
seen thirty months earlier; he played sparklingly before dragging a wide
one on. Fortunately for England, the instinct to assert proved contagious,
and Australia were swiftly three for 22: Watson, Cowan and Clarke all
going hard at the ball, Australia's captain bowled in lurching forward.
Chris Rogers was unluckily judged lbw with the slightest of nods from
the DRS, and only Steve Smith's luck and pluck contained the damage
thereafter. The day's overall analysis was a febrile fourteen for 290.

The second day featured cricket in every mood. At first, ball dominated bat, Australia losing five for 9 in 31 deliveries to the irresistible Anderson and Swann. But in thinking half an hour ahead, Cook allowed Agar to live in the moment, and he shone. The boyish newbie, and Australia, had an atom of good fortune, when he was seemingly stumped toe-on-line by Prior off Swann at 6, only to be reprieved by third umpire Erasmus; Australia would surely have struggled to make good an 85-run first-innings deficit. But with this one bound, Agar was free, and sailed into England's disbelieving bowlers with the glee and ingenuousness of youth. Every shot was displayed, propelled with a swing more reminiscent of golf than cricket. Phil Hughes, made to seem positively aged at twenty-four, adapted to his new role at number six with aplomb, and as the arrears were erased with ease the atmosphere became reminiscent of a testimonial match, with the teenage Agar the improbable beneficiary – every stroke was cheered, every run applauded, and an unprecedented Test match hundred by a number eleven seemed just a matter of time. At last, Agar swung lustily at a pull shot and picked out a deepish mid-wicket to conclude the last wicket partnership at a bewildering 163 from 187 balls.

Stealing back into the black, England lost two wickets, both in odd circumstances. Because the Hot Spot cameras were busy revealing to Sky viewers that Joe Root had been adjudged caught down the leg side without any corroborating mark on the bat, they were unavailable to adjudicate on the lbw appeal Aleem Dar on the field had rejected but which Erasmus off the field upheld, the third umpire leaving himself open to the charge of applying two different burdens of proof on the same day – both times at England's expense. The England Cricket Board was still apoplectic a day later when umpiring pratfalls rather evened themselves out. The crowd, at least, calmed down, and after tea was as subdued as it had earlier been almost carnivalesque, sensing that one or two more wickets might secure Australia a significant advantage but that every patient run by Cook and Pietersen drew the hosts back into the game.

The visitors struck back on the third morning, when Cook and Pietersen fell in short order after extending their painstaking stand to 111 at 2.22 runs an over, but Ian Bell proceeded to bat as nobody else in this game, at a tempo and in a style to suit himself. A slow starter in the hitherto damp northern summer, he blossomed beneath a warm sun, playing so blithely behind square as to make slaves of the bowlers serving up pace for his delectation. And with the second new ball came renewed freedom, enjoyed by both Prior and Broad as well.

Australia was to rue the wasteful use of an lbw referral against Bairstow (8), the ball from Pattinson speared down the leg side. That left them without a shot in their DRS locker when Stuart Broad (37) nicked Agar thickly to Haddin, the edge eluding the keeper's gauntlet but rebounding from his pad to slip. Contrary to some later assertions, the confusion of bat, ball and pad confounded the naked eye – Dar's not out was thus a perfectly fair decision, even if the replay rather mocked it. But with no recourse to the DRS, the decision stood, rather as did the cool, insouciant, subtly defiant, unapologetically professional Broad. Australia continued to toil wholeheartedly as Bell and Broad made their four-hour, 138-run stand the second best of the match. But there was a dawning sense that the match was now on an orderly course for home victory.

Watson and Rogers dented but did not disrupt that sense in a positive opening partnership of 84 on the fourth day, Watson striking eight barn-burning boundaries before getting entangled in his pads and the DRS. England then enjoyed a bonus wicket on the stroke of tea when Cowan surrendered his wicket to the part-timer Root by driving out of the footmarks, whereupon the hosts struck regularly. By now the luck was all England's: the tiniest of Hot Spot glows incriminated Clarke when he referred his caught behind; the hemi-demi-smidgen of the ball deemed within the width of the stumps when England referred an lbw appeal against Hughes was barely detectable to an electron microscope but made sense to Erasmus.

The last day dawned with England needing four wickets and

Australia 137 runs, Anderson and Haddin chewing away respectively at each. Theirs was a vintage contest. Anderson first prised out the adhesive Agar with a classic bluff, adjusting a fielder ostentatiously at deep backward square leg then sliding the next ball across and inducing a waft, providing Cook with the first of four chances at slip, three of which he held. Starc and Siddle followed swiftly.

When Cook turned to Steve Finn, however, Haddin took toll with premeditated drives and slog sweeps to untenanted boundaries. James Pattinson, an impostor at number eleven, played freely also, lifting Swann effortlessly down the ground for six. The granting of a further half-hour worked to Australia's advantage as their last wicket partnership assumed menacing proportions, and the resemblance to Edgbaston 2005 was now more than passing – a final Australian surge with the match seemingly in England's keeping.

A clammy-handed fielding effort continued the parallels, recalling Simon Jones eight years earlier. With Australia needing 26 to win, Haddin swept Swann to deep backward square leg where Finn had been languishing since his costly cameo. Finn ran gamely in, pitched forward, obtained a fair chunk of the ball, almost long enough to be paid the mark in Australian Rules football, but it was the wrong moment to be exploring a new career, and a boundary resulted. With Anderson in the dressing room seeking relief from cramp after 30 mighty overs, Broad brazenly stalled on the way back to his mark, to prevent a further over before lunch with a cynical footwear break – Diego Maradona would probably have called it the 'boot of God'. It didn't quite work, as Swann had to bowl another over anyway, albeit Haddin played out a maiden.

Cricketainment reared its pin head at the interval, through which a crooner sang patriotic songs, drowning what would have been a wonderfully tense hubbub. It's surely time for marketers to take the Benaud oath: I hereby promise that when I cannot add anything, I will add nothing. England resumed with only 20 to defend but with Anderson restored, and his first over upped the intensity again – a superb, testing maiden. The batsmen then clambered three when Pattinson squeezed an inside edge past leg stump from Swann, between two scampered singles the second of which restored Haddin to strike for Anderson's next over. Each ball now was being feted with fervent if anxious cheers, and the fifth met roars as it passed Haddin's bat. The bowler and fielders looked unsure, and Aleem Dar shook his head, but Cook went to the DRS as though by popular demand, which turned to unconfined joy as the replay confirmed the tiniest of inside edges. Somewhere, Stephen Fry was in hysterics.

Day One
WEDNESDAY 10 JULY

Close of play: Australia 1st innings 75/4
(SPD Smith 38*, PJ Hughes 7*, 21 overs)

'Staying positive' is usually presented as one of cricket's cardinal virtues. But after the hectic opening of the XL Ashes of 2013–14, both teams might do well to invest in the power of negative thinking.

One wicket after another at Trent Bridge today fell to a mix of hard-handed pushes and attacking strokes that were woolly if not outright wild, like the nervous humming of a happy tune to tamp down a rising sense of panic. Another forty-nine days are allocated for these back-to-back Ashes series; on initial indications, there will be time left for muck-up games with mixed teams.

Was it 'the hype', of which athletes are inclined to speak warily, as if it were a dangerous contagion or an alluring mirage? It's hard to believe something like that isn't at work when Alastair Cook and Ed Cowan, batsmen who lull themselves to sleep by counting leaves outside off stump, are reaching out a wicket's width to nick off. But attack these days is not so much a method as a default approved mode. Nobody goes into a game promising to play 'defensive cricket', to bore the opposition to distraction or block them into submission; no-one likes a party pooper.

The result was entertainment – 198 runs in boundaries accounting for almost three-quarters of the day's runs off the bat – but of a heart-in-mouth, sometimes ashes-in-mouth kind. The drinks trays should almost have been accompanied by cold compresses for fevered brows, applied to the accompaniment of whale song.

The toss was not an entirely bad one for Australia to lose, affording its baggy greenhorns valuable hours to ease into the series, with a bit of a run around this picturesque arena. Cool, dim conditions requiring illumination from Trent Bridge's lights kept the visiting bowlers fresh. Australia is left, of course, with the probable task of batting last, but at this match's present rate of progress that could be tomorrow.

It was at first England on whom the situation, and Peter Siddle, preyed. Siddle sojourned in Phuket after the Indian tour, and at Taunton looked a little like he was still on holidays. But he bowled this afternoon like a man refreshed, powerfully rhythmic, at a rasping speed and to a harrying line, subduing and penetrating like a veritable All Black, even if his fitness guru is actually an Australian Rules conditioning coach, Justin Cordy.

Local hero Richard Hadlee once said that he looked on an over like a pistol with six shots in the chamber. Siddle has acquired that capacity for rationing his effort over a period, rather than flogging himself to bowl his fastest ball on all occasions. There is no doubting his endeavour, yet it is an endeavour without strain, within the bounds of his energy and elasticity. After a tentative opening from the Pavilion End, the Victorian hardly deviated from full length and a fourth stump line, where tense bats stretched for contact. In his post-lunch spells of 6-3-17-2 and 3-1-5-2 from the Radcliffe Road End, his pitch map resembled a pebble-dashed pavement.

The crucial wicket, as on most occasions, was Kevin Pietersen, who had fanned at the ball before like a man keen to feel bat on ball after a hiatus – which he is. To the near-identical follow-up, he felt ball on edge instead, leaving with a glance over his shoulder of regret. The scoreboard shared his disappointment, getting stuck for four deliveries,

and not officially notifying Pietersen's dismissal until the following
over – electronic wishful thinking.

Overall, Siddle's was a triumph of variety for a bowler not always
credited with it. Full length accounted for Root, angle from wide of
the crease for Trott, late swing for Bell, wild swing for Prior – on the
batsman's part anyway. You'd have called it a *tour de force*, except that
Siddle would probably have given you his engagingly craggy smile and
asked disarmingly: 'Tour de France?'

Elsewhere the Australian effort was patchier, even if this incon-
sistency would not have entirely displeased their captain and coach,
leaving room for improvement and scope to tighten as the series progresses. Pattinson presented a fine sight, with his high-stepping run
and high-stretching front arm, but Starc picked up late wickets without impressing and the clammy-handed debutant Ashton Agar never
looked like breaking through.

Shane Watson bowled his first overs for Australia this year, going
through his full repertoire, of deliveries, and of anguished expres-
sions – not always welcome with him, given the possibility that
overanxious physiotherapists might mistake them for pain. It was good
to see him bowling, nonetheless. Bowling takes pressure off his batting, which in turn takes pressure off his bowling, which in turn takes
pressure off himself – all part of the delicate equilibrium of this hugely
gifted but highly strung cricketer.

After Watson began Australia's innings with three muscle-bound
boundaries off Finn, however, the bowler struck twice and almost a
third time as batsmen went unnecessarily hard at deliveries leaving
them. Clarke survived, but only a few deliveries more as Anderson
found conditions so much to his liking that he might have asked to
take them away in a doggy bag.

It was a scenario that gloomier Australians had envisioned – agitated strokes under clouded skies amid crowing Englishmen. They
would not have been entirely soothed by the appearance at the crease
of Steve Smith, a match at fidgeting for that great son of Notts, Derek

Randall – the young Aussie pats himself obsessively all over before each delivery like a man who has forgotten which pocket his keys are in.

In fact, Smith confirmed the progress he made in India, where his 92 at Mohali, in his first Test for two years, was arguably the best Australian batting of the tour. He struck five boundaries and a reverberating six, but also picked off eight singles, striking the right note of busyness and prudence. Australia actually have a tail that could take some budging here, down to Agar at number eleven, and it will assuredly not be amputated as easily as England's. But they, and everyone else here, may need to take a deep breath, and perhaps just dare to be dull.

Day Two
THURSDAY 11 JULY

Close of play: England 2nd innings 80/2
(AN Cook 37*, KP Pietersen 35*, 43 overs)

For all the heights that Australian teams ascended during their long period of global dominance, they made a routine of excellence that grew nearly humdrum. Since their gradual descent to cricket's midtable began, Australia has become a perversely more engaging side, human in its strivings, its highs somehow greater for the surrounding proportions of achievement.

Take nineteen-year-old Ashton Agar, whose 98 today turned this somersaulting First Test on its head . . . again. Here was a thrilling initiation in international cricket, and a stunning riposte to the surrounding Murraymania and British Lionising, pitching England's cricketers' into a triple-dip recession if not the country itself.

Tall, slim, fresh-faced, looking a little like an eastern prince at a western university while unmistakably Australian in his deportment and diction, Agar is the project player made good, who was playing second-grade cricket in Melbourne just eighteen months ago, and whose first contact with his current teammates was as a net bowler to them in Perth in December. A week ago, he was unsure if he would be remaining with the squad or heading off to join an Australia A tour of Zimbabwe.

The burden of expectation has yoked players throughout this match, so perhaps it is not completely surprising that the outstanding performance has come from the player of whom least was anticipated, and in his secondary skill at that. Agar was known to be able to bat: a first-class average of 33 from sixteen innings is not merely a trick of the statistical light. But his slot as last man was not a cunning ruse: it was a form of prediction that the teenager interpreted as permission for fun.

Nor was this a step-back-and-swish effort by a tail-end Charlie. Two sixes were launched down the ground with a full 360-degree swing of the bat. Three pull shots sailed through mid-wicket for four. One flick on the up through mid-on was signed off with back foot in the air. One cut, to level the scores, was so late it almost qualified as an epilogue. All were good strokes, executed with flair while fundamentally orthodox, played with a still head and full face of the bat.

Some of the best shots were the simply defensive ones – compact, unadorned, technically correct. Agar did something most batsmen in this match had hitherto failed to: he discriminated, applied no force where it was not required, took no chance where it savoured of danger. The only time he failed to do so, essaying a pull shot in the air when he knew the man at mid-wicket was back, cost him his wicket. Otherwise, he gave deliveries the respect they deserved.

Trouble was, from England's perspective, there were insufficient deserving of respect: while fielders jogged between overs in a vain attempt at conveying purpose, the home team neither attacked nor defended with complete conviction. Certainly neither Finn nor Broad appeared capable of landing consecutive deliveries in the same place. With three slips in place, they bowled straight and on the pads; with fielders at deep cover, they bowled short; with ring fields, they overpitched; in striving for the one ball that might take a wicket, they provided a host of scoring opportunities.

Swann's vaunted toxicity to left-handers was neutralised. And having bowled 18 of the innings's first 37 overs, Anderson struggled to penetrate in third and fourth spells of three overs each. In fact, if you wanted an insight into how acute is England's dependence on their spearhead, this was it. He should be accompanied to Lord's by his own personal surgeon and contingent of bodyguards.

All the same, without wishing to disturb the general air of bonhomie that rightfully surrounds Agar's feats, he embodies other factors at work in Australian cricket. He joins a lineage of instant Australian success stories in recent times – Pat Cummins, Jason Krejza, Marcus North, Nathan Lyon, Shaun Marsh, James Pattinson, Matthew Wade, David Warner, and Usman Khawaja – all of whom have either struggled or continue to struggle to repeat early proclamations of promise.

Immediate high-impact performances are arguably better for the media than for cricket teams, and they were not characteristic of Australian cricket at its peak. There were storied beginnings from time to time during the green and golden age, from Michael Slater to Michael Clarke himself. But it was an era of steady development and patient advances, during which steps back were as formative as leaps forward. Allan Border, David Boon, Mark Taylor, Steve Waugh, Shane Warne, Glenn McGrath, Ricky Ponting, Matthew Hayden, Justin Langer, Damien Martyn and, yes, Darren Lehmann all took time to find their feet in international cricket, and built top-line careers on deep foundations.

Which is why the more important innings for Australian cricket today may turn out not to be Agar's, a feat he can hardly be expected to repeat in a hurry, but Phil Hughes', whose enterprising but measured 81 not out was possibly his best and certainly most characterful Test innings since he was left out of the Australian side for Shane Watson almost four years ago.

It seemed to be in England's cricket hive mind that Hughes remained an exclusively off-side proposition. In fact, if he is not particularly graceful or fluent to leg, his strokeplay has grown a great deal more versatile. While Hughes struck eight of his nine boundaries to the off, he accumulated 35 of his 81 runs to the on, including 21 singles. He was subdued by Swann – 7 runs from 52 balls – but unrecognisable from the jerky, overwhelmed figure enveloped by India's spinners three months ago.

Without Hughes, Agar might have come to the wicket with another tailender, and perished quickly having a dart. With Hughes in calm control, there was a chance for Agar to prolong the innings, which flowered into a record partnership and the glimpse of a unique feat. There was a salutary lesson in this – that Australian cricket's revival cannot be accomplished merely one fairytale at a time.

Day Three
FRIDAY 12 JULY

Close of play: England 2nd innings 326/6
(IR Bell 95*, SCJ Broad 47*, 133 overs)

Both England and Australia have played in India in the last eight months. England won, surging back from behind; Australia, charitably, finished fourth, with the umpires and scorers having better series. So whom would you back in conditions at Trent Bridge as reliably Indian as Shahrukh Khan and hostility to the DRS?

The counterintuitive answer for much of these three days at Trent Bridge has turned out to be Australia, who have played disciplined and patient cricket in tune with the demands of a desiccated surface beneath a beating sun. At tea today, the visitors still had the better of this ceaselessly fascinating Test. After that, Ian Bell, who might be deemed an old India hand on the basis of his fine hundred at Nagpur in December 2012, drew the game back into alignment. Stuart Broad then did something recognisable wherever the game is played, tilting the match, if not the moral balance, firmly in England's favour.

Something about Australians and 'walking' invariably generates more heat than light. Let it be admitted: not even saintly Victor Trumper walked. Everybody knows it too. M.S. Dhoni is alleged to have said that he walks against everyone except Australia. So it might be best to content ourselves with the observation that this Test match has rather vindicated Dhoni's mistrust of the existing dispensations regarding umpiring technology: first a probably correct decision by Aleem Dar clumsily overturned by the third umpire; now a gaffe by Dar which the third umpire was powerless to remedy because Australia had depleted its referrals.

At least, as often seems the case with DRS misadventures, a rough-and-ready equation has been reached: Trott on 0 approximately equals Broad on 37. What do you know, eh? Umpiring 'all evens out', even when run through video. Either that or there's another secret technology, an ICC Even-Up-o-Matic, silently at work.

Earlier, Australia had toiled with enormous spirit. This was despite England starting the day with its most successful batsmen in India in harness, Cook and Pietersen, both guilty of playing at balls they ought to have left in the first innings, and resolved not to be twice convicted. Yet Australia matched them in patience, so that neither appeared completely at ease. Through his slowest Test fifty, Cook looked tense enough to gnaw through his bat; through his fourth-slowest, Pietersen played his defensive pushes with a pedantic, ostentatious and slightly grudging straightness.

In contrast to England on the second day, Australia offered an object lesson in the right lengths to bowl on this pitch; when Broad and Finn hit these, it was chance; when the four Australian pace bowlers did so, it was habit. It became impossible to remember an out-and-out Australian bouncer since Pattinson began the match with his 'vertical Harmison' over Cook's head – only on Wednesday, but now seeming like a fortnight ago.

Stump to stump was the corridor of uncertainty; just back of a length, where the occasional delivery was sticking in the pitch, was the range of riskiness. Yorkers, the quickest way from one end of this slowest of surfaces to the other, were an excellent and much-used variation. Even ten years ago, a spinner would have expected to bowl 40 overs on a third-day pitch such as this; now the skill in demand was reverse swing, which came and went in its mysterious fashion like a cat by night.

In the 26 overs he bowled, Ashton Agar played his part nonetheless, bowling slowly, temptingly, enjoying the necessity of batting restraint, and supported by fields that did not expect him to turn the ball round corners; only when the left-handed Cook and Broad were on strike was a bat-pad catcher employed, and an off-side sweeper was on patrol throughout his overs. His captain provided Agar with a maiden Test wicket by leaping to catch Cook, then showed further trust by granting him the last over before lunch, which probably caused the new teen idol to trend on Twitter again. Shane Watson bowled some invaluable 'dry overs', adding to the inertia he induced by a heavy-booted trudge to his mark at half the pace of anyone else in this game, his back as it receded resembling a fridge on casters being rolled slowly down a narrow hallway.

Australia had the game under such close control with England five for 176 and leading by only 111 that it was a surprise when Clarke replaced the ragged ball that batsmen were struggling to time in favour of a new Duke, which then provided so little sideways movement that Agar was back in the attack after half a dozen overs. New to the crease and short of recent runs, Matt Prior welcomed the brief interlude of bounce and hardness, and provided positive reinforcement for Ian Bell, who played perhaps his best Test innings – and there have been some excellent ones.

Bell is almost obsessively neat and compact in everything he does, with his fetish for bat twirls, cuff adjustments and guard notchings. He would roll his wrists turning a door knob. Only every now and again does he reveal his gifts, such as by the feathery late cuts he played to the third man boundary today, performed so unconsciously that they looked like rehearsals for shots rather than shots themselves. By close of play, Australia had taken one wicket for 150 runs with the second new ball, which England will have noted for when it comes their time to bowl.

Otherwise, Clarke's captaincy was hard to fault. Nor should he be too crestfallen. Should Australia end up losing their fifth consecutive Test in India, as it were, Clarke can console himself that they fought a great deal harder here than in the earlier four.

Day Four
SATURDAY 13 JULY

Close of play: Australia 2nd innings 174/6
(BJ Haddin 11*, AC Agar 1*, 71 overs)

At 2.40 pm today Australia were briefly listed favourites in this First Test. Not decisively or convincingly, more statistically, with the equation of 10 wickets chasing 227 runs verging on the plausible.

Did the Australians believe it? Did the English? Did it matter? Probably not much but maybe a bit. Odds posted by bookmakers are not much discussed in cricket dressing rooms – not those outside Asia anyway. All the same, this has been a Test in which expectations have had a way of impinging on the play: batsmen anxious to assert themselves, bowlers ever so slightly ahead of themselves.

Ironically, Australia had made a rather ragged and disjointed start to the day, Mitchell Starc opening with a colossal wide, Michael Clarke and Shane Watson allowing a chance to pass unmolested through the cordon. But England's tail had sold itself cheaply again, and Australia's first wicket partnership had swollen inversely, with Watson's bat resounding like a descending gavel.

Watson's discussion at drinks with partner Chris Rogers would have been along the lines of to 'keep going as we are' – the lulling noises of a fluent partnership at the point in its affairs which taken at the flood might lead on to fortune. Yet Watson, in perennial pursuit of that Test match feat that defines his career, would hardly have been human had he not wondered momentarily whether this was to be 'my day'.

In England's huddle, meanwhile, the atmosphere would have been rather different. Their performance had so far lacked the vitality commendably maintained by Australia on Friday, their subdued performance in the field mirroring the quiet crowd. Graeme Swann, the team's in-house minister for fun, looked unaccustomedly grim, failing to arrest two edged boundaries at slip, bowling slowly and with little drift, a fielder on the mid-on rope. As one sweep shot from Watson fairly detonated, Swann turned his back, either in order to forget it at once or to avoid eye contact.

Dry pitch? Home ground? For Swann they seemed an auspicious combination. But, again, there is something about it being regarded as 'my day' that can cloud the faculties. On the last day at Edgbaston four years ago, Swann was regarded as a banker to roll over Australia; instead he went wicketless, bowling as badly as any stage in his five years at the top. For all his perennial good cheer, Swann, one suspects, is an athlete who likes a little adversity, a wheel to put his shoulder against, odds against which to succeed.

As Broad ran in to deliver the first ball after resumption, Watson gave that finicky little touch he gives to his back pad out of concern it might impede its downswing. He received a good length ball decking back slightly, of a kind he had been dealing with successfully by playing straight, aware that England's intention was to beat a tattoo on his front pad. This time, however, he tried to work the ball, inclining his head slightly to the off and playing across the line. The thud of the ball was drowned by exultant English voices.

Adjudged lbw, Watson looked consternated, as though there had to be some misunderstanding, and hastily sought a referral. Confirmation of the decision left him downcast, doubtful. At what was he shaking his head as he vanished up the pavilion stairs? The pall of disappointment? Or the glimpse of hope?

Nobody conveyed the relief of Watson's fall more palpably than

Swann, whose face lit up when he paused at the top of his run and made eye contact with his county teammate Ed Cowan soon after. It was Joe Root who would dismiss Cowan driving out of the rough on the stroke of tea, but Swann whirled into his work for the rest of the afternoon with the whiff of wickets in his nostrils. His deliveries to trap Smith and Hughes were spun with booming confidence; he also bowled an execrable full toss to Clarke, to which Clarke attempted an execrable sweep, the result being a dot ball altogether without merit. The wheel had turned. So had the odds.

There remained the excellent Rogers. Neat, grooved, arms in tight to his body, Rogers is an efficient strokemaker, with a low centre of gravity and a high temperature of ignition, toting around the expertise accumulated at four major and two minor counties. His backlift is a flex of the wrists, his follow-through barely more than a poke. Where Watson craves the feel of bat on ball, like a man chasing kisses, Rogers leaves when he can, and appears to draw strength from it, adding each no-stroke to a tiny tally of micro-advantages. He is cool too. When Dharmasena mistakenly gave him caught at the wicket, he called for a referral as perfunctorily as a diner calling for the cheque.

Might the odds fluctuate yet further? Does this match have a further trick to play? This is a pitch on which it has been harder to get in than stay in. There have been four first-ball dismissals, thirteen partnerships worth five runs or fewer. That suggests wickets falling in a clatter, while leaving open the faint possibility of a pair getting set. It would be a turn-up for the books. But on this match, those books have exerted a strangely tidal and not altogether reliable effect.

Day Five
SUNDAY 14 JULY

Close of play: Australia 2nd innings 296
(110.5 overs) – end of match

You wouldn't want to play poker with Stuart Broad, but you might with Brad Haddin. On Friday afternoon, Broad, indifferent and inscrutable, stood his ground after a nick to Haddin that almost left a gash in the ball en route to slip. At 2.25 pm today, however, Haddin imparted his own edge, far subtler, to a delivery from James Anderson, and immediately gave a sense that the jig was up.

As the appeal reverberated, he gave the umpire a quick, anxious glance. As it was rejected, he looked down and away. When he walked up to his partner in their stirring last-wicket partnership, James Pattinson, Haddin did not flash him one of the laconic smiles he had allowed himself from time to time during the day. And Broad's *sangfroid* notwithstanding, the body language of a batsman aware he's in trouble still possesses powerful qualities as a 'tell' – so powerful that the ICC might conceivably add a kind of 'Guilt-o-meter' to its technological bag of tricks. It would be at least as reliable as Ball Tracker.

Cricketers seldom enjoy exactly what they deserve, but Haddin certainly deserves better than to be remembered as the man who lost this Test match for Australia after going so close to being the man who won it. While there are of legend no second acts in American lives, he has proven that there are second opportunities for Australian cricketers.

Fourteen months ago Haddin seemed to be slipping into a twilight when he returned from a tour of West Indies for personal reasons – a grave family illness – leaving the gloves in custody of a lively apprentice, Matthew Wade. Haddin to Wade looked a natural line of succession, an opportunity for the old-stager to accept the thanks of a grateful nation for services rendered, and give way in time-honoured fashion to the younger man. He had done his duty. He had business at home. Time for a change.

But in any other terms than sport, Haddin was a young man, just thirty-four, and begged to differ. He returned to domestic cricket, led well, batted punchily, kept tidily. Eight months ago, I saw him make a quicksilver leg-side stumping in a Sheffield Shield match while standing up to the sprightly seam bowling of Trent Copeland. The skills were still there, if and when needed.

It turned out that even more than skills, what Australia needed was know-how. Haddin has been the upside of the retirements of Ricky Ponting and Mike Hussey, for he has taken the gloves back from Wade in order to provide the kind of hard-bitten, green-and-gold implacability this team is perceived to lack. Interestingly, on the eve of this Test, Shane Watson divulged in a ghosted column that Haddin suffers acutely from nerves, to the extent that he finds it difficult to eat during games. They must be the kind of nerves alleviated by the crossing of a boundary rope, because he seldom exudes anything on the field other than self-control and enterprise. It became obvious as the last day unfolded why Steve Waugh advanced the counterintuitive notion last summer that Haddin might play for Australia as a batsman. He looked here as good as ever: an impermeable bastion in defence and sweet timing in attack, with a timely reappearance of his signature drive down the ground in the air.

As Sunday dawned, we were almost back to where we began on Wednesday, the weather overcast, the sky dim, the floodlights on, the ground quiet and still after the morning rendition of 'Jerusalem', which is becoming to Test cricket what 'Bohemian Rhapsody' is to karaoke – something fun once rendered utterly stale by repetition. Alastair Cook opened with Anderson and Swann, his best bowlers – an entirely natural choice which also reveals an English weakness, because everyone knows they are his best bowlers, and pressure is subtly relieved when anyone else is turned to.

So it proved. Anderson bowled superbly, confirming his transformation from a classically English swing bowler to the best paceman in the world in dry conditions. He is as classically English now as chicken tikka masala. But when Anderson gave way at last after his leonine 13-over spell, Haddin pounced on the pedestrian and diffident Finn. When Haddin faced the next over from Swann, it was with five fielders on the fence. Suddenly it was Cook who looked beleaguered, almost benighted.

Haddin had willing helpmates. The task for the student prince Ashton Agar was far tougher than the one set him on Thursday. Half the overs in the first hour were maidens, with little room for his glorious 360-degree swing of the bat. In Swann's second over, Agar danced down the wicket, miscued a flail to Broad at mid-on, dithered over a single for a misfield, and all of a sudden in mid-pitch looked gangling, boyish and incongruous before scurrying back to his ground. In Broad's second over, Agar wound up gloriously, bat around his ears, and flogged the ball forward of point for four, bringing salaams from the wattle outcrop of Fanatics in the new stand but only a subdued ripple of applause from elsewhere – spectator allegiance now had a more obviously partisan aspect than three days earlier. The roar that erupted when Agar nicked Anderson to slip was itself a kind of tribute, the eager prodigy having been transformed over the course of this Test into a worthy opponent.

But even after his dismissal, the residual spirit of Agar continued nourishing the idea that everything remained possible. After all, if a teenager can almost score a hundred on debut at number eleven, then almost no possibility is precluded: recall for Mark Ramprakash, a spin-bowling coaching appointment for John Howard, or a game for the ashes of Margaret Thatcher seem almost probable by comparison.

In James Pattinson, Haddin found a final splendid consort, an arch competitor and a competent technician, who could easily pass for a specialist batsman at a slightly lower level of the game, because he *was* one until a teenage growth spurt encouraged him to take up bowling.

And, astoundingly, almost 40 per cent of Australia's runs in this game were added by the respective last wicket partnerships. If records for this ever existed, they have been rewritten.

Haddin knew Pattinson well enough to indulge him with the strike. Swann came to know Pattinson well enough not to toss the ball up again after being wellied down the ground for six. At the luncheon adjournment, Australian appetites were heartier than English. But there would be no second act in Australia's day, and its confirmation barely needed video assistance. One look at Haddin's face was sufficient.

The Decision Review System
MATTERS ARISING

Tucked away in a corner of the programme for the Trent Bridge Test are a series of potted interviews with the match officials in which they are asked among other things whether they remember games for 'decisions or players' feats'. It's great performances that count, avers Marais Erasmus. 'If I'm not noticed,' he says, 'it means I have got things right!'

It's good advice, and worth citing not only because of Erasmus's inability to keep to it on the Friday of this Test. This was a wonderful game of cricket that deserves to be remembered for the excellence of its skills and the drama of its moments. But there's also a danger that those recollections will be overshadowed by the umpiring – not because of its quality, although that was assuredly an issue, but because of its involuted complexity.

There were thirteen referrals in this Test: five were upheld, eight struck down. England were better at them: they were three and one. Australia's record was two and seven. Which, of course, cost them dearly when it came to Stuart Broad's impersonation of Bill Lawry, who proverbially never left the crease if there was still one stump standing, for they had no referrals left.

But should a game of cricket be *so* susceptible to the influence of technology? Judging if and when to seek video adjudication is certainly a skill, but wouldn't we prefer matches to be decided by prowess with bat and ball? And aren't we there to watch a game rather than to dicker over the microns by which a delivery might have pitched outside leg, or whether 45 or 55 per cent of a digital ball is striking a cyberstump? It's getting to the point where teams will be selecting specialist referral consultants, their effectiveness to be statistically measured on an official metric, with successful referrals to be announced musically – 'Jerusalem' for England, obviously, perhaps 'Tie Me Kangaroo Down, Sport' for Australia.

Imagine just for one moment that the Trent Bridge Test had ended with the same telltale nick by Haddin, the same perfectly reasonable not-out decision by Aleem Dar, and England with no referrals remaining. Would we have been satisfied that justice had been served? Would we have regarded it as a win for 'accurate umpiring'? How big an apology would the ECB have wanted from the ICC? Wartime reparations would probably have looked a bagatelle by comparison.

The Decision Review System is changing the game in other, subtler ways too, upsetting calibrations of long standing. Off spin to left-handers has grown more effective – ask Graeme Swann. The forward lunge in batting is likewise less effective – ask Shane Watson.

Watson is a member of the batting school raised to believe that getting in a big stride inures one to lbw decisions. But it doesn't any more, or not, at least, to the same degree. Ball-tracking technology has instilled the belief among umpires that many more deliveries hitting the pads would also hit the stumps than we used to believe – in effect the first enlargement of the stumps since they grew to their current statutory size in 1931. It was clear from the off in Australia's second innings that England were aiming to hit Watson's pads, confident that even in the event of an appeal being turned down they could pursue the adjudication through the referral system. As it happened, Aleem Dar adjudged the delivery from Stuart Broad to be hitting leg stump, and Watson's rueful look after his vain referral spoke volumes. Five years ago, he probably wouldn't have been out. Likewise his partner Chris Rogers in the first innings.

This isn't necessarily a problem. The 1935 change to the lbw law had similar repercussions, batsmen having to unlearn the 'pad play' that had become popular. But imagine if Ricky Ponting was beginning his career now. How far would he progress with that forward thrusting pad?

There is also emerging a sense of parallel games: cricket involving DRS, and cricket not. When we see, as we did at Trent Bridge, how profound an impact DRS can exert on the conduct of a match, how do we assess cricket without it? First-class cricket? The Indian Premier League? Non-DRS international cricket, which is by definition the most lucrative form because it involves India? And, as they say, whither honour? It takes a bit of chutzpah to stand as still as Nelson on his column when you've just left a splinter in the ball that's now in slip's hand, but Stuart Broad has demonstrated its feasibility.

To be fair, while 'walking' is sometimes imagined to be part of an abiding cricket honour code stretching back to antiquity, it belongs more properly to the realm of what Eric Hobsbawm called invented tradition. Simon Rae, in his excellent history of unfair play, *It's Not Cricket*, finds negligible evidence for walking before World War II, and concludes that the custom was only a vogue in English cricket for the two decades after, where he suspects it represented a last efflorescence of gentlemanly conduct as the distinction between amateur and professional narrowed to vanishing point.

Even during its heyday, Rae reports an ambivalence about the politesse, recounting an incident in a Test at Cape Town in 1964–65 when Ken Barrington walked after being given not out for a caught at the wicket, and occasioned howls of execration: 'Ugly new low in sportsmanship'; 'an ostentatious act which bordered on gamesmanship'; 'it seems the England players are quite capable of umpiring the match themselves'. Rae quotes the quivering judgement of former Springbok Jackie McGlew: 'You must never take control of the game out of the umpires' hands.'

Broad certainly left that commandment of McGlew's unviolated. But in the age of DRS, what he left in the umpire's hands was the equivalent of a grenade with the pin pulled out. A system designed to eliminate 'howlers' protected one, and set a new benchmark for player impenitence to which others will surely aspire; a good umpire and good man had his career travestied because he will forever be associated with a rare mistake, and a superb game of cricket, while not spoiled, was sadly sullied.

FIRST TEST Trent Bridge, Nottingham 10–14 July 2013
Toss England **England won by 14 runs**

ENGLAND	1st Innings			2nd Innings		
AN Cook*	c Haddin	b Pattinson	13	c Clarke	b Agar	50
JE Root		b Siddle	30	c Haddin	b Starc	5
IJL Trott		b Siddle	48	lbw	b Starc	0
KP Pietersen	c Clarke	b Siddle	14		b Pattinson	64
IR Bell	c Watson	b Siddle	25	c Haddin	b Starc	109
JM Bairstow		b Starc	37	c Haddin	b Agar	15
MJ Prior†	c Hughes	b Siddle	1	c Cowan	b Siddle	31
SCJ Broad	c Pattinson	b Pattinson	24	c Haddin	b Pattinson	65
GP Swann	c Hughes	b Pattinson	1	c Clarke	b Siddle	9
ST Finn	c Haddin	b Starc	0	not out		2
JM Anderson	not out		1	c Hughes	b Siddle	0
EXTRAS	(b 6, lb 5, w 8, nb 2)		21	(b 2, lb 13, w 1, nb 9)		25
TOTAL	(59 overs; 281 mins)		215	(149.5 overs; 660 mins)		375

AUSTRALIA	1st Innings			2nd Innings		
SR Watson	c Root	b Finn	13	lbw	b Broad	46
CJL Rogers	lbw	b Anderson	16	c Bell	b Anderson	52
EJM Cowan	c Swann	b Finn	0	c Trott	b Root	14
MJ Clarke*		b Anderson	0	c Prior	b Broad	23
SPD Smith	c Prior	b Anderson	53	lbw	b Swann	17
PJ Hughes	not out		81	lbw	b Swann	0
BJ Haddin†		b Swann	1	c Prior	b Anderson	71
PM Siddle	c Prior	b Anderson	1	c Cook	b Anderson	11
MA Starc	c Prior	b Anderson	0	c Cook	b Anderson	1
JL Pattinson	lbw	b Swann	2	not out		25
AC Agar	c Swann	b Broad	98	c Cook	b Anderson	14
EXTRAS	(lb 15)		15	(b 11, lb 10, nb 1)		22
TOTAL	(64.5 overs; 294 mins)		280	(110.5 overs; 467 mins)		296

| AUSTRALIA | | | | | | | | | |
1st Innings	O	M	R	W	2nd Innings	O	M	R	W
JL Pattinson	17	2	69	3		34	8	101	2
MA Starc	17	5	54	2		32	7	81	3
PM Siddle	14	4	50	5		33.5	12	85	3
AC Agar	7	1	24	0		35	9	82	2
SR Watson	4	2	7	0		15	11	11	0

| ENGLAND | | | | | | | | | |
1st Innings	O	M	R	W	2nd Innings	O	M	R	W
JM Anderson	24	2	85	5		31.5	11	73	5
ST Finn	15	0	80	2		10	3	37	0
SCJ Broad	19	4	60	2		23	7	54	2
GP Swann	6.5	0	40	1		44	10	105	2
JE Root						2	0	6	1

| FALL OF WICKETS | | | | |
Wicket	Eng - 1st	Aus - 1st	Eng - 2nd	Aus - 2nd
1st	27	19	11	84
2nd	78	19	11	111
3rd	102	22	121	124
4th	124	53	131	161
5th	178	108	174	161
6th	180	113	218	164
7th	213	114	356	207
8th	213	114	371	211
9th	213	117	375	231
10th	215	280	375	296

Umpires: Aleem Dar (Pakistan) and HDPK Dharmasena (Sri Lanka)
Referee: RS Madugalle (Sri Lanka)

THE SECOND TEST: Lord's

Preview
RIFT VALLEY

'Let's be honest, very rarely do you get everyone pulling in the same direction in a dressing room.'

No, that's neither Michael Clarke nor Shane Watson discussing their mutual dislike, now outlined in documents filed in support of a wrongful dismissal case against Cricket Australia by their former coach Mickey Arthur. It's actually Graeme Swann in his 2012 autobiography, admitting that he did not always find Kevin Pietersen the easiest teammate, and very far from the easiest captain.

Yes, these things happen. Swann also adumbrated an even more colourful feud during his years at Northants, where the fiancée of keeper Toby Bailey cancelled their wedding in order to date his teammate Russell Warren. Not surprisingly, this dispute divided the dressing room, and more, the cricketing Yoko Ono in question being close to Swann's then girlfriend. Swann divulges that one player, Malachy Loye, would not even talk to Warren in the middle, which must have made running between wickets challenging.

The friction between Clarke and Watson, since hashtagged Mickeyleaks in a vast improvement on Homeworkgate, is rather more prosaic and less palpably divisive. It's a kind of open secret that they aren't close, or even particularly friendly, despite, or perhaps because of, two years as captain and deputy of Australia in Test and one-day international cricket, with the mistrust brought into the open by Watson's suspension from the national team in India by Clarke and Arthur.

The disclosure on the eve of a Lord's Test that Clarke once called Watson a 'cancer' is a colourful additional detail: it is not a reference to his star sign, or to a forthcoming astrological rotation policy. Add in the detail of Clarke's estrangement from Andrew Symonds and Simon Katich, Watson's erstwhile opening partner, and you have a racy story that could run and run.

Yet not all tensions, as Swann hints, are alike, because not all teams are. Those between captain Kim Hughes and the formidable axis of Rod Marsh and Dennis Lillee weakened a vulnerable Australia in 1981; those between Shane Warne and the pairing of Steve Waugh and John Buchanan were contained and to a degree harnessed by mighty Australia in the late nineties through the early noughties.

You could mount an argument based on this that middling teams have greatest need for cohesion and harmony; the best can rely on their stars aligning at telling moments because that is what stars do, and because winning tends to maintain an equilibrium of contentment. But strong teams also feel it, especially when they underperform the sum of their abilities. Australia's coach Darren Lehmann has some insight here. Twenty years ago, he formed part of a Victorian Sheffield Shield team with everything going for it bar success, thanks to a notorious dressing room and dysfunctional leadership. It was, Lehmann observes in his autobiography, 'the best first-class team I have ever seen and yet we failed to achieve half of what we should'.

So what's the story here? In his own autobiography, Watson lays bare some of the reservations entertained about him, recounting the outcomes of an 'honesty session' at John Buchanan's celebrated boot camp nearly seven years ago, where teammates confided their candid views that he was 'too intense' and 'a whinger'. That reputation continues to follow him, reinforced most damagingly in recent times not by Arthur, but by the man who sacked him, Cricket Australia's Pat

Howard, when in March he commented that Watson 'acts in the best interests of the team sometimes'.

Watson's problems are not entirely of his own making. Many of his vulnerabilities derive from his injury-related comings and goings, for he has played only just over a third of the Tests and about half of the one-day internationals in his period as an Australian cricketer. But while it's not Watson's fault that he's had to make more comebacks than Cher, it has aggravated a tendency to insularity, which Cricket Australia sought to counteract by appointing him vice-captain, to little avail. And the surprise would be had this not inflamed Clarke, who toils on despite a bad back that occasionally causes him to move as though sealed in a full body cast.

Clarke is sensible enough to understand that there are issues of circumstance here as well as an apparent variance of personalities. It has in general been an unhappy, frustrating period in Australian cricket, whose complications have had many causes and authors, as Clarke implicitly acknowledged in his attempt to scotch Mickeyleaks at Lord's on Tuesday: 'I can't remember for a long time the team being as united as we are right now.'

Clarke will know, too, that tensions inhere in cricket teams because of the members' acute interdependence. Batsmen can do nothing without partners, bowlers nothing without fielders, captains nothing without respect. A cricket team on a long-duration tour, such as the Australians at the moment, is like a great caravan travelling a long but well-trodden route, its members relying on one another for support, company and amusement. Mickeyleaks may even do them good, enabling individuals to talk more openly about matters that people would naturally prefer to avoid.

That said, cricket dressing rooms generally are different places to even five years ago, buffeted by the incessancy of competition, the possibilities of corruption, the tendency to squads rather than teams, and the T20 revolution with its inequality of incomes and privileging of the virtuoso individual: England's predicament with Pietersen sprang, of course, from his rapturous romance with the Indian Premier League.

In some dressing rooms, I dare say, Kwame Nkumrah's noble senti-ment is turned on its head, and the forces that divide are stronger than those that unite. Certainly, common purpose, rather than arising nat-urally, now needs creating, something England have acknowledged in their in-house slogan, 'the team is not a hire car' – that is, not a vehi-cle merely for the occasional convenience of individuals. This Lord's Test, then, perhaps comes at just the right moment for the Australians. Because if a Lord's Test is not a purpose to unite individuals, then nothing is.

Summary

THE EMPTY CITADEL

The Lord's Test is rather like the Boxing Day Test at the MCG, in the sense that feats in it have disproportionate value while failure tends to reverberate – better to drop your bundle somewhere hot and far away in the middle of football season. The Second Test of 2013 suggested that when it came to losing, Australia was picking its moments badly. They fell apart as publicly and abjectly as against the same opposition in Melbourne thirty months earlier.

Although Joe Root and Ian Bell conjured up more runs between them than Australia in both innings, England's match winner was Graeme Swann with nine for 132 from 52 overs on a pitch that did him no favours but against batsmen who did. Swann did little more than he usually does in the first innings, deliver a tight spell asking a few questions; Australia's batsmen broke down as though they were being interrogated by Smersh. He then chipped away on the fourth day, and without bowling anything unplayable secured victory at Lord's in the last over available – England's fiftieth Test win at Lord's.

Australia made two changes to their Trent Bridge XI, discard-ing the unlucky Cowan for the coach's Queensland protégé Usman

Khawaja, and spelling the spasmodic Starc in favour of the spirited Ryan Harris. The last named made an immediate impression on the first day, bustling out Root and Pietersen after the early fall of Cook, then upending the well-set Trott with a ball too short to glance, too full to pull and too quick to do other than top edge to backward square – not since McGrath's palmy days had an Australia bowled so incisively at headquarters.

Shortly after lunch, having won the toss, England were indifferently placed at four for 127, only to strike back through Bell and Bairstow, and a Siddle no ball that spared the latter when his stumps were scattered on 21. Bell moved in a smooth, almost stately fashion to a hundred in four and a half hours off 203 balls: his third in consecutive Ashes Tests, linking him with Jack Hobbs, Wally Hammond and his teammate Stuart Broad's father Chris. There was no bang or clatter, but he showed just how difficult a batsman he can be to contain. Though Australia strained to deprive him of off-side width, Bell still scored more than half his boundaries in the arc from backward point to cover point; when they straightened their line, he accumulated sixteen singles and a couple of threes between mid-wicket and backward square leg, including with a shot of undramatic originality fast becoming a trademark, awaiting the ball at the top of its arc and tugging it to the on side with a half-pull, half-cuff. As the contact occurs above head height, the top edge is the danger, but somehow never eventuates. It is executed with such natural control as almost to constitute a nurdle.

Bairstow showed spirit and spunk in helping Bell add 144 in 259 balls, even if some of their work went by the board when Smith struck thrice with his leg breaks in twenty-two deliveries as the long day waned. When Bresnan was caught at the wicket off the first ball of the next morning, however, it was the last thing to go right for the Australians all day, by the end of which they were not simply heading but plummeting towards defeat.

First, England's last two wickets added 72 with cheerful

abandon, Broad and Swann as relaxed as a post-coital cigarette. Watson responded with clumps of his own, only to step across on the verge of lunch and be adjudged lbw twice – as at Trent Bridge, first on field then off. Coach Lehmann would later blame the referral on Watson's partner Rogers, which seemed an unnecessary expedient to save the batsman's blushes. Whatever the case, it sent a weakening tremor through Australia's order, which by tea was in ruins at seven for 96. Rogers made a mess of a full toss on his county home ground and failed to seek a review he should have; Hughes flayed flat-footed at Bresnan and sought a review he shouldn't have. Khawaja looked overwhelmed, Smith unsure, Clarke unsteady, weathering a fusillade of short balls from Broad before being torpedoed on the crease. Agar was marooned and Haddin becalmed, leaving the tenth wicket to provide Australia's second biggest stand of 24. With an advantage of 233, England could afford to lose three cheap early wickets to Siddle before the close, and Australia could not afford to miss Root (8) when a nick from Watson bisected Haddin and Clarke.

The costliness of that miss haunted the visitors through the third day as the 22-year-old Root laid down the basis of a huge innings – 'erecting a tent with infallible pegging then posting inexorable sentries', as Robertson-Glasgow once wrote of Phil Mead. Australia's bowlers were paid due respect in the knowledge that with just a three-hour remission they would eventually feel the pinch as the afternoon wore on. Taking no chances and giving no more, Root added 45 and 34 in the first two sessions, then 81 in the last, Bresnan, Bell and Bairstow providing the company, and younger brother Billy acting as twelfth man the impudent encouragement. 'He was probably nastier than Shane Watson,' Joe reported. 'He was just being his cheeky self, trying to wind me up. Telling me how slowly I was batting and how he would be smacking it to all parts.' England's youngest Ashes centurion at Lord's was in sight of turning double-centurion when he succumbed to his first frivolity: a dilscoop improbably caught at third man.

Having wasted time that fourth morning, England declared with a 582-run lead which, it was quickly revealed, they hardly needed. Watson abjured a referral after being hit on the pads, failing to counteract inswing; Rogers abjured a stroke altogether, failing to pick the straighter one; a straighter one also accounted for the strokeless Hughes, who again squandered a review. Khawaja played some pleasing strokes without suggesting permanence; Clarke worked his way to a half-century without achieving fluency. When both fell to Root's round-arm off breaks, the tail could delay the inevitable but not avoid it; even Australians in the press box cheered when the agony was ended by Pattinson's lbw. He would be seen no more during the series, having experienced a recurrence of long-term stress fractures. Australia was suffering something similar.

Day One
THURSDAY 18 JULY

Close of play: England 1st innings 289/7
(TT Bresnan 7*, JM Anderson 4*, 89 overs)

Four years ago at Lord's, the wheels fell off a young and callow Australian attack so spectacularly that Australia spent the rest of the tour driving by the rear-vision mirror. It was entered in the category of Australian cricket events that Must Never Happen Again, and in some senses the team has been readying for today ever since.

Ryan Harris has been integral to those preparations. It was felt that if Australia could just get him there, quality would out. If that meant a retinue of medicos travelling just behind him, in the fashion of a support crew in the Tour de France, then so be it. And so it proved.

Michael Clarke spent Cricket Australia's investment thoughtfully: 5-2-9-2, 4-1-12-0, 4-1-7-1, 4-0-13-0 were Harris's spells, all from the pavilion end, all at good pace, and with a gratifying, surgically reinforced spring in his step. He caused Kevin Pietersen to take his leave after four deliveries, daintily tucking his bat beneath his arm as he walked for a nick, which was as good as things got for the visitors.

Towards the end of a protracted day after a hot afternoon, Clarke had three strokes of fortune with Steve Smith's leg breaks, last glimpsed endangering short leg fielders at Worcester, and here greeted a little casually. They dissolved the excellent partnership of Ian Bell and Jonny Bairstow, and gathered up Matt Prior for good measure. Compared to four years ago at Lord's, then, this turned out to be an excellent day for Australia; mind you, compared to four years ago at Lord's, the Dardanelles campaign started well.

Thirty-four-year-old Harris is a remarkable bowler, having led the conventional paceman's career in reverse, starting life as a fourth seamer and graduating steadily to the new ball, the equivalent of working your way from backing vocals to front man. He has the presence now of an ageing rocker, mellowed and domesticated by the years but still capable of belting out a mean rendition of 'Livin' on a Prayer' – which, in a sense, is how he has endured, with the help of medical science, faith and perseverance.

Harris's powerful legs have long been undermined by suspect knees and ankles. Since August 2012 he has also been easing his way back from shoulder arthroscopy, and shoulders are what Harris is all about. You could not squeeze past him in a doorway. He returns to his mark with a jaunty cheerfulness. You imagine him whistling on the way.

Rumour has it that on Wednesday the England Cricket Board were keen for Mick Hunt to shave the pitch of its five o'clock shadow of grass. Fortunately, nobody issues orders to cricket's Duchy of Grand Fenwick, and Australia were not displeased to have the first opportunity to ascertain the surface's responsiveness. Bowling to a full length to allow for the bounce, Australia benefited by two early lbws.

After lunch, Harris, who discomforted Trott with short deliveries when they met in Australia, did so again. Trott's indeterminate pull shot gave Harris his fiftieth wicket in thirteen Tests, which would qualify as breakneck progress were these games not spread over three and a half years. And frankly, except on the slowest pitches, Trott shouldn't get too many deliveries in his half for the next six months – his forward thrust invites it.

Unfortunately for Australia, James Pattinson could not get comfortable with the slope at either end, and had he been watching the game on television would have been tempted to adjust the horizontal hold. Likewise, Ashton Agar rather struggled with his action, which from so wide of the crease lends his trajectory a certain sameness.

Resourceful captain that he is, Clarke made do and mended. He chivvied his men along all day, moved the field around alertly, jogged from slip at one end to the other, where he periodically exchanged jests with Shane Watson, providing the kind of photos round which caption contests are designed.

Watson, who took five wickets here against Pakistan three years ago, took his first wicket of the year for Australia, the coveted one of Cook. Nonetheless, it will be interesting if Watson is compelled to bowl twenty overs in this innings and does not come off when he opens, for one might hear again those low-level murmurings about his being overworked as a bowler with deleterious consequences for his batting. Australia will always be in the position of wanting a little bit more from Watson – and, to be frank, he owes them.

There was no Mitchell Starc or James Faulkner: so much for the theory of harnessing the slope to exploit Cook's alleged vulnerability to left-arm pace. And while Siddle's sixty-eight striving overs in nine days are an excellent advertisement for vegetarianism, he was slow to start, and his best delivery, straight, full and fast to Jonny Bairstow, was illegal.

That no ball afforded the Australians their first long look at Bairstow. Good judges fault his technique, which is bossed by his bottom hand. Yet as Ricky Ponting observed earlier this season, there is 'something' about him. It's not X factor perhaps so much as Y chromosome. In the spirit of his gamesome father, he looks, quite simply, born for the cricket field.

In any case, Bell has enough technique for two batsmen. His bat hardly departs its groove. When he plays a defensive shot, the ball drops like a shot partridge. When he strokes the ball off the back foot, the additional effort is virtually imperceptible. He expressed satisfaction before the match at his improvement in 'grinding out innings'. Today, as at Trent Bridge, he ground pure fillet mignon.

Bell did not play in the corresponding fixture here four years ago. His career was on hold, his average hovering enigmatically around 40 after nearly fifty Tests. Since the start of 2010 he has averaged 59 and compiled eleven centuries. The years have not been so kind to Australia, but today, thanks to Harris and to Smith, they looked up just a tad.

Day Two
FRIDAY 19 JULY

Close of play: England 2nd innings 31/3
(JE Root 18*, TT Bresnan 0*, 20 overs)

Scientists yesterday announced a development in a famous experiment at Trinity College, Dublin, called the 'pitch-drop', designed to test the viscosity and fluidity of this form of tar. Sixty-nine years after it was set up, a drop of suspended pitch finally fell into a beaker, and was caught on a time-lapse camera. It is being described as a 'drop heard round the world', a bituminous Higgs boson.

At Lord's today, a cricket experiment continued, not quite as long running but almost as paved with anticlimaxes: the effort to turn Shane Watson into a Test batsman, now into its 43rd attempt. So much time, effort and resources have been poured into this sporting prac that it must surely one day yield results. But this was not the occasion, and his 30 was a cameo to sum up a career: the clumping early boundaries, the accretion of dots, the obdurate front foot stride to the ball seaming back, the look of befuddlement at the granting of the lbw.

In mathematics, the most frequently occurring variable is called the mode; when it comes to batting, it might almost be called the

Watson. No-one in Test history has succumbed so regularly in the band between 30 and 60; no batsman has fallen lbw in such a high proportion of innings; this is consistency blurred into straightforward monotony. As in the second innings at Trent Bridge, the event was here accompanied by a review – an experiment like one of those you used to pull in your school chemistry classes with the random addition of liquids in search of the perfect stink bomb. And it left its reek all over the Australian innings.

Occurring as it did off the last ball pre-lunch, Watson's compound error meant that Australia lost a session it could to that point have regarded as shared. Was it selfish? The instinct for self-preservation is fundamental to batting and hard to reprove. It was certainly poor cricket, and contagiously so, for Australia seemed mindful after lunch of their eroded buffer against umpire error.

Chris Rogers elected not to review when he should have, Hughes reviewed when he shouldn't have, and Clarke as a result had no review left. As Australia's captain simply walked off on his dismissal for lbw, it looked almost archaic. What, no meeting, no comparison of notes, offer of eyewitness impressions or virtual reality simulation? Did we ever do it this way?

In these Ashes so far, the DRS has become a confounding influence on Australia, perhaps because it runs against the grain of that antipodean nostrum about cricket being a simple game, and discretion does not suit a team prone to doubt anyway. The first time Watson played in a Test under DRS, against West Indies at the Gabba, he was adjudged lbw to Jerome Taylor for 0, and eschewed a review that would have spared him. It's almost as though he is still searching for redress, determined to repeat this particular experiment until he obtains the right results.

Between times, Usman Khawaja, included here in Ed Cowan's stead at number three, fretted and strutted for thirty-five deliveries, was issued a reprieve by slip, then squandered same with a skip and a sky – echoes perhaps of a coach's advice to be positive come what may.

Likewise the run-out of Ashton Agar, whose 'play without fear' philosophy extended to his running between wickets, where fear, or at least circumspection, is not entirely to be scorned. Australia had scored 5 runs in the preceding eight overs, and was 265 in arrears – a scenario that called for a quick single as much as it did for a switch hit with the bat held by the blade.

In his defence, Agar has been in international cricket less time than David Warner's moustache. Back to Watson, who has no such excuses, and actually quite the opposite, because the world has been handed to him exactly as he wished: the opportunity he publicly coveted to open the batting, the chance to bowl as and when it suits him, even his preferred place in the field. Before the Second Test, of course, Watson was fingered by his erstwhile coach Mickey Arthur as the origin of many of the team's discontents. What he embodies more properly is the divided nature of the game down under. In full flow, he looks like Australian cricket as it would wish to regard itself: bold, exhilarating, intimidating. In the next breath, he can look like Australian cricket today often is: skittish, brittle, entitled, neurotic. And indulged: in the last two years Watson has averaged less than 25 in 29 Test innings. He retains passionate, almost evangelical advocates, Shane Warne and Ian Chappell among them, who have enjoined the selectors at intervals to couple him with Warner as a dream-ticket opening partnership. Yet no player in modern cricket shows so clearly that innings are more than just a collection of strokes, however easy on the eye. Graham Gooch draws a crisp distinction: he says that he doesn't coach England in batting so much as in 'run-getting'. Watson does not seem to 'get' runs, in either sense of the word 'get'.

To fill the breach at the Nursery End in England's second innings, Clarke threw Watson the new ball – not actually the worst experiment, for Watson the bowler shows a creativity that Watson the batsman seldom does. His ninth ball, heading down the slope, took an edge that bisected his captain and his successor as vice-captain – the elements of a triangle seemingly unable to connect. And so the experiment continues, the only law for which it has so far provided evidence being the one concerned with diminishing returns.

Day Three
SATURDAY 20 JULY

Close of play: England 2nd innings 333/5
(JE Root 178*, JM Bairstow 11*, 110 overs)

In the lead-up to this Second Test at Lord's, Cricket Australia's CEO James Sutherland expressed delight at the gelling of the national team with its new coach Darren Lehmann. In the three weeks since Lehmann's appointment, Sutherland said, the scene had been transformed: it was a 'different team' in a 'different place', and he was 'really excited about the place this team is in'.

Which place was he talking about? The Royal Garden in Kensington is a finely appointed hotel, to be sure. But really? Yes, *really*. 'It's not just . . . one or two relationships – I'm talking about the whole team environment,' Sutherland continued. 'You can see it in the way they're moving around the hotel, you can see the way they're walking onto the ground.'

Well, that's it, then. Is it too late to change the venue of the Third Test to a hotel? There, evidently, you see the *real* Australia, nailing those lifts, executing their skill sets at the breakfast buffet, putting it in good areas with the concierge. And walking onto the ground? The way the players handle those gates, and effortlessly avoid tripping over the boundary ropes – why, it's clear how much they have gleaned from Lehmann, justly famous for his walking onto grounds, first one leg, then the other, socks on, shoelaces tied.

Because what's happening for Australia after the hotel and the walking bit remains stubbornly problematic. After the previous day's sixteen-wicket pile-up, traffic conditions in the Second Test today reverted to something smoother and saner – and Australia just weren't in it. They were held at bay all day by a batsman who looks too young to star in a Harry Potter movie, Joe Root, and confounded by the black magic of the slow-motion replay depriving them of a key wicket, Ian Bell's. One wonders how confidently the visitors were moving round their hotel in the evening – rather like they were themselves in slow-motion would be my guess.

Anyone, of course, can make a duff prediction – mine of England winning these Ashes 3–1 is now looking like deranged optimism. But if Sutherland genuinely believes that Australia is suddenly a 'different team' in a 'different place' then he is on a different planet. What this Second Test has shown in cruel relief is not just the diminished condition of Australian cricket but the wishful thinking that surrounds it – thinking that is arguably now an obstacle to its restoration.

Football clubs famously incline to a similar mentality, where in adversity the coach is first under the bus. Except that not even football clubs talk of instant change, of formerly dead eyes suddenly developing killer glints, and of the cocky strut in a hotel foyer preluding imminent restoration of former greatness. But in Australian cricket, such fantasies are growingly abundant.

In January, most conspicuously, Shane Warne published on his website what soon became known as the Warnifesto, a bullet-point digest of how he would revive Australian cricket's fortunes, with a list of his preferred picks, a bunch of official jobs for favoured confrères, and a good old bellyache about the selectors' little-loved rotation policy.

At the time, CA pooh-poohed it. The Australian team was going just fine, thanks, and Warne's remarks were deemed just Warnie being Warnie. But although much has since changed in Australian cricket, it appears that several of his 'time to go back to basics' prescriptions were unconsciously digested. In with Darren Lehmann, part of Warne's own mooted hierarchy: 'Boof understands the game as good as anyone and has a great outlook on the game, he's a good balance of old school and what the needs are of the current day player.' Out with rotation, which Warne argued would 'never work'. Back to Shane Watson at number one; out with Ed Cowan and Mitchell Johnson, inter alia.

Which is not to say that Warne is a bad judge, or that Lehmann is a poor coach, or that rotation did not have a host of foreseeably unfortunate entailments. It is that CA seems by its words and deeds to have abandoned its former gradualism in favour of a quick-fix mentality better suited to radio shock jocks and tabloid newspapers. Pick the kid: thus Ashton Agar. Gather the old stagers round and partake of their lore: thus the presence round the playing group this week of Warne, Steve Waugh and Glenn McGrath. Out with the players on whom years have been spent getting them here: thus kiss-offs for Cowan and Nathan Lyon, after they battled through defeat and distraction in India. Let's do it the old Aussie way, with a laugh, a joke and a post-play coldie.

This also serves to stave off more serious questions, such as: how strong is our first-class system?; what is the impact of carving two months out of the middle of it to play domestic T20?; does our Centre of Excellence work as advertised?; why in the whole of Australia is there not a single young batsman capable of playing as today did 22-year-old Root, with such patience and aplomb, attempting nothing exotic until he was well in, otherwise methodically turning the strike over until the field seemed like one big gap?

This was actually old-fashioned Test match batting: 140 in 58 overs in the first two sessions, 162 from 32 overs in the last, as the bowlers unsurprisingly flagged, having only had three hours off in the three days, thanks to Australia's bedraggled innings. Australia used to excel at it; it now comes as naturally to them as translating Linear B into Latin in iambic pentameters.

The non-dismissal of Bell was entirely ludicrous, Smith's catch at backward point being as obvious as a Dan Brown plot until technology obscured it. It led at least to one moment of candour, an anonymous poster on the Cricket Australia Twitter stream speaking his or her mind: 'That decision sucks ass. #bullshit.' It's actually one of the more sensible remarks to emanate from CA recently. Needless to say, it was hastily and apologetically withdrawn.

Day Four
SUNDAY 21 JULY

Close of play: Australia 2nd innings 235 (90.3 overs) – end of match

Until the last Ashes series here, Australia had not lost a Test at Lord's for three-quarters of a century. It was cricket's own international inter-generational Occupy movement. No Aussie mounted Father Time to plonk a baggy green on his head or attach a can of Foster's to his scythe, but they might as well have.

Then, four years ago, Australia went down, albeit with some semblance of fight; now the citadel has fallen altogether, and been dis-covered deserted. Australia has clocked up some vintage defeats over the last few years. MCG 2010. Newlands 2011. WACA 2012. But Lord's 2013 has been as shabby and public a humbling as any of them. Victor Trumper! Donald Bradman! Shane Warne and by now proba-bly Elizabeth Hurley! Your boys took one hell of a beating!

Meanwhile, late-night television viewers in Australia were being beguiled by the charms of golf, and it must have looked pretty tempt-ing by comparison: prettier countryside, funnier pants, and neither DRS nor lbw, although beware Shane Watson taking up the game because he'd probably start kicking balls off the tee rather than driv-ing them.

Speaking of Watson, which is where Australia's travails seem invariably to begin, yet again the mountain laboured and brought forth a mouse. 'Watson lbw' is fast becoming the 'Hughes c Guptill' of the English summer. He could sell advertising space on his pads, so prom-inently are they featuring in each day's play.

Today's dismissal offered a minor variation on the theme, with Watson outside the line of the ball as it came back down the slope rather than playing across it – perpetrating a new error in an effort to avoid an abiding one. The result was the same, with the growing impression of a batsman spooked by the recurrence of events. Ray Robinson described how Bodyline never quite left Bradman's mind thereafter, how 'now and again a fast ball rearing at him caused in Bradman's mind an unnerving flashback to the days when he was cricket's hunted stag'. It's hard to avoid a sense that the ball seaming back into Watson now brings memories tumbling forth, the ghost of lbws past. Here, on his dismissal, he looked up and his partner was again Chris Rogers, whom their coach rather gratuitously dobbed in as instigator of Watson's car-crash review on the second day. The glances exchanged were as pregnant as the Duchess of Cambridge. At last Watson began moving off, even more weightily than usual: at the pace he was going, his partner may well have caught him up, for Rogers fell only nineteen deliveries later.

This was its own peculiar interlude, Rogers admitting a ball from Graeme Swann to his off stump, front knee bent like an obsequious courtier. When technicians as proficient as Rogers are falling lbw to full tosses, as in the first innings, and letting go straight ones, as in the second, then something is seriously amiss. And it is surely a topsy-turvy state of affairs when a batsman who has played three Tests, Rogers, is drafted to help a batsman who has played forty-three, Watson, fulfil his potential. Australia has committed to maintaining this push-me-pull-you opening partnership for the series, but on present trends it might prove what in politics is called a 'non-core promise'.

Watson and Rogers were not alone, of course, for there was a lot of passionate equivocation about. Later in the day, Brad Haddin pushed a knee-high full toss from Joe Root painstakingly to mid-wicket – a fine positive cricketer neutered by the occasion. At length, he padded up fatally to Swann. Smith, Hughes and Agar departed remonstrating with their fates and the DRS but might as well have been blaming the Bilderberg Group.

Australia's solitary positive was provided by Usman Khawaja, who recorded only the second fifty by a batsman in the visitors' top four this series. Were the highly strung Khawaja a racehorse, you would throw a blanket over him and hold out a sugar lump, but there is no doubting his thoroughbred lines – his defence is crisp and neat, and not even Michael Clarke plays so daintily off his toes. The chief criticism of Khawaja in recent times has been that he does not provide teams with much beyond his batting, and some grounds for that complaint still exist. No umpiring career lies ahead of Khawaja if his referral advice to Rogers in the first innings and Hughes in the second innings is anything to go by. But he coped coolly with an off-stump rough that looked deep enough to fall into. His main problem was timing: his runs were two days late.

Otherwise, events were another stark repudiation of the prevailing Cricket Australia wisdom that fortunes can be revived simply by appointing as coach a wily old stager who tells everyone to go express themselves. Mickey Arthur has complained that his dismissal damaged his reputation. This Test has arguably enhanced it.

Australia can play better than they have showed here. If their batsmen could give their bowlers more than three hours off in three days, they just might. As it is, a macabre statistic is that their tenth-wicket partnership is the most reliable component of their batting, having provided 31.6 per cent of their runs in this series. If this happened at your club, you would reverse the order. If it goes on happening, Australia might as well.

The trouble for Australia is that England can also play better. So far in this series, Alastair Cook, Jonathan Trott, Kevin Pietersen and Matt Prior, responsible between them for 1823 runs at 82.86 in 2010–11, have eked out an aggregate 313 runs at 20.9. That discrepancy is not sustainable indefinitely. Still more worrying is what may lie further out. The Australians will be back here for a Test in two years. It is supremely unlikely that any of Clarke, Harris, Haddin and Rogers will be among them. Who will be in their places? Where Australia once ruled, Father Time is now against them.

SECOND TEST Lord's, London 18–21 July 2013
Toss England   **England won by 374 runs**

ENGLAND	1st Innings			2nd Innings		
AN Cook*	lbw	b Watson	12		b Siddle	8
JE Root	lbw	b Harris	6	c Smith	b Harris	180
IJL Trott	c Khawaja	b Harris	58		b Siddle	0
KP Pietersen	c Haddin	b Harris	2	c Rogers	b Siddle	5
IR Bell	c Clarke	b Smith	109	c Rogers	b Smith	74
JM Bairstow	c and	b Smith	67	c Haddin	b Harris	20
MJ Prior†	c Haddin	b Smith	6	not out		1
TT Bresnan	c Haddin	b Harris	7	c Rogers	b Pattinson	38
JM Anderson	c Haddin	b Harris	12			
SCJ Broad	c Haddin	b Pattinson	33			
GP Swann	not out		28			
EXTRAS	(lb 11, w 4, nb 6)		21	(b 15, lb 8)		23
TOTAL	(100.1 overs; 448 mins)		361	(7 wkts dec; 114.1 overs; 464 mins)		349

AUSTRALIA	1st Innings			2nd Innings		
SR Watson	lbw	b Bresnan	30	lbw	b Anderson	20
CJL Rogers	lbw	b Swann	15		b Swann	6
UT Khawaja	c Pietersen	b Swann	14	c Anderson	b Root	54
PJ Hughes	c Prior	b Bresnan	1	lbw	b Swann	1
MJ Clarke*	lbw	b Broad	28	c Cook	b Root	51
SPD Smith	c Bell	b Swann	2	c Prior	b Bresnan	1
BJ Haddin†	c Trott	b Swann	7	lbw	b Swann	7
AC Agar	run out		2	c Prior	b Bresnan	16
PM Siddle	c Swann	b Anderson	2		b Anderson	18
JL Pattinson	not out		10	lbw	b Swann	35
RJ Harris	c Pietersen	b Broad	10	not out		16
EXTRAS	(b 4, lb 1, w 2)		7	(b 4, lb 5, w 1)		10
TOTAL	(53.3 overs; 226 mins)		128	(90.3 overs; 375 mins)		235

AUSTRALIA 1st Innings	O	M	R	W	2nd Innings	O	M	R	W
JL Pattinson	20.1	3	95	1		20	8	42	1
RJ Harris	26	6	72	5		18.1	4	31	2
SR Watson	13	4	45	1		12	5	25	0
PM Siddle	22	6	76	0		21	6	65	3
AC Agar	13	2	44	0		29	5	98	0
SPD Smith	6	1	18	3		14	0	65	1

ENGLAND 1st Innings	O	M	R	W	2nd Innings	O	M	R	W
JM Anderson	14	8	25	1		18	2	55	2
SCJ Broad	11	3	26	1		21	4	54	0
TT Bresnan	7	1	28	2		14	8	30	2
GP Swann	21.3	5	44	5		30.3	5	78	4
JE Root						7	3	9	2

FALL OF WICKETS Wicket	Eng - 1st	Aus - 1st	Eng - 2nd	Aus - 2nd
1st	18	42	22	24
2nd	26	50	22	32
3rd	28	53	30	36
4th	127	69	129	134
5th	271	86	282	135
6th	274	91	344	136
7th	283	96	349	154
8th	289	104	–	162
9th	313	104	–	192
10th	361	128	–	235

Umpires: HDPK Dharmasena (Sri Lanka) and M Erasmus (South Africa)
Referee: RS Madugalle (Sri Lanka)

THE THIRD TEST: Old Trafford

Preview
THE CAPTAIN'S CARES

Lists of the 'most read' articles on news websites are usually only good for corroborating the triviality of our times. But a week ago the rolling chronicle of viral videos and celebrity wardrobe failures at the online home of Australia's most powerful newspaper, the *Daily Telegraph*, afforded an unexpected glimpse of the collective cricket consciousness: the most popular story was an archived report of the now well-worn yarn of Michael Clarke's contretemps with Simon Katich in the dressing rooms of the Sydney Cricket Ground.

In evaluating the debacle of Australia's performance at Lord's, readers in search of a smoking gun had converged instead on a smoking chokehold – the one in which Katich briefly suspended Clarke when they differed over when the team victory song might be sung after a Test in January 2010. To think that Australian cricketers used to get hung up on *when* to belt out 'Under the Southern Cross'; after six consecutive defeats, they might now be in danger of forgetting the words.

But did the desire to revisit this story hint at a public mood shift? After all, when you tire of blaming the selectors because that's old and you can't really blame the coach because he's new, while all the talk of structures and culture sounds a bit esoteric, there's something to be said for falling back on the time-honoured satisfaction of blaming the captain.

It need hardly be said that this would be unfair, an easy out, a revival in the undertone of captious innuendo that has never been completely inaudible during Clarke's tenure: people always have this friend who knows this bloke who read this email about this story that says this thing about . . . y'know . . . Clarke being a bit of a dick. He wears nice clothes. He has rich friends. He must be suspect. It's meant to be the English who are uptight, but Australians can be just as censorious of their cricket heroes.

That said, what are we to make of Clarke's Ashes of 2013? Australia's skipper had a modest Test at Lord's that actually could have been worse. Had Matt Prior not snatched at a second-innings stumping, Clarke's last seven Test innings would have been worth a bedraggled 87 runs. Although he turned the reprieve into a stolid half-century, Clarke's muted performances this summer have been the leading indicator of Australian decline, even more telling than Shane Watson's version of the hokey-pokey, in which you put your left foot in then take your whole self out.

Much was written about the delivery with which James Anderson hit Clarke's off pole at Trent Bridge, which was retrospectively imbued with magical properties. But the ball that really told a tale had been bowled in the previous over by Steve Finn, the potential hat-trick delivery at which Clarke thrust his hands as desperately as a Test novice, and was fortunate not to nick. It was the kind of shot that sends a tremor through a dressing room, causing the next man in to tense, and floods the fielders with seratonin.

In his previous Test, Clarke, batting rather reluctantly at three, had gone hard at his first ball from Ravi Jadeja, and been stumped far from home; there was a hint at Nottingham of similar frailty, with Clarke, this time at number four, flushed from the pavilion too early for comfort. At Lord's, Clarke then reverted to his favoured slot at number five, only to arrive in both innings with crisis already spreading. He played superbly in these situations in the southern summer against South Africa and Sri Lanka, decisive and daring from the get-go regardless

of the scoreline, taking advantage of scoring opportunities offered by
attacking fields. But at that time Clarke still had the rainy-day fund
of Mike Hussey's runs to draw on at number six, and Matthew Wade
ticking over nicely at number seven. Since then, Hussey has retired
and Wade been retrenched. To his teammates, Clarke is now it *and* a
bit, and if that's not inhibiting, arguably it ought to be.

What about Clarke's leadership? If an Australian captain in
England is no longer required to saunter with sovereigns and deliver
empire-building speeches, he will still seldom enjoy a private moment,
and the mantle of being 'Australia's only world-class player' has proved
for Clarke an increasing hardship. It hasn't only been his shortage of
runs that has left him a somewhat diminished figure. Clarke spent
most of his time after arrival in England surrounded by medicos tending his back. He wasn't in the vicinity when David Warner swung his
woozy punch. He wasn't in the loop when his coach Mickey Arthur
was defenestrated. He was, of his own volition, no longer a selector,
but did not sound altogether comfortable when Arthur's replacement
began instigating changes to the team, making a point of asserting his
overriding responsibility for the batting order.

During Australia's bowling endeavours he has striven to look as
busy as ever, ringing changes and wrangling fields, but the kind of
Nelson touch or Napoleonic luck he used to show has been lacking. He has caught well, but declined to bowl himself. At times it
has been tempting to try and read his mind. When Stuart Broad did
'a Broad' – and if Vinoo Mankad can be lumbered with the bowl-
ing-end run out, then Broad is surely entitled to a similar vernacular
immortality for his crease adhesion – Clarke's response showed either
an impressive self-command in a trying situation or a resigned self-
acceptance as a leader doomed to disappointments. Ricky Ponting
would never have accepted 'a Broad' with such equanimity; the stench
of burning martyr would afterwards have been overpowering.

This, then, is a crucial Test for Clarke's leadership. Statements of
authority come in different forms: Barack Obama gives a speech, Silvio

Berlusconi throws a bunga-bunga party, Vladimir Putin either strips to the waist or kisses a big fish. For Clarke, gestures will no longer suffice. He needs to place his stamp on this tour at Old Trafford, or risk the stamp being placed on him.

Summary
RISING, DAMP

If not quite a dead Test, the Third at Old Trafford could hardly in advance have been described as very well, with England needing only a draw to retain the Ashes, and Australia to prevent this needing to make it the first of three consecutive victories. But by the time the likelier of these scenarios had duly transpired, the visitors were feeling rather better about themselves, with the running of the game for most of its duration, and rain to blame for their inability to prosecute a win more thoroughly. England needed nearly 300 runs and Australia seven wickets to win when the weather closed in on the final day, momentum and moral ascendancy entirely with the latter. David Warner, Mitchell Starc and Nathan Lyon, included for the overlooked Phil Hughes and the injured James Pattinson and Ashton Agar, all enjoyed moments too.

England had the luxury of an unchanged side, but Australia the greater luxury of the toss, and set their stall out on an arena showing the benefits of a recent makeover. The Point, a lush new cricket stand-cum-convention centre, put the twenty-first century on show. The players had sadly forsaken their dressing rooms in the old pavilion, which Neville Cardus described them descending from like a 'white waterfall', in favour of luxurious new digs across the opposite side of the ground, topped out by a commodious media centre. Above all, the square had been tilted at 90 degrees, to run, after more than a century and a half, north–south, which tells you something of the frequency of sun in Manchester and also the power of tradition. When local boy

James Anderson aborted his run on the way to bowl his first delivery, it was as though he feared taking a wrong turn, and he remained a little out of sorts the rest of the day.

Rogers, who as it happened had hardly played in Manchester despite his many years of county cricket, appeared contrastingly very much at home. Having looked the part in the first two Tests, he at last delivered the lines, fluently and convincingly, taking the full-length cues England's pace bowlers offered, and soliloquising to 50 in 49 deliveries. Only as a century gleamed ahead did Rogers lose impetus and at last his wicket, for the third consecutive time to Swann, England's chief threat on another slow surface. Clarke by then had found his feet after a sticky beginning and was using them lightly, not so much finding gaps in the ring field as revealing them. The short ball continued to trouble him, but required from bowlers such a stupendous effort that a sustained barrage was out of the question. Late in the day, with a twenty-fourth Test century under his belt, he rediscovered some of his touch of the Australian summer, and even some of his youthful brio: he grew up playing indoor cricket, and you detect it now and again in his method, the way his strokes flow into motion, the follow-through seeming to carry him the length of his first run.

The innings' main talking point, however, was the officiation – a curate's egg without the good parts. The decision that befell Khawaja, where third umpire Kumar Dharmasena somehow upheld a catch at the wicket given by Tony Hill when the batsman had simply missed it, proved to be a mere prelude. Smith's chequered 89 was like Montaigne's life – full of misfortunes that never happened. To sum up: Smith was 0 when hit on the pads playing back to Swann, and was reprieved by Hill then Dharmasena, who overlooked the ball's predicted impact with leg stump; Smith was 14 when he solidly nicked Anderson to Prior, but no Hot Spot was detected and Marais Erasmus's not-out decision stood; no reviews remained, therefore, when Smith was palpably lbw on 24 to Broad, but Hill's instincts failed him again. Yes, three experienced umpires, hundreds of thousands of dollars of training, millions of dollars of equipment, and a batsman can still cram four innings into one. At other times, Smith played quite competently, even attractively, but a century would have been a travesty, so it's perhaps just as well he holed out. Between times, in helping his captain add 214 from 408 balls, he had the satisfaction of ensuring that Australia would not lose a seventh consecutive Test match.

Nor was it only umpires feeling technology's superintendence. Pantomime boos swept Old Trafford as Warner emerged to bat again for Australia fully fifty days since his banishment, and the strains of the *Rocky* theme emanated from Billy Cooper's trumpet; Warner then looked slightly punch-drunk after nicking to slip via Matt Prior's pad, groggily insisting on a futile review despite his captain's clear misgivings. A tricky situation for both batsmen; one wonders whether Clarke might have been sterner had Australia been more precariously placed, or Warner surer of his position; as it was, he knowingly acquiesced in the squandering of a referral for the sake of a temporary accommodation. Game theory almost needs a whole new subgenre to incorporate DRS-related conundrums. Another arose before the close when nightwatchman Tim Bresnan effectively adjudged himself caught behind despite there proving to be no evidence of his having hit the ball. Who needs the Prisoner's Dilemma or the Centipede Game when you can have the Non-Striker's Nuisance?

Australia did not pause when Clarke himself departed after an innings of almost seven and a half hours with 23 fours, nor did England regroup: rather one could almost have been persuaded that the series roles had been reversed, that the visitors were in the ascendant and the hosts under the cosh. As Starc took up the scoring slack, he and Brad Haddin looted an unbeaten 97 from 117 uninspired deliveries, as bowlers' lengths wavered and fielders' attention wandered. England then staggered through to stumps, losing two wickets for 52, with Alastair Cook lucky not to be a third by nicking off to Lyon.

For their endurance on the third day, England had mainly to thank Kevin Pietersen, who exhibited no sign of the calf strain he had been nursing ahead of the game, and only one of the grievance he holds about his temporary estrangement from his teammates a year earlier – and he confined that to the press, to whom he gave a sullen audience under sufferance afterwards. At the wicket he exuded circumspect command, as though he had already designated the day for a century, and was basically checking it off his to-do list. Only when Lyon came on did he ramp up the intensity, bashing the spinner back towards the city centre, and temporarily from the attack. Otherwise England's innings was a lengthy tactical withdrawal – well planned and scrupulously staged, but a withdrawal nonetheless. Cook lasted almost four hours, Bell two and a half, and the innings itself nigh on ten. It was grim stuff: 155 scoring shots from 834 balls, barely one an over.

Mind you, the running was Australia's to make, and when it came their second turn they struggled a little to make it in the face of some skilful defensive bowling from Anderson, Broad, Swann and Bresnan, and some obvious time wasting from just about everyone. No batsman could do better than a run a ball, even Warner, promoted to opener again, and getting off some succulent shots in his 41 from 57 balls before holing out, amid jubilation, to his old sparring partner, Root. Clarke looked flustered, even indignant, when the umpires fussily assessed the light and called everyone in, as well he might, given how inattentive they had been to England's slothful over rate. But had he not regarded Manchester's weather with some foreboding, he was about the only one. Rain then fell much of the night over which he made his declaration, setting England an improbable if not outlandish 332 to win.

Everyone – teams, umpires, crowd, media – seemed surprised to be playing as early as 11.30 am on the final morning. That included Cook, who compounded a leaden-footed lbw with an unavailing review in the first over; Trott and Pietersen became Haddin's sixth and seventh victims of the match. The game's last delivery, a whizzer from Siddle, left Bell with a memento on his right thumb, and a flea in his ear from some suddenly garrulous Australian fielders. But minutes later the players were off the field again, and the rain teeming. When England took its lap of honour on recapturing the Ashes after play's abandonment three hours later, it was amid a damp and diminished faithful, and involved a sprinkler this time meteorological rather than choreographical. Not as dead as it might have been, the Third Test ended nonetheless with the makings of a nasty cold.

Day One
THURSDAY 1 AUGUST

Close of play: Australia 1st innings 303/3
(MJ Clarke 125*, SPD Smith 70*, 90 overs)

'You're messing with my career, Darrell,' Mark Ramprakash complained to Hair of that ilk when disgruntled to be given out in a Lord's Test some years ago. Right or not, at least Ramprakash knew who to blame.

As Usman Khawaja walked off just before lunch at Old Trafford today, he could only shake his head at his plight, and inwardly shake a fist at 'the system' – a technological/bureaucratic nightmare that has become almost a third competitor in this Ashes series.

Yes, the DRS had another of those days when it looks like your grandma trying to make a call on a smartphone and accidentally downloading a snuff movie. Khawaja, a young man fighting for his career, was a victim; Steve Smith, ditto, was a beneficiary. Australia came out ahead, but the game overall was the loser, for cricket's continuing officiation crisis overshadowed a stoic, battling hundred from Michael Clarke well escorted by Smith.

In the case of Khawaja, umpire Tony Hill made an honest mistake – a caught behind from a turning delivery that left an uneasy Khawaja in an ungainly position and was the subject of a convincing appeal. Doubt abounded, replays multiplied ambiguities, and technology should have provided rapid remedy. Yet despite no definitive evidence to speak of, third umpire Kumar Dharmasena elected to uphold the decision, on what basis one can only surmise.

Hill was then perhaps the only person in the ground who saw no reason to give Smith lbw playing back to Swann when the batsman could only have been closer to his stumps had he been inside them. Smith was 0, and after 3 runs in two innings at Lord's was staring into a career abyss. Not that it's an unimpeachable guide, but Ball Tracker confirmed widespread initial impressions by projecting an impact flush on leg stump. Nonetheless, Dharmasena deemed the decision to be an 'umpire's call'. That it was: a *bad* call.

Frankly, these were two 'howlers': the umpiring equivalents of Peruvians coming from Peruvia, and Gaul being quartered into three halves. Yet rather than subtract them from the game, the DRS cubed them. And from somewhere within the Board of Control for Cricket in India there emanated a deep, Mephistophelean chuckle.

The latter decision deprived England of a referral which would have come in handy when Hill, now speculating that Socrates died from an overdose of wedlock, ruled Smith not out lbw when the ball would have struck the dead centre of the wicket. The only consolation was that Broad was the bowler, a case of the ICC's unacknowledged Auto-Square-Up-o-Scope exerting its influence again.

In and around this risible nonsense, Clarke produced of necessity what he had been churning out on demand until a few months ago: a hundred, albeit after a torrid beginning. Rather as he has all summer, Australia's captain struggled for fluency in his first 30 runs, playing at wide ones, letting straight ones go that just cleared the stumps, ducking under short ones while leaving his bat in harm's way. At length he asserted himself with three boundaries down the ground in six deliveries from Swann, two in the air using his feet. Clarke's advance on spinners is not as bold as some others' – he takes quick, short steps rather than forming the prescribed 'x' with his legs – but the point is to disturb the bowler's length rather than annex territory, and this did the trick as it usually does.

Once settled, Clarke felt his powers coming back. Three boundaries off Broad bespoke his class: a superb pull in front of square,
a deft parry over the cordon, and a feathery glide through a vacant
third slip, all from quite similar deliveries, short and on the line of the
body. It was reminiscent of Len Braund's line about bowling to Victor
Trumper: 'I put 'em where I like, then he puts 'em where he likes.' With
Clarke on 99, Swann set a 3-6 field, and bowled straight at the stumps
from round the wicket. The Australian captain found a gap anyway, his
jog through belying the momentousness of Australia's first century of
the summer. Twice reprieved, Smith flourished in his slipstream. Today
might be this Test's best batting conditions, and 300 runs could look
ever more imposing.

Otherwise the day's most effective batting was by Chris Rogers,
who made most of the early running, punchy and positive, playing late
and crisply. Unlike most of his teammates, Rogers does not go looking
for the ball; rather he waits, plays it tight into his body, his concentration accentuated by a helmet pulled down as low as a bookkeeper's
visor. Aware of Rogers' comfort on the back foot, England's pace bowlers attacked him on a full length, from over and round the wicket.
He counterattacked with driving so firm and fluent that Alastair Cook
had recourse to an off-side sweeper. After lunch, Rogers lost a little
strike and impetus, and Tony Hill (correctly) judged him lbw while
turning to leg, thereby offering the basis for a rueful joke: Why is a
stopped clock better than Tony Hill? Because at least it is right twice
a day.

Hill should not shoulder too great a degree of blame for today.
Umpires have made mistakes since time immemorial. But if DRS is
not about correcting obvious errors then it is worth nothing at all. And
those who insist that the 'people are the problem, not the technology'
deserve to be stuck in a room full of computers and asked if they are
happy now. The technology will *always* have to be used by people. The
challenge is to fit it to them. Heaven knows, perhaps we should consider what local hero Dick Tyldesley urged for Roses matches: 'No

oompires and fair cheatin' all round.' Just about anything would be better than what we have.

Day Two
FRIDAY 2 AUGUST

Close of play: England 1st innings 52/2
(AN Cook 36*, IJL Trott 2*, 30 overs)

If it was not the ball of the century, it was at least the ball of the afternoon. Nathan Lyon's third delivery in Ashes cricket pitched off, bounced, turned half a bat width and took Alastair Cook's edge, en route to first slip: a collector's piece of finger spin.

Not an hour earlier, Shane Warne, in his dual role as commentator and emeritus professor of spin, had described Lyon as Australia's best slow bowler. Perhaps his coach, seldom seen without a Sky earplug in place, had passed this felicitation on; perhaps it was Warne's well-publicised pre-match pow-wow with the team's spinners; perhaps it was just a good delivery, of which the underrated Lyon has bowled a few in the two-year, 22-Test career that was interrupted by his omission from the Test team at Trent Bridge.

The delivery did not furnish a wicket; it did not even represent a chance, officially. The nick eluded Brad Haddin's gauntlet and looped from just above his knee into space in front of slip, where Michael Clarke, arms flailing like a drowning man, was unable to time his dive and interpose a hand. It had to be chalked up as a moral victory, which in a ball is the story of this Third Test for Australia.

More moral victories followed: beaten edges, scuffed pads and muffled defensive shots, all cues for upraised arms and stifled cries. There was smart fielding, even the spare Lyon and the owlish Chris Rogers throwing themselves around, and Joe Root went 34 balls without adding to his initial single. With a scoreboard showing Australia having declared at seven for 527, it might have been footage from one of those trainwreck Test matches from the 1990s that Sky has been showing between fixtures on its dedicated Ashes channel, where England is six for 27 chasing three for 600 every time you tune in.

For all the epic nature of his 187, then, Michael Clarke may have made his seminal contribution to this match before a ball had been bowled, by winning the toss and securing Australia first use of this excellent pitch, which Cardus would have described as 'fit to be watered by a bowler's tears', although the England Cricket Board probably frowns on even that these days.

Australian runs on the board have put a different complexion on the contest, affording rest to their bowlers, scope to their captain, and comfort to their camp. Had England been lucky at the toss of the coin, custody of the Ashes might already have been determined; as it is, hope springs eternal in all those moral victories.

Clarke's innings, meanwhile, simultaneously resolved and deepened the mystery of his consistent prior failures at number four, where before this Test he had scored 667 runs at 20.8, versus 5771 at 63.41 at number five. That is, these failures seem to have no rational explanation, save perhaps that during his previous occupancies at number four he was otherwise out of sorts, and at number five has perhaps faced a little more spin. Beyond that, it would be a fertile area of inquiry for Malcolm Gladwell.

One of Cook's few obvious schemes was to post a short cover, where Clarke was caught during the Oval Test four years ago, but the chance it elicited burst through Swann's yielding hands. Otherwise, apart from the indulgence of three consecutive fours from Bresnan, Australia's captain took no liberties, happy to offer paternal oversight to Steve Smith's advance on a maiden Test hundred.

Smith owes his place in the touring party to concerns about his captain's fitness, and probably his place in this XI to his captain's continued advocacy: that being so, Clarke would have derived as much satisfaction from Smith's runs as his own, and shared his chagrin at falling short of the landmark. Smith's miscue to get out was as premeditated as it was unthought through, like an attempt to repeat a scientific experiment without heeding the admonition not to try this at home.

Warner then emerged to gusty boos in his semi-official role as cartoon villain, complemented by a moustache that looked like it had been scribbled on his face with an HB pencil, and left amid jubilation after the unaccountable call for the referral of a clear edge to slip – another strange interlude, courtesy of cricket's ghost in the machine, the DRS. For the day's hinge point, however, no remonstration with the video gods was necessary: it was a decidedly low-tech drop, Matt Prior grassing Brad Haddin (10) off Anderson, taking a bottom edge on the wrist as he doubled back awkwardly to his left. Australia would then have been six for 380, and England in with a chance of limiting the extent of Australia's march past 400: say it soft, but England's 2012–13 player of the year seems to be suffering a version of the notorious curse of the cover of *Sports Illustrated*.

As it was, a few bold blows from Haddin pushed Cook into default defensive mode, and with three and four fielders back, the playing expanse of Old Trafford suddenly looked a lot like Australia's coastline: big, invitingly porous and difficult to police. When Clarke at length chopped Broad on, he walked off grimly, as though there were runs for the taking, which the angular Starc proceeded to seize with some uninhibited blows down the ground.

If England were not quite inert in this period, they were not especially ert: the bowling was lacklustre, the outcricket underwhelming, the leadership indistinct, with more fruitless consultations than an episode of *Yes Minister*. The surge in energy and purpose when Australia entered the field was a striking contrast, and earned its reward with the wickets of Root and Bresnan to add to their moral victories; had the chance Cook offered gone to hand, the resemblance to a day of Ashes cricket in the 1990s would have been complete. In the context of a 0–2 deficit, of course, moral victories will not suffice. But they are a start.

Day Three
SATURDAY 3 AUGUST

Close of play: England 1st innings 294/7
(MJ Prior 6*, SCJ Broad 9*, 120 overs)

Due to treatment for a calf injury, there was some doubt that Kevin
Pietersen would play in this Third Test. Which, said England's management, was *not a problem*, because everything was *under control*. The
stand-by batsman, James Taylor, had just made a hundred against the
Aussies at Hove, and would make an *ideal replacement*.

It was one of those bureaucratic procedures whose boxes were very
important to tick – minimise the potential loss, convey the impression
of smooth continuity – despite virtually nobody believing a word. Can
anyone conceivably think other than that Pietersen is second only to
James Anderson in Ashes irreplaceability? Not, surely, after today.

Yes, there is so much to find irritating about him – the prodigality,
the histrionics, the warhorse prance, the fancy ink, and the tendency
to, as Sam Goldwyn put it, bite the hand that lays the golden egg. It's
a year since he turned one of his finest innings into the pretext for a
boorish public sulk. But my word, no modern batsman can complicate
opponents' lives so quickly, and no member of England's order causes
Australians such confusion. Only James Taylor's family wanted Taylor
to play at Old Trafford more than did the visitors.

Australia's prospects looked rosiest fifteen minutes from lunch when
Starc strangled Alastair Cook down the leg side, Haddin diving parallel
to the ground to catch the deflection in an outstretched right gauntlet.
It was reminiscent of Haddin's snare off Mitchell Johnson at the SCG
in January 2010 to get rid of Salman Butt – nine months before *News of
the World*'s snare got rid of Butt permanently – and the high point of an
outstanding day by the Aussie keeper which should not go unremarked.

Pietersen was confronted immediately by two short mid-wickets – a bluff as it happened, for Ryan Harris persevered wide of off stump and almost induced a nervous edge. Pietersen followed with a similar wave at Starc, swishing his bat angrily afterwards, and a wander down the wicket to Watson, thereby squirting the ball to fine leg, that would have amused the instigator of the old KP Genius Twitter account.

With Pietersen, though, the worst and best can be just a ball apart. Soon after, he pulled consecutive deliveries from Starc for four – balls not that short, but through whose line his bat swung with the swift sureness of a beheading axe in *Game of Thrones*. And not even Viv Richards worked the ball to leg with the force and fluency of Pietersen – mind you, had Richards had use of Pietersen's bats the mid-wicket boundaries would have needed reinforcement with crash barriers.

After lunch, Pietersen had his first look at Nathan Lyon, and liked what he saw, striking consecutive sixes down the ground with that gimlet eye and 360-degree swing. Lyon pushed long on, three-quarters of the way back already, to the fence; Clarke ostentatiously brought the fielder back in, then further in for Ian Bell, who responded with his own six down the ground as if insulted.

This is what is known today as 'batting with intent', which sounds like a low-grade cricket offence, such as bowling with malice aforethought or fielding with menaces. But short of volunteering to bowl to Pietersen with his left arm, Lyon had no answer, and gave way. By the time he returned, Lyon's arc was flat, his pace monotonous, and the bowler who took nine Indian wickets in his previous Test was nowhere in evidence. Later he could be seen rehearsing his action, as though searching for something that had felt right in the nets but in the middle had deserted him. His head must by now be humming with advice.

Pietersen needed help too, of course, and received it mainly from Bell. As self-contained as Pietersen is expansive, Bell is in love with cricket's simple movements. He replays defensive shots not to finetune them, but for the sheer devilment. His Legoman swivels and pivots suited the Legoland backdrop of New Trafford's big shiny red box, The

Point. It was a surprise when Ryan Harris seamed one back to puncture his defence. His stumps to that stage had seemed as permanent as Richard Branson's smile.

It wouldn't have been a day of Ashes cricket without a video conundrum, Pietersen (64) being hit on the pad well down the pitch by Watson, and what appeared a bare majority of slip and keeper declining to refer when the bowler looked at least mildly engaged. A technology that started life as a television gimmick and has since been invested with the predictive powers of Nate Silver then suggested that the ball would have made contact with leg stump, causing coach Darren Lehmann and analyst Dene Hills to gesture to their team with raised fingers – New Age dissent, as it were, which might frankly have been better left *within* the dressing room, but which was indicative of brittle relations between officials and players that this game has done nothing to help.

Pietersen later referred an lbw that might have been not out had the ball suddenly dematerialised after striking the pad, but otherwise was a perfect bullseye. Was there a nick? Was there not? Was there a spot, or a noise, or a deviation if we slowed the footage down to a frame an hour and sat there till kingdom come? Dismissals are becoming like too-clever technothrillers with too many characters and plot twists. For heaven's sake, you want to cry, just kill the guy already.

The situation, with the follow-on still at a tantalising distance, actually needed no further intrigue, and, unlike England, Australia made its last hour in the field its best, thanks to Mitchell Starc's savviest spell since arriving here. This put the day in still clearer perspective: Pietersen scored 113 off 206 balls while six other batsmen scratched 129 off 334. England have found that they can live with Pietersen in the nick of time. Because, if it wasn't obvious before, they can't live without him.

Day Four
SUNDAY 4 AUGUST

Close of play: Australia 2nd innings 172/7
(MJ Clarke 30*, RJ Harris 0*, 36 overs)

Five days sounds ample time to determine the better of two cricket teams – the better of rivals in anything, for that matter, given that marathons only take hours, and general elections just a day. But it is amazing how quickly Test matches can slip away. All those breaks. All those pauses. All that concentrated inactivity. Time may not fly, but it marches inexorably.

For Michael Clarke at Old Trafford today, time was of the essence. How much did his batsmen need, to set a target alluring to England? How much would his bowlers need, to round up their opponents? How far was he to factor in Manchester's dark satanic weather?

There are conflicting theories about third-innings declarations, none of them definitive. The perils of overgenerosity are usually illustrated by the famous case study of Garry Sobers, who with a cavalier call allowed England to canter to a Test win at Port-of-Spain. Asked by a customs official at the team's next destination whether he had anything to declare, he replied: 'Not any more.' Yet Ray Illingworth made a habit of declaring slightly earlier than opponents anticipated, so that they would try to bat sensibly, and he could use bat-pad fielders for his slow bowlers – he, of course, being one of them.

With his team trailing 0–2, Clarke had the running to make, and would have heard all the urgings that he had to be 'prepared to lose in order to win' – not least, one imagines, from his friend and familiar Shane Warne, now arguably closer to the Australian captaincy than he ever was during his playing career. By the same token, Clarke might not have been altogether sanguine about the prospect of losing a game of which Australia has had the better since the toss. A record of seven consecutive Test defeats would be a burden for a team at an impressionable stage in its renewal. These Ashes are a long game, with the teams also building towards five Tests down under, and confidence over the course will count.

Clarke also needed time for another purpose: respite for bowlers who had toiled for 140 overs, on a pitch as hard as marble, and in the main beneath a hot sun. So he equivocated, and Australia got a little lost, as can happen in even the best-intentioned third innings.

The decision to open Australia's second innings with David Warner was described as 'tactical', perhaps to cluster the left-handers at the top of Australia's order, and perhaps also to extend Shane Watson's breather ahead of his second-innings overs. Yet one would have thought this situation made to Watson's measure at the top of the order: the opportunity to approach a Test innings as a one-day scenario, a task at which he excels, with a hard ball on a flat surface.

As it was, Australia neither zigged nor zagged. Warner found some fluency, and Khawaja looked momentarily more comfortable for batting off stump to Swann after experimenting with leg stump in the first innings, even if the consequences of the tactic caught up with him when Swann circumvented his defences round his legs. Smith hit a couple of peachy sixes, too, but the ambivalence of Australia's approach was embodied in his run-out, attempting a second when his captain was thinking only of a long single.

Somehow in their pomp, the XIs of Steve Waugh and Ricky Ponting always had plenty of time; they almost made it seem to stand still. So here was another mark of this current side's developmental phase, that even with a 159-run lead they were not quite capable of taking the game by the scruff of the neck. The likes of Hayden and Gilchrist would in similar circumstances have by now shaken it half to death.

Time today put Alastair Cook in a different predicament. His men set out to fill it every which way, in a kind of variation on Parkinson's Law, overs expanding to fill the maximum time allowable for their completion. Had strategy meetings lasted any longer, someone would have been appointed to keep minutes. Bowlers trudged to their marks. Fielders never took a short cut when there was a long way round. England contrived to bowl 22.3 overs in an afternoon session shortened ten minutes by rain, and 6.3 overs in the next 36 minutes. Species have evolved faster. The quickest England moved all day was at 4.26 pm when the umpires decided that the light was an issue, whereupon they set new PBs for spontaneous ground evacuation and feet up-putting – Andy Flower has probably had them practising it.

Light is actually the one arena in cricket where the on-field umpire's influence has been strengthened, and his subjectivity entrenched: you can't refer the light. The decision of Marais Erasmus and Tony Hill to curtail play may have been a case of umpires enjoying what little authority they have left. To be fair, the gloom was soon so stygian that not even Shane Warne's smile could have relieved it, and by 5 pm the clouds had burst anyway.

To continue to be fair, it could be inferred from the DRS that cricket has all the time in the world. An argument frequently made in favour of the system is that it has curbed dissent, yet in one sense the opposite is true – dissent has been normalised and domesticated, because what are the earnest conclaves that occur after every decision but a form of approved disputation, brought about mainly because umpires were not born with bats' ears and X-ray vision?

The indignation potentially built into the process was apparent today when the suspicion of a nick from Warner (19) was referred upwards for forensic analysis, litmus testing, carbon dating, etc. When it was knocked back, England's players looked surly and disgruntled, as is increasingly bound to happen when dressing rooms are simultaneously watching replays, and adjudication processes are winding on so laboriously. Cricket is becoming ever more like Gene Hackman's eavesdropper in *The Conversation*, poring ever more frantically over the same evidence, and growing ever more disoriented by each apparent clue: we are all Harry Cauls now.

Day Five
MONDAY 5 AUGUST

Close of play: England 2nd innings 37/3
(20.3 overs) – end of match

During one of the long hiatuses at Old Trafford today, Sky rummaged
round its archives and replayed highlights of the unforgettable last day
of the Ashes Test here in 2005 – also a draw, albeit involving a proper
breathless hush rather than the squelching tedium amid which this
Third Test ended.

The roles eight years ago were completely reversed, with Australia
the hunted and England the hunter, destined to corner their quarry at
Trent Bridge then hold them at bay at the Oval. What a difference the
years have made, of course; but how different, too, are those respective
positions of pursued and pursuer.

Not that the Ashes rivals are ranked first and second in anything
save the Ashes these days, but it wouldn't be surprising were England
experiencing something like 'the hollow feeling' that John McEnroe
confessed to when he seized Bjorn Borg's tennis crown thirty years ago.
The phrase 'undisputed number one' sometimes rolls off the tongue as
though it is tautologous when the opposite is true: no-one faces more
stress than the favourite; nobody presents a larger target than the front
runner. The status of Ashes front runner is a relatively recent sensation
for England: one wonders how well it sits with them, and their quietly
spoken captain.

When England officially retained the urn with the abandonment
of the game at 4.40 pm, the players looked happy enough, acknowledging the few remaining spectators through the still-falling rain.
But they will be conscious of having won not so much by playing
well as by playing well enough while Australia plunged to woebegone depths. The home team's shortcomings have been made good by

made-to-measure pitches and by a certain professional grimness, from the pragmatic cynicism of Stuart Broad to the cynical pragmatism of their over rate here on Sunday.

Certainly they displayed not a glimmer of interest in pursuing their 332-run target here today, and there was a degree of wishful thinking in some of the morning lamentations about Manchester's weather. With England three for 27 under clear skies, radars were suddenly being studied like the thick arrows on a map of the Battle of Waterloo, the role of Blucher's corps taken by the dense cloud mass advancing from the southwest.

There was some disorderliness about England's decline too. Alastair Cook referred more in hope than expectation, and Kevin Pietersen in what looked like indignation, further inflamed by the decision's upholding upstairs. Time for another 'please explain' letter to the ICC? Or have the England Cricket Board already used theirs this summer? In any event, this has been a bad game not only for the DRS but for England's vaunted reputation with it. They now seem just as perplexed as everyone else, remonstrating with it like a bank customer swearing at an ATM that won't surrender their cashcard.

The top floor of the local headquarters of Kellogg's, visible over the terraces on Old Trafford's western side, has been emblazoned throughout with a banner bearing a target and the explanatory legend: 'Hit this, Joe Root!' It has looked more and more ironic. Root's batting in this game was less in tune with his youth than with his Yorkshire heritage, nine scoring shots in 114 balls, an unconscious channelling of how Douglas Jardine used to regard batting against Bill O'Reilly: 'I've given up all the shots that get me out, and now I don't have any left.'

Not that conditions were ever easy. Bowlers nibbled it about for the duration of play, and the pitch showed excellent carry for a fifth day, the clearest example of which was a wicked Siddle lifter immediately after lunch, from which Ian Bell withdrew his thumb like he'd just slammed a door on it. Inevitably, a pit crew sprinted to the middle: the physio accompanied by two players from each side with drinks for colleagues who had been on the field for all of three minutes.

Pretty soon, everyone was back in the warm and dry anyway, where they were to remain. No word was heard afterwards of a potential injury to Bell, which is just as well for England, given their reliance on him this summer. Who would have thought in 2005 that the sight of his grooved shadow batting and constant bat twiddling would become so reassuring to local fans?

It is easier at the moment, in fact, to get a fix on Australia than it is on England. Australia are a battling, mid-table team with a good captain, a fine seam attack and a jumble of young batsmen being rotated furiously. For a team that has won six and drawn two of the last nine Ashes Tests, by contrast, England is a puzzle: conscientious and efficient but not exactly overwhelming, and as a combination rather less than endearing.

At their best they are effective; under pressure they can look nonplussed, as during the Agar–Hughes partnership at Trent Bridge and the Clarke–Smith partnership here, and even a bit peevish. Fine batsman that he is, Cook rather lacks his predecessor's polish and aplomb. Fine cricketers that he leads, there is little hint about them of a dynasty: one questions, for example, how much cricket lies ahead of Graeme Swann, who will turn thirty-five soon after the tour of Australia.

Later in the day, Sky reverted to highlights of the first day of the Boxing Day Test of 2010, the zenith of England's dominance of Australia. It is the way this team would like to be remembered: relentless, uncompromising, unyielding. England assuredly won that series; it is more the case this summer that Australia have lost. And the pursued cannot always rely on the pursuer falling short.

THIRD TEST   Old Trafford, Manchester 1–5 August 2013
Toss Australia   **Match Drawn**

AUSTRALIA	1st Innings			2nd Innings		
SR Watson	c Cook	b Bresnan	19	c Pietersen	b Bresnan	18
CJL Rogers	lbw	b Swann	84	c Prior	b Broad	12
UT Khawaja	c Prior	b Swann	1		b Swann	24
MJ Clarke*		b Broad	187	not out		30
SPD Smith	c Bairstow	b Swann	89	run out		19
DA Warner	c Trott	b Swann	5	c Root	b Bresnan	41
BJ Haddin†	not out		65	c Broad	b Anderson	8
PM Siddle		b Swann	1			
MA Starc	not out		66	c Swann	b Anderson	11
RJ Harris				not out		0
NM Lyon						
EXTRAS	(lb 6, w 2, nb 2)		10	(b 4, lb 2, w3)		9
TOTAL	(7 wkts dec; 146 overs; 649 mins)		527	(7 wkts dec; 36 overs; 176 mins)		172

ENGLAND	1st Innings			2nd Innings		
AN Cook*	c Haddin	b Starc	62	lbw	b Harris	0
JE Root	c Haddin	b Siddle	8	not out		13
TT Bresnan	c Haddin	b Siddle	1			
IJL Trott	c Clarke	b Harris	5	c Haddin	b Harris	11
KP Pietersen	lbw	b Starc	113	c Haddin	b Siddle	8
IR Bell		b Harris	60	not out		4
JM Bairstow	c Watson	b Starc	22			
MJ Prior†	c Warner	b Siddle	30			
SCJ Broad	c Haddin	b Lyon	32			
GP Swann	c Haddin	b Siddle	11			
JM Anderson	not out		3			
EXTRAS	(b 3, lb 17, nb 1)		21	(w 1)		1
TOTAL	(139.3 overs; 598 mins)		368	(3 wkts; 20.3 overs; 95 mins)		37

ENGLAND

1st Innings	O	M	R	W	2nd Innings	O	M	R	W
JM Anderson	33	6	116	0		8	0	37	2
SCJ Broad	33	6	108	1		7	2	30	1
TT Bresnan	32	6	114	1		6	0	25	2
GP Swann	43	2	159	5		15	0	74	1
JE Root	4	0	18	0					
IJL Trott	1	0	6	0					

AUSTRALIA

1st Innings	O	M	R	W	2nd Innings	O	M	R	W
RJ Harris	31	9	82	2		7	3	13	2
MA Starc	27	5	76	3		4	2	6	0
NM Lyon	35	12	95	1		3	0	8	0
SR Watson	15	7	26	0		2	2	0	0
PM Siddle	29.3	7	63	4		3.3	0	8	1
SPD Smith	2	0	6	0					
MJ Clarke						1	0	2	0

FALL OF WICKETS

Wicket	Aus - 1st	Eng - 1st	Aus - 2nd	Eng - 2nd
1st	76	47	23	0
2nd	82	49	74	15
3rd	129	64	99	27
4th	343	110	103	–
5th	365	225	133	–
6th	427	277	152	–
7th	430	280	172	–
8th	–	338	–	–
9th	–	353	–	–
10th	–	368	–	–

Umpires: M Erasmus (South Africa) and AL Hill (New Zealand)
Referee: RS Madugalle (Sri Lanka)

THE FOURTH TEST: Riverside

BACK TO SQUARE FOUR?

There are advantages to Australia having lost the Ashes. We can go back to discussing things that *really* matter, like . . . er . . . Shane Watson. His position in Australia's long-term plans must shortly become an election issue. Interest rates? The NBN? These pale by comparison with the urgency of the need to find a role in which Australia's most gifted cricketer can succeed.

Well, it certainly matters to Watson, anyway. And it's possible that this has become part of the problem, Watson approaching his continued underperformance at Test level with an intensity that prevents him remedying it. While a player's on-field manner is hardly an infallible guide to their innermost thoughts, Watson's demeanour is so unchangingly mirthless that it cannot be irrelevant: the heavy tread, the ever-downcast eyes, the pendulous top lip that could suppress a smile if Grandma caught her tits in the mangle.

I dare say you would be downcast, too, had you Watson's record in the last two years: seventeen matches, 20 wickets at 31.35, 773 runs at 24.15, including one half-century in his last *twenty* innings. But then Watson has always been the same, occupying first slip like a piece of scenery, trudging back to his mark like a French soldier retreating from Moscow. Surely no cricketer has presented such a potentially explosive range of skills in a less dynamic or appealing package. Afford a player sufficient opportunities, of course, and they are bound to succeed, and there will be all manner of self-congratulation when Watson does. But will anyone do the sums on what it might have cost the Australian cricket team in the meantime? Now there's talk that Watson might drop down the order which he campaigned so assiduously to climb just a few months ago. Watson is even borrowing Julia Gillard's last election slogan: 'I'm happy to play anywhere to be part of an Australian team that is certainly moving forward.' 'Moving forward' and not falling lbw, one presumes.

At his press conference after the Old Trafford Test, coach Darren Lehmann was asked whether Watson could still be grouped in with Australia's best six batsmen, and he couched his reply in terms of Watson as an all-rounder. It was another response that would not have been out of place on the Australian campaign trail, where candidates are counselled to answer the question they want rather than the question that has been asked.

Lehmann has a point too: Watson's unflattering figures, one for 114 from 61 overs, bely how well he has bowled on this tour, always accurate, often sharpish, a boon to his captain and to his team's other fast bowlers. England's lack of the same economical relief bowler was exposed at Old Trafford as its pace attack toiled listlessly in Australia's first innings, taking two for 338 from 98 overs. But there's something about Watson's untouchable status within the Australian XI that says as much about modern cricket, with its clerisy of coaches and myriad matrix managers, as it does about Watson.

For fifteen years or so, Watson has been Australian cricket's pet project. All the king's horses and all the king's men only tried to put Humpty Dumpty together once; with Watson it has been every other week, in search of the ideal gameplan-implementing, skill-set-executing cyborg. For those charged with his maintenance, therefore, Watson exerts a sort of fascination. 'I would have failed as coach of Australia if Watto doesn't end up with 10 Test hundreds, he's that good,' said Lehmann's predecessor, Mickey Arthur. 'We've got to push him and give him the direction.' Not, you'll notice, a challenge to Watson to fulfil his potential, but a challenge to his enablers to 'push him and give him direction' – a noble-sounding but rather self-overestimating sentiment that effectively exonerates Watson of responsibility for his own performances.

Watson is also strangely in tune with the game's media complex, with its fondness for the kind of explanations of events that irk Nassim Taleb: post-hoc rationalisations with a ring of plausibility. Watson is the perfect subject for professional observers with a repertoire of technical elucidations, enhanced by their stunning facility for summoning up replays, and for slicing and dicing stats, which reduce the player to a kind of static mechanism, susceptible to the adjustment of expert hands.

One group subtly reinforces the other. After a Test like that at Lord's ten years ago, Watson would have been the first man picked for the subsequent tour match at Hove, and been told to go out and score 150. The solution this time was to spend a week 'working with the batting coach on a few things' – watching video, drilling his technique, smashing throwdowns. This is cricket become too clever by half. Batting is not just a set of movements in which to achieve biomechanical proficiency. It's a holistic craft requiring constant exploration and experience, as well as kinaesthetic reinforcement. Greg Chappell has made the keen observation that when he was beginning his career, players spent 90 per cent of their time playing and 10 per cent practicising, and that the ratios are now reversed. Watson, I fancy, is a victim of this phenomenon, perhaps because of an understandable anxiety about injury that makes him loath to play any match he does not absolutely have to, but also an innate tendency to overanalysis: he would benefit from less time talking and thinking about batting, and more time doing it.

The best way to learn the business of converting starts is, amazing to say, by converting starts – by experiencing batting through the 40s, the 70s, the 90s, and pushing on after hundreds. Solving batting problems by batting? It's so crazy it might work. In the meantime, though, the only election slogan that suffices for Watson is the obvious one: 'It's Time.'

Summary
THE QUICK AND THE DEAD

Umpiring had been a talking point throughout the first three Tests of the 2013 Ashes; in the Fourth, the talking did not even wait for the match to begin. Its preliminaries were overshadowed by the reactions to a Channel 9 news story about the reliability of Hot Spot being compromised by silicone tape on the edges of bats, with attention drawn to the conspicuously spotless edge of Kevin Pietersen's bat when he was adjudged caught behind in the second innings at Old Trafford. Imputations, denials, tweets, statements: it kept the cogs turning for a few days anyway.

Perhaps the most surprising aspect of this story, though, was that it was not called Batgate, given that the story was about what was and was not recorded by tape and given the low bar set for '-gate' suffixes by Homeworkgate – after all, as Matthew Parris recently observed, Watergate would these days be called Watergategate. All we were reminded of was the ridiculousness of vesting authority for decision-making in a technology never designed for that purpose. In the event, the Fourth Test was the one least shaped by adjudication. There were some bizarre moments, notably Tony Hill giving an lbw with the players already off the field, Ryan Harris having repented his referral: the umpire as wallflower. But Aleem Dar had an excellent game. You didn't notice? Just so.

Riverside also offered perhaps the best pitch of the summer, or at least the most interesting, with quick bowlers able to nibble it about throughout and slow bowlers gaining some assistance. The bounce was consistent, too, and on the last day scary indeed, as Stuart Broad bore down from the Lumley End, turning a bum-nipping Aussie run chase into a high-fiving English rampage, bettering Anderson's ten for 158 at Trent Bridge and Swann's nine for 122 at Lord's with eleven for 121. Clocked by the radar at between 91 and 93 mph, he should really have been assessed by the Beaufort Scale.

England was first to find batting a precarious occupation, their innings a listless, sometimes strokeless affair. Jonathan Trott was the only batsman to achieve any sort of shotmaking ease, looking good, as for most of the summer, until he got out bat-padding a nondescript ball from Lyon to short leg. Pietersen went into his shell too quickly, Bell tried to burst from his too soon, and Cook simply never left his, labouring almost four hours over 51, until he perished padding up to the recalled Jackson Bird. Two normally enterprising batsmen in Bairstow and Prior took 116 balls to eke out a partnership of 34, only to succumb within three overs of one another. It was fine 'dry' bowling from Australia, if rather arid batting from England, that certainly did not achieve its objective of taking control of the game. It took England's pace bowlers to retrieve them a share, reducing Australia to four for 76 shortly after lunch on the second day.

Throughout this faltering progress, Chris Rogers held firm, taking strike as if armed for urban warfare with what looked like a square of carpet underlay on his arm and a phone book down his shirt. Deep in his crease, striving to resist as he was tugged and drawn into playing outside his safe zone, he somehow kept accruing runs – cuts, glides, nudges, nurdles, thick edges, inside edges. Content to be beaten in return for remaining active, he avoided becoming simply a stationary target. Pressure eased when Watson, after an anxious first half-hour, slotted into his new nook at number six and began loosing some retaliatory strokes, forcing England onto the defensive. By tea, the colony of Fanatics in the temporary terraces had been restored to cheerful voice and beersnake-lengthening humour.

After the break the game tightened, as Australia glimpsed a lead, England probed for a breakthrough, and light towers switched on to counteract the gloom somehow intensified the contest – it was like a suspect getting the third degree. For much of the series, 35-year-old Rogers had played as you'd expect of a batsman with sixty first-class centuries; Swann's quizzical spell reminded you that there remained the business of Rogers' maiden Test hundred to be made. Gifted a full toss, he disposed of it gratefully to go to 96, but remained there for the next half-hour. He didn't quite nail a cut, and picked out point; he played a couple down in front and let a couple go; he tried finding space on the on side and turned the face too early; then he did it again; then he and Watson almost had a moment between wickets. Deep breaths all round.

An appeal: Watson out, nicking unluckily down the leg side. By now Rogers seemed to be ageing by the ball: when he played and missed at a cut he bent his head for a few penitent seconds. He was almost still reliving it when he swept the next ball for four to reach his milestone, and celebrated as soberly as his balcony did noisily – no exultation, just relief. Finishing at five for 222, just 16 in arrears with five wickets remaining, Australia could take some quiet satisfaction from their day as well.

At last, England got a little busy. Some bolshie blows from Harris apart, Australia's tail contributed little. And while England lost three in erasing their arrears, they were clearly exhibiting more purpose, and Pietersen and Bell embarked on setting Australia a fourth-innings target with an impressive sure-footedness. Pietersen caught the eye, as he cannot help, with his long limbs, tiptoe walk, and seemingly delicate grip of a shiny bat; with every ball there is a sense of imminent possibility. Bell, nonetheless, cast a shadow at least as long, although he's actually easy to look away from. He is predictably efficient, imaginably controlled; you feel like you could pop out to the shops, or the pub, come back in a hour or two and still find him doing much the same, playing similar strokes, forming the same physical shapes. Being next man in when they are at the wicket together must be an alternately churning and lulling experience. Bairstow did not do quite enough again when called on, but Bell batted serenely into the evening, his progress interrupted only when Harris came round the wicket for a final short-pitched burst, lifting him off his feet, and on one occasion sitting him on his backside. Otherwise his third century of the series had an easefully recumbent character, Bell as relaxed as a man warming at his fireside.

And although Harris burst through Bell, Prior and Broad first thing on the fourth morning, Australia struck another line of resistance in Bresnan and Swann, who laid cheerfully about them as England's last two wickets added 55. To deepen the visitors' frustrations, Bresnan (12) let a straight ball from Bird hit him on the knee roll and was somehow reprieved both downstairs then upstairs; Swann (17) then shovelled Lyon down long on's throat only for Smith to gag. Little things they were at the time; like overlooked clues in a whodunnit, their importance emerged later.

Having survived four awkward pre-lunch overs, then sat through an hour of rain which was to push the game into the twilight, Australia's openers looked their 299-run target right in the eye, the powerful left hook of Warner and the counterpunching left jab of Rogers a potent combination. Warner used timing to cut and drive Anderson and Broad, strength to plonk Swann into the crowd, inside out. Rogers was, again, all nous and nerve, watching an edge go to ground; seeing off one referral, deploying another; soft bottom hand one ball, hard bottom hand next. England's appealing had a tone of imprecation, and the openers a brisk solidity as they shook hands on raising their three-figure stand amid the 27th over. At last, after building through three consecutive maidens, Swann tempted Rogers to push out, and Trott accepted the chance at slip. Australia moved on smoothly after tea, one wicket down nearly halfway home as Warner took toll of a flat spell from Anderson, but there was a sense from here on that the game might be won and lost in a short time.

Although Broad would be responsible for the demolition, it was Swann and Bresnan who created the initial breach, the former trapping a motionless Khawaja, the latter startling Warner with bounce. At once the game was afoot; English chins and chests stuck out, English chatter made stump mics blush. Enjoined to 'spice it up', Broad passed Clarke's groping bat with the first ball after drinks and poleaxed off stump, and Australia suddenly looked like an undermanned riot squad trying to kettle a seething crowd, with pressure points all over. Smith gloved a bouncer onto his stumps, Watson and Haddin both reviewed lbws to no avail, leaving Harris with no recourse had he sought it. To all intents a county ground, Riverside rocked for half an hour like a Test match colosseum, the crowd reading Broad's velocities off the video screen with audible relish. Dar and Hill consulted their light meters when Broad dropped short at Lyon, but stumps went everywhere next ball anyway, and the bowler took a breather after a spell of 9-2-21-5. Cook coolly turned to spin from each end for six overs while the sun was cloudbound, to ensure play continued, then recalled his quicks as it re-emerged, Broad delivering the coup de grâce when Siddle spooned a drive to mid-off. The margin of victory, 74 runs, looked the healthier for those morning runs, even if the morning itself now seemed like days ago. Certainly, nobody was talking about Batgate, which is one of temporary controversy's appeals: it is only ever filler material, for which the need disappears in the event of anything resembling good cricket.

Day One
FRIDAY 9 AUGUST

Close of play: England 1st innings 238/9
(TT Bresnan 12*, JM Anderson 16*, 90 overs)

Alastair Cook described himself as 'desperate' for a big score on the eve of this Fourth Test. For a batsman of such accomplishment, and a captain who generally takes such pains to neuter his remarks of all meaning, it was a curious lapse into candour. Because, as it turned out, he wasn't kidding. For more than three and a half hours today, his pre-emptive adjective looked uncannily well chosen; the innings certainly left despair in its wake.

The intent was clear enough. What the pros say of a golf major is also true of a Test match: you can't win it on the first day but you can lose it. Batting till the brink of tea for 51, as Cook did, was all about precaution against defeat. At that pace, however, the innings needed to wend its way deep into the second day to achieve its objective, and it fell well short. If anything it confirmed the curious irresolution that has infiltrated England's cricket since Australia's disintegration at Lord's, which may be momentary, but has given Michael Clarke's team rather more hope than they might have anticipated at this stage of the tour.

Even at his best, of course, Cook belies everything you've grown up reading about the natural elegance of left-handers – a right-handed Cook would be too ugly for words. His voluminous double backlift foreshadows violence, only for the bat swing to almost peter out, like a fist drawn back to deliver a haymaker that stops an inch from your face. Often the strokes are like little last-second twitches, the weight not quite committed, the bat applied with utmost reluctance. Then the look away to leg, the unconscious redrawing of the notch of his guard, and the quiet husbanding of energies preparatory to doing it all again.

Early on, Cook sets to defend his stumps, to resist all temptation outside the line of his eyes. He'll use the pace of the ball to nudge straight and off his legs; otherwise, with a little jink across his stumps, he leaves, and leaves, and leaves. Had a likeness been commissioned in honour of his monumental feats in Australia in 2010–11, the figure would have been posed shouldering arms.

During this series, however, Cook has been even less animate than usual: 196 runs from 583 deliveries. The Australians have starved the cut and the pull he deployed to such effect on true surfaces down under thirty months ago. He has been left to back his patience against that of the visitors – a contest that on the face of it should favour him.

'My Test career suggests I do score runs, so hopefully it's just a matter of time,' he commented on Thursday, accentuating the positive, and the temporal.

Yet the trouble with such an approach is that a scoreline of one for 75 from 35 overs can easily become three for 80 from 40 with two new batsmen at the crease. England did not subside so far today, but part of their cricket incurred risk whilst seeking to banish it. Cook's dismissal, playing no stroke to a nip-backer from Jackson Bird, was a fitting conclusion: he that lives by the scabbard shall die by the scabbard.

The main beneficiary of England's quiescence was Nathan Lyon, a supernumerary at Trent Bridge and Lord's, then a bit player at Old Trafford, who, had this been a three-Test series, might have continued the recent trend of his career into post-Warne trivia territory. His prospects did not seem rosy when Kevin Pietersen launched him down the ground for some early boundaries, and Clarke whisked the spinner from the attack for half an hour. Pietersen was hereabouts at his most mercurial, pushing to point soon after and blithely setting off for a run, abandoning Cook (41) to fate: a direct hit from Warner, who otherwise was electric in the field, would have marooned England's captain by metres.

But Lyon versus Pietersen has already acquired the quality of a parable, the good little'un against the great big'un, or a fairytale, Jack seeking to scale the beanstalk. When the off spinner resumed, Pietersen addressed him with exaggerated caution, as if to prove that he too was capable of gravitas, or perhaps that he was not to be guilty of the 'arrogance' of which Australia's in-house kidologist Shane Warne accused England a few days before. The result was a muted, slow-motion, forward-prodding demise, which Pietersen will replay in his head for a day or two, and Lyon perhaps a bit longer.

Thereafter, nobody seemed capable of playing the ball as distinct from the situation. Bell came out as if determined not to be daunted, to play like a batsman with two hundreds under his belt in the series. When that way led into indiscretion, Bairstow adopted a posture of strokeless defiance that similarly rebounded on him. From round the wicket, an angle he used profitably in India, Lyon obtained drift and drop if not inordinate turn.

The rain that saved England's blushes at Old Trafford had also saved Australia's attack from undue wear and tear, and Harris and Siddle sustained their pace and their discipline through the final session as their team tightened its grip. Bird made the most of the moistest wicket Australia has seen so far, where batting conditions will probably be at their best tomorrow – conditions Australia's batsmen might already be using but for a late flexion of England's tail.

These are awkward days for England, with nothing much to gain from two dead Tests, having achieved their mission of recapturing the Ashes, while Australia have nothing to lose, able to deem the matches irrelevant should they disappoint but able to tap them for improbable encouragement should they turn out well. Michael Clarke's team have had the better now of five of the last six consecutive days of this series. Should that tendency continue, Alastair Cook might be plumbing different depths of desperation.

Day Two
SATURDAY 10 AUGUST

Close of play: Australia 1st innings 222/5
(CJL Rogers 101*, BJ Haddin 12*, 74.4 overs)

'Maybe my future's over here,' Chris Rogers ruminated last year, as he piled up runs for Middlesex while his home state of Victoria hesitated over offering him a contract, believing him to be out of step with the march of Australian cricketainment. At the last, he was grudgingly awarded a contract at the lower end of the scale, receiving less than several juniors with superior strike rates and cooler hair.

But Rogers was right: his future *did* lie in England, his old-fashioned values having acquired a retro chic with the retirements of Ricky

Ponting and Mike Hussey. Australia's selectors were belatedly on the lookout for batsmen who placed a price on their wickets in terms of runs rather than rupees, and nobody fitted that description more exactly than the unassuming 35-year-old left-hander. His century at Riverside today was thus one he deserved rather more than Australian cricket did, although Australian cricket these days will take what it can get.

For a batsman who has done so much waiting in his career, no wait can have been as pregnant as the half-hour he spent on 96 – long enough to look in, back and also down, like the trapeze artist who cannot help but sneak a peek at the void below. Rogers had made sixty previous first-class hundreds, but somehow lost his way at Old Trafford when a three-figure score was there for the taking – this was like learning to walk having already learned to run.

Rogers is a meticulous cricketer. As the last English wicket fell in the morning, he had bolted for the pavilion to allow time for his Clark Kent-like routine of removing his glasses, inserting his contact lenses and slipping into his gear. But the lip cream and battered forearm guard suggest a degree of superstition, a belief in ritual and repetition. As he negotiated nineteen scoreless deliveries from Graeme Swann, he held fast to his processes in the way a younger batsman might not have, before seizing the opportunity finally offered. In a sense, this was the innings Rogers was brought to England to play, not only for his own sake, but for others'. An Australian specialist batsman without the name Clarke or Hussey has not scored a Test hundred since the first day of the Adelaide Test nine months ago: the team will not turn any sort of corner until a century-making habit catches on.

This was also one of those days when batsmen must reconcile themselves to being beaten every so often, as one must accept falling over as part of learning to ice skate. Rogers took the rough with the rougher, and with soft hands that kept his edges from carrying to the cordon. Having played the cover drive so effectually at Old Trafford, he here renounced it altogether, collecting just 10 runs forward of the wicket on the off side, including the disposal of a Swann full toss.

Either side of lunch, Broad kept squaring Rogers up in defence with balls zipping across him; twice the batsman inside-edged sketchily to fine leg as balls came back the other way; he went to 50 in the act of being dropped at slip as a ball seamed away, raised Australia's hundred even as he was cut in half by one that jagged in. But a couple of wild drives at Anderson in the 60s, and bottom-handed bunts in the 90s were the sum of his indiscretions.

Rogers had altogether admirable support from Shane Watson, whose 68 was the opposite of his usual innings, which of custom begins with a bang and a crash only to end in anticlimax. For once, his hangdog air looked entirely appropriate, given the scoreline of four for 76, and he betrayed nerves by jabbing lugubriously at invisible undulations and blemishes, leaving his ground so early in one instance that the ball had barely reached Prior, who semi-seriously rolled the ball towards the stumps. Then as he emerged into double figures, Watson worked two boundaries off his legs, and pulled in the air over midwicket – brave shots, but cool evaluations of circumstances. He was in the 50s before executing one of his signature clumps through cover; the way he turned strike over between times was actually more encouraging.

The most frustrating aspect of Watson has been not that he doesn't deserve his place in the Australian team, but that he actually does, not necessarily because of his spasmodic performance, but because there is nobody better – another commentary on Australian cricket's rocky modern condition. Even here, as Watson has been struggling with the bat, his preference has been justified by continued excellence with the ball – thus the endless hankering to find a role to suit his talents. It would be the most exquisite irony if that role turned out to be the same one for which he was initially selected: as a number six or seven bowling valuable relief overs.

It looked like a day England might prosper when the cloud cover remained intact and David Warner and Usman Khawaja neither quite played at nor quite left Stuart Broad. Mind you, when it comes to neither one thing nor the other, nothing quite outdoes the Decision Review System, which split hairs jesuitically over a Broad appeal against Rogers (20) who was given out caught behind on the field then not out lbw off the field, Hawk Eye suggesting no contact with the bat and only the slightest projected contact with the bails. It's getting so that the interrogation of decisions is like the reconstruction of a crime scene, even if *DRS: Durham* doesn't have quite the same gloss as *CSI: Miami.* Perversely, the decision was righter and fairer than most others this summer, although it would be funny to hear Pippa Middleton try to explain to Americans why.

Thereafter, despite the cheap removal of Clarke, England's cricket again lacked spark. The bowling was inconsistent, the fielding indifferent, the wicketkeeping untidy, the captaincy unremarkable: it says something about Cook that when he tries something different, like giving Trott three overs of bald medium pace, the result resembles county cricket in the 1960s. That's another aspect of old-fashioned values. Sometimes they just look . . . old-fashioned.

Day Three
SUNDAY 11 AUGUST

Close of play: England 2nd innings 234/5
(IR Bell 105*, TT Bresnan 4*, 74 overs)

This has been a dry summer, overhead, underfoot and with the ball, Australia's pace attack, in the persons of Ryan Harris, Peter Siddle and Shane Watson, taking 'dry' bowling to new degrees of desiccation by conceding barely 2.5 runs per over between them.

It has been bowling perfectly attuned to curbing an English top six disinclined to seize initiative at the best of times, only Kevin Pietersen among them scoring at better than 50 runs per hundreds balls in Test cricket. It has also been the kind of cricket of which Australia was not capable in 2010–11, when its plans centred on the speed, width and varying humours of Mitchell Johnson, to whom the dry life came as naturally as it did to Shane McGowan. Disciplined lines and thoughtful fields have been rewarded in other respects too: Brad Haddin today took his catches in the series to twenty-four, having in Australia thirty months ago collected just eight.

Just yesterday, however, Australia's austerity regime began to reach its limits. Pace bowlers wrung for the second time this summer by back-to-back Tests started to run dry physically. As the ball aged and softened in the afternoon, hamstrings, quadriceps and intercostals tightened, and the body of Watson, which has not borne such a series workload in five years, finally rebelled. The spirit was willing but the flesh was, as Brett Lee once said, 'running on fumes'.

It was a close-run thing, because early signs were that the policy was still wreaking an effect. In a ten-over spell broken by lunch, Harris rumbled in as relentlessly as an outback road train, powering down an off-stump highway and at last running Joe Root down. Since his big day out at Lord's, Root has been ever more backward in coming forward, scoring from only 17 of the 185 balls he has received, three of which have also dismissed him – a temporary eclipse, in all probability, but a real one all the same.

Harris kept on keeping on too. For such a husky unit, his mobility is exceptional. He power walks back to his mark, and throws himself round the field and off his own bowling, even if you can miss it because it is so affectless. On one occasion, having zigged in his follow-through, he zagged right to intercept a crisp straight drive, rose immediately from the ground and turned on his heel to accept his cap and jumper from the umpire then marched purposefully to fine leg without so much as dusting his right flank. Later, he dived to check an on-side clip from Ian Bell, chased all the way to boundary and dived again to save a single run, pulling the ball back with an outstretched hand as his body vaulted the boundary rope. Alec Bedser wouldn't have attempted it – although, of course, Harris wasn't expected to walk home to Woking in his bowling boots in the evening.

Straining to break the bonds Harris clamped on them, Cook and Trott also succumbed to old weaknesses, the cover drive and the half-hook. Barely in the black with seven wickets remaining, England were in danger of wasting a tidy morning's work evicting the last five Australians inside fifteen overs. But when Harris was relieved, Bell and Pietersen found the going freer, collecting their runs at a healthy 3.2 an over without taking needless risks. Accreting ever more heavily behind point as his opportunities in front of square have been curtailed, Bell has demonstrated growing versatility as a strokeplayer this summer. He took such toll of the bowling to third man that Australia might conceivably have posted a fourth, fifth and sixth man, even if Clarke in the main kept the boundary unpatrolled – a rare omission from a skipper who so seldom misses a trick.

Only after Bell had been in occupation for a couple of hours did he hazard his pet cover drive – compact, grooved, as familiar now as a popular catchphrase. Wagon wheels scarcely do Bell justice, for they cannot convey how often he finds space in fields inaccessible to others, how regularly he sets two fielders in pursuit because the ball has bisected them so perfectly. Roughed up by Harris from round the wicket late in the day, he did not seem so much disturbed as pleased to be fully occupied.

Even at somewhere below his best, as he was today, Pietersen defies containment, turning length balls into half-volleys with his forward stretch, seeking gaps on the on side from fourth stump deliveries, never averse to a challenge. He played the day's most dynamic strokes, hooking Siddle superbly first behind then in front of square to the boundary, with so long to play the shots that he almost looked to be lying in ambush. Finally he breached a technical canon of his old coach Duncan Fletcher, that you should play off spin by staying leg side of the ball and hitting through the line, otherwise you risk playing with half a bat – which is exactly what Pietersen proceeded to do, tamely front-edging Lyon to cover. By then, though, England was as comfortable as Watson was uncomfortable, undergoing treatment for an indeterminate 'right hip/groin pain'; Siddle and Bird looked like they wouldn't mind a rest either.

In sight of stumps, Bell found an especially galling gap, between keeper and slip – the gap of eight Tests and nearly eight months since Australia's last victory veritably yawned. The visitors have hardly been alone in appearing weary in this game: even Anderson's frictionless gears are showing signs of corrosion. But it was a harsh setback for a team that has had the better of six of the seven preceding days of the series without experiencing a scoreline benefit. The new ball tomorrow morning looms as a last chance to redeem a summer so far dry of success.

Day Four
MONDAY 12 AUGUST

Close of play: Australia 2nd innings 224
(68.3 overs) – end of match

It was director Erich von Stroheim whom they dubbed 'the man you love to hate'. This Ashes has outdone Hollywood in providing two such men, and today at Riverside was their day: David Warner and Stuart Broad, cricketers who fit right into an Ashes panto pantheon, perfect bait for boos.

They have rather more than that in common too – both are high-strung cricketers who have known phases of distinct ordinariness in their careers; both are high-impact players who can win matches in an hour. This might have been a different series had Warner not gone walkabout in Birmingham and been available to play for Australia from the beginning, although perhaps only slightly different, because England have in Broad a type even rarer in this age of 'good areas' and 'asking questions': a bowler of genuine speed.

Today was actually England's best win of the summer: not as exciting as Trent Bridge or as overwhelming as Lord's, but following a genuine contest, with the last two days a considerable improvement on Old Trafford. It is next to impossible to maintain total intensity over the duration of a five-Test series, let alone a ten-Test cycle, but England perceptibly raised their effort a cog in and around tea, to give Australia a sense of the level they must attain to win Test matches.

They needed to, and they knew it. The DRS might have had another patchy Test here, but it has a certain efficacy as a kind of real-time barometer of players' innermost thoughts. In the third over of Australia's chase, there was one such interlude, James Anderson appealing for lbw against Chris Rogers, only to see Tony Hill shake his head.

Those who have watched this series will know that Tony Hill shaking his head is usually only an interlocutory stage in the arrival at a decision – something to get out of the way before the serious stuff starts. On this occasion, however, Hill was correct; he even looked correct to the naked eye, the ball appearing to pitch outside leg stump.

After the Trent Bridge Test, much was said about England's mastery of the DRS. They had a process, a checklist, a designated on-field consultation committee – they probably had a management diagram and kaizen performance matrices. Yet Alastair Cook made the gesture as integral to these Ashes as the sprinkler dance was thirty months ago, and the replays began rolling in the third umpire booth and across the big screen.

For once there was no need to consider how the device might be improved by think music: the miscalculation quickly became clear, and so, perhaps, did the underlying anxiety. England had almost 300 to defend, against a batting line-up that's had more changes than the Sugababes, but did they sense already an underlying trickiness to the task, that they would risk one of their precious reviews on something so speculative?

Their apprehension became understandable when Warner scored freely, almost breezily, speeding Australia to their first 50 in 75 balls and their second in another 85. Whatever he's like after dark, he has an undeniable presence at the crease, a busy, bustling, happy-go-lucky air – you could almost hear him emit a Muttley-like snigger after he hit Graeme Swann's second ball for six today. As in the field, he surged between wickets as though to breast an imaginary tape.

While he reserves his trademark switch hit for T20, Warner has one Test match shot all his own, where he rocks onto the back foot and brings the bat down with a force and intent similar to a butcher using a meat cleaver – at his best, only an off-side sweeper, of which Cook finally had to avail himself yesterday, has a chance of intercepting this shot. It is testament to the percussive force of the modern cricket bat, but also to an eye uncannily quick to detect and deal with errors of length.

It took the day's best ball to unseat him, a rasping chest-high lifter from the undersung Tim Bresnan, who thereby justified his selection ahead of the horses-for-courses pick of Graham Onions. The way was then open for Broad, who is saved from irritating England fans perhaps only by his propensity for irritating Australian fans. Whatever your allegiance, his highs are now as high as any cricketer in the world. Just weeks ago, Broad went 326 deliveries between wickets. In that same span today he could have bowled Australia out about six times over. And if he bowled the ball with which he dismissed Clarke a hundred times, I fancy he'd do him more often than not.

Dennis Lillee's fitness guru Frank Pyke once said that the ideal fast bowler would be a 'beautifully coordinated giant', not only because of the advantage of his height but the length of his arms, thereby providing the leverage conducive to real pace. No bowler on either side fits this bill better than Broad, 196 cm in the socks he reveals during one of his periodic pit stops to adjust his boots. He is best appreciated from side on, where the sweep of his arms and the brace of his front leg can be seen levering off one another, generating speeds that yesterday neared 150kmh. His flaw is a reluctance to bowl full, for he is loath to be driven, but after tea he attacked the stumps as much as the batsmen: two bowleds, three lbws and a catch at mid-off tell the tale.

There was some seriously fine bowling in this match. In the morning, to finish with innings figures of seven for 117 from 28 overs, Ryan Harris pursued England's tail like an implacable bounty hunter, ending with something like a shootout as Bresnan and Swann fired with random gusto. The 79 England added for its last three wickets was to prove more than useful; it might even have been essential.

Nathan Lyon completed a match analysis of seven for 97 from 42.1 overs, which in the post-Warne era nearly justifies a ticker-tape parade, but this was overshadowed by a more melancholy personal landmark. Since he became Australia's 'song master', leader of the victory chorus of 'Under the Southern Cross', after being hand-picked by predecessor Mike Hussey, Lyon has not once been called on in this capacity. In that time, Australia has lost seven of its eight Tests. There is a certain malicious pleasure in being a villain, but it's better always to be a winner.

FOURTH TEST Riverside Ground, Chester-le-Street 9–12 August 2013

Toss England   **England won by 74 runs**

ENGLAND	1st Innings			2nd Innings		
AN Cook*	lbw	b Bird	51	c Haddin	b Harris	22
JE Root	c Haddin	b Watson	16		b Harris	2
IJL Trott	c Khawaja	b Lyon	49	c Haddin	b Harris	23
KP Pietersen	c Haddin	b Lyon	26	c Rogers	b Lyon	44
IR Bell	c Harris	b Lyon	6		b Harris	113
JM Bairstow	lbw	b Lyon	14	c Haddin	b Lyon	28
MJ Prior†	lbw	b Siddle	17		b Harris	0
TT Bresnan	not out		12	c and	b Harris	45
SCJ Broad	c Warner	b Harris	3	c Smith	b Harris	13
GP Swann	c Lyon	b Harris	13	not out		30
JM Anderson		b Bird	16	c Haddin	b Lyon	0
EXTRAS	(b 5, lb 1, w 3, nb 6)		15	(b 4, lb 5, w 1)		10
TOTAL	(92 overs; 399 mins)		238	(95.1 overs; 405 mins)		330

AUSTRALIA	1st Innings			2nd Innings		
CJL Rogers	c Prior	b Swann	110	c Trott	b Swann	49
DA Warner		b Broad	3	c Prior	b Bresnan	71
UT Khawaja	c Prior	b Broad	0	lbw	b Swann	21
MJ Clarke*	c Cook	b Broad	6		b Broad	21
SPD Smith	c Prior	b Bresnan	17		b Broad	2
SR Watson	c Prior	b Broad	68	lbw	b Bresnan	2
BJ Haddin†	lbw	b Swann	13	lbw	b Broad	4
PM Siddle	c Cook	b Anderson	5	c Anderson	b Broad	23
RJ Harris	lbw	b Broad	28	lbw	b Broad	11
NM Lyon	lbw	b Anderson	4		b Broad	8
JM Bird	not out		0	not out		1
EXTRAS	(b 2, lb 11, w 1, nb 2)		16	(b 6, lb 5)		11
TOTAL	(89.3 overs; 410 mins)		270	(68.3 overs; 293 mins)		224

AUSTRALIA									
1st Innings	O	M	R	W	2nd Innings	O	M	R	W
RJ Harris	19	3	70	2		28	2	117	7
JM Bird	22	9	58	2		20.3	6	67	0
SR Watson	13	6	21	1		6.3	1	22	0
PM Siddle	18	6	41	1		17	4	59	0
NM Lyon	20	7	42	4		22.1	3	55	3
SPD Smith						1	0	1	0

ENGLAND									
1st Innings	O	M	R	W	2nd Innings	O	M	R	W
JM Anderson	25	8	65	2		16	1	73	0
SCJ Broad	24.3	7	71	5		18.3	3	50	6
TT Bresnan	19	3	63	1		13	2	36	2
GP Swann	18	5	48	2		18	6	53	2
IJL Trott	3	0	10	0					
JE Root						3	2	1	0

FALL OF WICKETS				
Wicket	Eng - 1st	Aus - 1st	Eng - 2nd	Aus - 2nd
1st	34	12	17	109
2nd	107	12	42	147
3rd	149	49	49	168
4th	153	76	155	174
5th	155	205	221	175
6th	189	224	251	179
7th	193	233	251	181
8th	198	245	275	199
9th	214	258	317	211
10th	238	270	330	224

Umpires: Aleem Dar (Pakistan) and AL Hill (New Zealand)
Referee: RS Mahanama (Sri Lanka)

THE FIFTH TEST: The Oval

HUSSEY'S LEGACY

The Oval is the oldest of England's Test grounds, having hosted the country's very first Anglo-Australian cricket encounter; it is also by convention the venue of the last match in each English Ashes series. The latter being so, it is no stranger to notionally 'dead' Tests, often demonstrating that reports of their demise have been exaggerated. If it comes to it, Sir Donald Bradman's farewell was in a 'dead' Test, and seemed no less dramatically vibrant because of it; likewise the triumphs of Derek Underwood in 1968 and Dennis Lillee in 1972, and even Phil Tufnell in 1997, none of which could influence custody of the urn.

But Australia arrives here to meet England on Wednesday for a match reflective of the ground's dual character: for a 'dead' Test that needs to be the first of the rest of the cricket life of Michael Clarke's team. The present 0–3 deficit reflects how badly Australia has played this summer, but not how well for quite prolonged stages; a 0–4 deficit, in the event of a further defeat at the Oval, would be a correspondingly cruel fate. To future generations, however, such nuances will mean nothing. The latter scoreline would imply a gap in quality between the teams even more cavernous than in 2010–11, when Australia, thanks to Mitchell Johnson and Ryan Harris, were at least able to take a Test off an opponent that otherwise routed it thrice by an innings.

Winning something at last, by contrast, would amount to more than a consolation prize, such as England was able to secure at the Oval in 1993 and Sydney in 2003 after being comprehensively bested. It would break the self-reinforcingly barren streak of eight winless Tests accumulated through India and England that is now obviously preying on a callow team. If it wouldn't provide momentum – and this series has offered ample further evidence of cricket's defiantly anti-Newtonian qualities – it would arrest what might be called Australia's *nomentum*: the doubt that gnaws at its cricketers, and can undermine them all at once, as in the middle session of the second day at Lord's and the final session of the fourth day at Riverside.

Anatomising Australia's defeats this year is a bit like what it must be to psychoanalyse Woody Allen: out of all the abundant troubles, traumas, phobias and anxieties, which to choose? The serial choppings and changings? The procession of number threes? The deteriorating consistency of Michael Clarke with the bat? The depressing consistency of Shane Watson with the pad? Thus one hesitates to add another, except that Riverside brought it into sharp focus: an underestimation of the importance of the number six role in the team's batting order.

It's no fluke, I suspect, that the final collapse in Australia's fortunes has been coincident with the unexpected retirement of Mike Hussey during this year's Sydney Test. In the last three years of his career, Hussey carved out a crucial role as redeemer-in-chief. Clarke clocked up the individual statistics; Hussey became the master partner, the striker of alliances, the bulwark against the aforementioned *nomentum*.

Australia has been losing wickets in bunches for some time now, especially, since the dissolving of the mighty opening partnership of Matt Hayden and Justin Langer, at the top. But until Hussey's departure it had not really been losing them in bushels. Now when a slide begins there seems to be no arresting it, and no point round which to rally. Seven batsmen have filled the number six slot in the last eight Tests for a total of three half-centuries in sixteen innings. The player who made the best fist of the task, Phil Hughes, whose fine unbeaten

81 in the position at Trent Bridge enabled Ashton Agar's dream debut, has not filled the role since.

The current incumbent, Shane Watson, was given the breach to fill after failing as an opener. Nor did he bat there in the subsequent tour match at Northampton. Perhaps he lost the game of rock-paper-scissors by which the Australians seem to have determined their batting orders this season. Yet at Riverside, Watson actually showed the position's pivotal nature to good advantage: he was Chris Rogers' soundest support in the first innings, making the most of a sunny day and a soft old ball to steer Australia to a lead; by becoming part of the roadkill in the second innings, he then guaranteed there would be no fightback.

Hussey, then, has proven to be one of those cricketers best appreciated in their absence. He was always known to be important – it's only now that we fully grasp the multiplier effect of his contributions. For while a solid number six may not be an obvious matchwinner, he will assuredly make you harder to beat. And at the moment Australia has no need greater than to stop losing.

So to the Oval, *fons et origo* of Australia's Ashes story 131 years ago, and also where Australia last lost the Ashes, along with its status as number one Test nation, this time four years ago. That match was also the occasion on which, after an indifferent series, Hussey scored a skilful and spirited Test century to rejuvenate his career. Here's a message for Michael Clarke's men to believe in: that renewal is possible in even the most unpromising of circumstances.

Summary
ENGLAND RAINS SUPREME

Given the reliance the English place on weather as a conversational subject, it's not surprising they created a game in cricket acutely in thrall to the elements, where sun, cloud, rain and gloom can be news as good for some as bad for others. The Oval served up a classically

English Test, where what was set up by an excess of rain was ruined
at last by a lack of light – and perhaps also by a lack of administrative
common sense that makes an archaism like 'player safety' a consideration in an age when cricketers enjoy only slightly less protection than
former wiseguys testifying against the Mafia. In the end, a draw was
arguably the fairest result. Australia hardly deserved to lose after having much the better of the first three days, and England did not quite
deserve to win despite re-emphasising their bottom-line superiority on
the final day. Clarke and Cook having shown willing, it was, perhaps,
their shared triumph.

Some feeling entered into the preparatory sparring when Stuart
Broad gave a damnfool interview in which he praised himself for not
walking at Trent Bridge, citing it as evidence of his team's 'win-at-
all-costs mentality'; Darren Lehmann responded with a damnfool
interview accusing Broad of 'blatant cheating' and exhorting Australian
fans to 'send him home crying' during the Ashes of 2013–14, and there
was a general comparison of umbrages. Little harm was done, save
by Cricket Australia, who in failing to do anything made it a case of
dumb, dumber, dumbest. Interesting times.

Otherwise, England's lead being unassailable at last, and the English
Premier League having commenced, there was an end-of-school-term
feel to the match's preliminaries. Clarke talked experimentally before
the match of including Matthew Wade as an ersatz number three;
Cook seemed set on Chris Tremlett, in the wings since Old Trafford.
In the end, Australia called up James Faulkner, probably on the say-so
of long-time booster Shane Warne, and England capped second spinner Simon Kerrigan and third seamer-cum-batsman Chris Woakes,
apparently because of a last-minute mowing of the pitch. Australia,
who named their squad a full day in advance, had more to show for
their decisiveness, even if the main thing they got right was by accident: the promotion of Shane Watson to number three because of the
desire for an extra bowler, and the toss, affording first use of a surface
that might almost have been laid in adobe brick.

When Watson was 8, Anderson nipped one into his front pad in the fashion so familiar all summer long, but Aleem Dar shook his head, and England elected not to refer – wisely, as it turned out, for the black box spat out a simulation showing less than half the virtual ball striking the vapour stump. Watson had been given out at Old Trafford in almost identical circumstances, albeit the ball was slightly newer here, and Anderson apt to swing it just that little more. In other words, it was a good decision that could easily have gone the other way, and on such infinitesimal margins can a day, even a career, hinge. Watson was soon striding from strength to strength. Once Anderson and Broad had been seen off, he collared the debutants Kerrigan and Woakes gladly, taking 6 fours each from their opening spells; he fell on Kerrigan like Homer Simpson on a plate of donuts. With figures of 2-0-28-0, the hapless Kerrigan was not so much rested as spared, and would be allotted only half a dozen more forgettable overs in the match.

When he had finished mauling the newbies, Watson was 76 from 71 deliveries, and with a sniff of a pre-lunch hundred; he settled for a hundred further runs from 175 deliveries, with a lull or two, including 41 minutes in the nineties, about ten of them recovering from being struck behind the left ear as he reeled back from a Broad bouncer. All the while he strove not to commit his front leg too soon and to play plumbline straight, profiting to the on side as England targeted his pads, and gradually turning a weakness into a strength: he scored 91, including 35 singles, in the quadrant of the field from mid-on to square leg, but only 34, with just three singles, in front of square to the off. Anderson's restored thrust kept England in touch until midafternoon, and Broad again discombobulated Clarke with the short ball. But when Smith settled in with Watson, the sun blessed their partnership. They looked an unlikely duo between wickets: Watson jogs like a soldier in full pack, Smith zips from end to end as if on a skateboard. Otherwise they fed off one another, Watson enjoying the back-up, Smith the front-up. Both put their luck to good use, Watson in being dropped at slip by Cook off Anderson at 104, Smith in having been thrice reprieved by the umpires at Old Trafford. The former was unfortunate in picking out Pietersen at deep backward square leg with a flat hook after more than five and a half hours, ending the partnership at 145 from 266 balls; the latter buckled down in the last hour to ensure his presence on the morrow.

After the nightwatchman Siddle had fallen following a delayed start, Smith added 65 from 89 balls with a careful Haddin, then reached a maiden Test century with the maximum impudence: a six down the ground from Trott's amiable mediums. He had gone close before, if never so convincingly: it was the final leap of a player who had been edging ahead little by little. Australia's tailenders sold themselves dearly and gaily too, helping Smith put on 107 in 96 balls, and leaving Cook nonplussed before he had to take Root in to see through the day's eighteen concluding overs.

As it unfolded, England's batting exhibited the same qualities as the pitch, being hard, slow and featureless. Dull? Maybe, although the patience and intensity of the third day was uninteresting only if one thinks of entertainment purely terms of big hitting and/or batting collapses. The superb Harris, whom Australia had given thought to resting, reached his highest speeds of the series: day in, day out, there had been no better bowler on show all summer. It was also a sight to see a batsman as instinctively dominant as Pietersen resist his predisposition for more than three hours, and a batsman as youthful as Root carve out a groove for almost four. It also, kind of, worked, in the sense that 176 was the highest score at which England's third wicket had fallen all summer, and Australia's bowlers were waylaid in the field for a full day ahead of a probable last-day assignment bowling England out. Some interplay twixt Pietersen and Clarke added colour to proceedings, and some chutzpah from the ebullient Faulkner a soundtrack. 'Any time they feel threatened they sort of go in their shell and play pretty defensive cricket,' he complained of the Englishmen, if, with his team 0–3 in the series, not exactly from a position of strength.

London awoke to rain on the fourth morning, and it never budged, leaving Australia to fret about contriving a target, and England to consider taking one up. With only thirteen wickets having fallen in the match so far, prospects for the fifth day were hardly rosy. But now defeat had been almost ruled out, England were prepared to search for the initiative, and began to wrestle Australia for it. Led by Prior and Swann, their last six biffed and scrambled 130 from 168 deliveries; led by Broad and Anderson, they kept Australia's slogging within bounds, Swann pitching in with the crucial wicket of Watson after he had been dropped at mid-off by Broad on 0. And Clarke's anxiety to conjure a result – 'to be prepared to lose in order to win' as his confrère Shane Warne kept repeating on Sky like an advertising slogan – showed through at tea when he offered a scenario from which only England could really win.

There was much exuberant praise for Clarke 'making a game of it' afterwards, and it did make for a more exciting last session than anyone could have expected, but it was a gauntlet rather desperately thrown down. Because, needing to score 227 at less than a run a ball, England picked it up and started using it to slap him round the face. Cook and Trott took on an attack in which Harris was limited by a hamstring strain and Siddle by accumulated weariness, pacing the opening to a nicety; Pietersen then surged to history's fastest Ashes 50, in 36 deliveries, at which stage in his previous innings he was still in single figures. Suddenly, Clarke could see a scoreline of 0–4, and it must have felt like someone had walked over his grave; suddenly, defensive cricket became a game that two could play, and it was Australia whose overs were dragging out, Australia whose fielders were taking long detours, Australians who were taking a long time over not much. 'Same old Aussies!' chorused the inhabitants of the OCS Stand. 'Always cheating!' Ah, the classics.

It was Clarke's newest cap who came to his aid, Faulkner also learning to embrace defensive cricket with three excellent overs full of his T20 variations – slower, quicker, fuller, wider – then catching Trott and Pietersen as they tried to work to leg, the lbws also finely judged by Dar. England was in no danger of defeat, but in Bell and Woakes had two new batsmen with far-flung fields to find boundaries through. That they found the space to add 36 in 26 deliveries was altogether commendable, but when Bell was run out by Starc in his follow-through, hurling down the stumps ahead of the striker's scurry home, the light was discernably poor – worse on the reading, in fact, than that in which the teams had quit Old Trafford on the fourth evening, to Clarke's chagrin. *Exeunt omnes*, with a bit of badinage passed between Prior and the Australians, perhaps about defensive cricket.

The other Clarke, Giles of the ECB, issued a thunderous release, which can be distilled to 'same old ICC, always bungling' – ironic, of course, seeing that he is one of the body's most powerful executive board members, and belongs to the aforesaid classic category. But hey, the lateness of the hour was good for the fireworks, if not for deadlines: thus it was that Aussie pressmen were still hard at work when several English players reportedly revived the sprinkler dance in more rudimentary form. At least Stuart Broad didn't try to justify it as evidence of a wee-at-all-costs mentality, while Darren Lehmann kept his own counsel. Some lessons had been learned.

Day One
WEDNESDAY 21 AUGUST

Close of play: Australia 1st innings 307/4
(SPD Smith 66*, PM Siddle 18*, 90 overs)

Australian cricket fans are on the hunt for what David Warner's brother calls 'escape goats', and sooner or later they're going to have to stop kvetching about Stuart Broad – their coach Darren Lehmann included.

That being so, Shane Watson's mighty 176 at the Oval today could hardly have come at a better moment. He presents the disenchanted with an inviting target: he bats, he bowls, he broods; he carries himself like Marvin the Paranoid Android making a cameo appearance in *Baywatch*. When Michael Clarke agreed during his pre-match press conference that 'maybe' some toughness had been lacking in Australia's cricket this summer, it had an echo of the judgement that Watson was 'sometimes' a team player emitted by a Cricket Australia official six months ago.

Above all Watson can make it look easy. Even the briefest glimpse of him at the crease suggests a player of high, if sometimes rather mechanical, quality. He loads up massively on the back foot, like the plunger on a pinball machine being retracted to propel the silver sphere into the playfield. With the ball in flight, his front foot seems almost to hang in space, in search of a safe landing area; it savours of all the time in the world, even if it has ended rather too often in recent times with his left pad in harm's way.

Watson did all this again today. The difference was that he went on doing it. This was a smart innings. Watson slotted some early boundaries to soothe his nerves; he also missed some good deliveries he needed not to nick. He flourished his trademark off drive but also on-drove a four with a flexing of the wrists, a conspicuous act of straightness. As England probed away at his pads, he scored two-thirds of his runs to leg, with discretion and attention.

Watson also identified key moments and won them convincingly. First he challenged a teasing Swann by striking him for a calculated straight six, whereupon the spinner swapped to round the wicket and pursued a more defensive line. Then he took punitive toll of England's two debutants. When James Anderson gave way to Chris Woakes after an hour, it was like the difference between an invasive body search and a perfunctory frisking. Woakes could find nothing like a reliable length, was alternately too short and too full, and generally too amiable. Watson pulled one half-tracker off the front foot so jubilantly as to rotate more than 360 degrees. Had he hit it harder he might have corkscrewed into the ground.

Coming in off a diffident step, Simon Kerrigan looked happy

enough for the ball to arrive at the other end, let alone with any rotation. 'Pie chucker' did not begin to describe it; these were nothing so butch as pies, they were more mini-quiches or vol-au-vents. What Monty Panesar unleashed on those hapless nightclub bouncers in Brighton had more venom and purpose.

The most impressive stage of Watson's innings was post-lunch, however, when he took care to consolidate the position he had built up. Having sprinted to their second fifty in 47 balls, Australia took 128 over their third, as Watson spent 41 painstaking minutes inching his way through the last 10 runs of his hundred. He would have been pardoned nerves. Watson in the nineties has been like English cricket in the nineties: an accident waiting to happen. Yet he was prudent rather than hesitant. The defensive shots were well grooved and well groomed. While his captain was being bombed from short of a length at one end, Watson dug himself a secure foxhole at the other. And after tea, Watson did as a Test batsman should once past a hundred – set himself to double down, while taking toll of tiring bowling with a soft ball about whose shape England went through their now standard charade.

In achieving a third Test hundred so commandingly, of course, there is a sense in which Watson deepened rather than resolved his enigma, delivering at precisely the moment Australia ceased to indulge him. His promotion to open the batting, after a long phase of his agitating for it, was the first executive decision of Lehmann's tenure. The role in which he has at last succeeded, by contrast, was arrived at by default: when all the other places were filled, number three was what Watson was left with. This, of course, has been the poisoned chalice in Australia's top order – and he put it to his lips like it was Krug from a supermodel's Manolo Blahnik.

Did Watson need to feel the wall at his back? Was he better pressed into service without the scope to ponder where he might do better? Was he empowered by batting in a first innings and the relief from bowling? Let the theorising begin, for if the factor could be identified, extracted, bottled and refrigerated, Lehmann would carry it round in his personal esky.

It's not clear whether Lehmann had been partaking of the contents of said esky when he addressed his pre-match comments regarding Stuart Broad to an Australian radio station, but they weren't his shrewdest of the tour, and stand in rather stark contrast to the dignity and pragmatism of the Australian camp's original response to Broad's Trent Bridge stayputitude.

Mind you, Lehmann's remarks were no more ludicrous than those to which they were a response: Broad's attempt to turn his cynical opportunism into an emblem of flinty hardness. Welcome as Broad is to stand his ground till kingdom come when given not out after nicking one, he shouldn't expect an iota of credit for doing so. While he might not deserve to be an 'escape goat', nor does Broad deserve to escape scot-free.

Day Two
THURSDAY 22 AUGUST

Close of play: England 1st innings 32/0
(AN Cook 17*, JE Root 13*, 17.3 overs)

It's surprising more batsmen don't go to their hundreds with sixes. Think about it. You're well set. Invitations are usually being dangled. The field is usually up, and the air might be the safest place to hit the ball. Doug Walters earned immortality by doing it once, Ken Barrington a reputation by doing it several times.

It's the fear of ignominy and self-recrimination, of course, that generally holds cricketers back. You'll punish yourself less for perishing through too much care rather than too little – or that's the way conventional thinking runs. So it requires reasoning that's a little counterintuitive to choose the more aggressive option. But Steve Smith has always been a rather counterintuitive, if not counter-exemplary, cricketer, and a six was the way he chose today to raise his maiden Test hundred.

Here's how Smith might have summed it up. He was 94. Four fielders were bunched on the off, saving one; mid-on had also been brought in to police leg-side singles; Jonathan Trott was trundling in from the Vauxhall end like the shade of Brian Close rolling his arm over on a shirtfront at Weston-super-Mare. Little guide was offered on how to proceed by Smith's brief Test career, twice in which he has fallen in sight of three figures: he was stumped toe on line on 92, stretching tentatively forward, in Mohali five months ago, and caught on 89, head in the air, in Manchester three weeks ago. So hey, why not live a little? After all, only about forty overs remained of a truncated day – the more reason not to draw matters out unnecessarily. As the lusty up-and-under came to earth half a dozen rows back in the OCS Stand, Smith gestured cheerfully to dressing-room comrades. Off came the helmet to reveal his improbably cherubic features.

These may actually be a bit of a handicap to Smith, still only twenty-four and nobody's idea of a bristling, bustling, implacable Aussie hard nut. He still resembles one of those precocious nine-year-old scamps who rules his backyard, badgering his siblings and parents to bowl to him; setting off between wickets, he lowers his head and pumps his arms like he's running away after retrieving the ball from next door's Alsatian.

The first time Smith was chosen against England, in fact, it was with the instruction to play up to that mischievous persona, to lighten the Australian camp's dark mood with a joke or two – something he rather naively revealed, and on which England predictably pounced. 'Tell us a joke, Smiffy,' James Anderson would say slyly whenever they were in proximity.

Smith's cricket remains unreconstructed. He waves his bat towards fourth slip as the bowler approaches, then actually aims it towards point as the bowler releases, as though he's giving directions rather than shaping to play a stroke. As the ball nears his zone, however, Smith seems to jerk into position like a puppeteer has yanked his strings, and his bat descends with convincing force: a straight drive from Woakes, a square drive from Broad and a cover drive from Anderson today defied the moist outfield to hold them up. Shane Watson hardly struck the ball harder on the first day than Smith on the second. As the field dispersed, with at times as many as six fielders on the perimeter, Smith hit gaps hard, challenging the older Brad Haddin and Ryan Harris to keep up.

Like Australia's, Smith's tour has been a chequered one. He might not have been chosen for the Oval at all had he not enjoyed effectively four innings at Old Trafford thanks to the pardons of Tony Hill and the protocols of the DRS. Yet he has ended up contributing runs or wickets in four of the five Tests, which is rather more than most of his teammates, and the nearest he came to offering a chance here was squeezing home on 89 responding to a call for a single from Haddin, Trott throwing at the striker's stumps with too much elevation and too little conviction – neither team, incidentally, has had much luck, or indeed shown much skill, at hitting the stumps direct this summer, for all their interminable practising of the activity.

Otherwise, this was assuredly a frustrating day for the visitors, who perhaps sensed that they'd left their best till last and also dampest. 'Grrr, rain at the Oval,' growled Shane Warne, clearing his throat on Twitter in the morning. 'Anyone know if this rain will go away & play can start or is it set in all day?' The strains of 'Jerusalem' were not to be heard until 2.25 pm; if forecasts can be believed, we may be fortunate to hear them at all on Saturday.

Later in the day the great man could be heard complaining on Sky about England's lassitude bowling their overs. Rightly so, too. In the hour after tea, England were capable of barely a ball a minute, going about their task with all the vigour of participants in one of those work-for-welfare schemes where one man digs a hole and another man fills it in. Nothing counterintuitive to see here – just good new-fashioned professionalism.

As Australia's pace bowlers hurried through their abbreviated late shift, Michael Clarke swinging them round busily in search of a breakthrough, Smith might actually have been worth a bowl – partly to keep the light-conscious umpires sweet, partly for a further pleasing glimpse of the less obvious.

Day Three
FRIDAY 23 AUGUST

Close of play: England 1st innings 247/4
(IR Bell 29*, CR Woakes 15*, 116 overs)

There's a nice story in Matt Prior's autobiography about the aftermath of England's marathon batting effort, led by Alastair Cook and Jonathan Trott, to draw the Brisbane Test of 2010. Prior describes his team's long-time batting coach Graham Gooch surveying the Gabba scoreboard across which the visitors' total of one for 517 was emblazoned. 'That's what every scoreboard should look like,' said Gooch with satisfaction.

There have been few such causes for celebration for Gooch this summer: it has been a low-scoring Ashes on slow pitches that have militated against utter batting dominance by either team. But for all its occasional austerity, today at the Oval was about as effective a day as England's top order has enjoyed during the series.

All pitched in, none stood out; there were none of the 'daddy hundreds' Gooch values most, but this was a communal effort. It started, in a way, with Gooch himself, out there at 9 am hurling balls at his batsmen with his familiar sidearm, as indispensable to him as the bullwhip to Indiana Jones. Not that there's anything heroic about Gooch, with his round shoulders, top-heavy physique, slightly hangdog air – nothing anyway apart from his record, of forty years at the top, tens of thousands of runs, and hundreds of thousands of kilometres of travel in cricket's name. What John Arlott said of Maurice Tate applies no less to Gooch: he has not so much played cricket as lived in it.

No Ashes series in history has been undertaken with such extensive backroom staffs: selectors, coaches, assistant coaches, specialist coaches, conditioning coaches, analysts, physiotherapists, media professionals. This development, furthermore, has occurred in a relatively short time: as recently as 2005, Australia toured here without a bowling coach, and England's use in that role of Troy Cooley was regarded as a shaft of organisational genius.

Yet despite the elapse of nearly two decades since he played his last internationals, Gooch fits this system almost perfectly. A batsman who had his technical travails, he was among the first to use a specialist consultant – not that he ever had the title or a formal role, but Gooch's Essex teammate Alan Lilley was his batting go-to guy for much of his career. A roly-poly young cricketer, Gooch also set himself apart in his time with a zeal for physical preparation. Perhaps the closest he has come to a coaching *mot* is the observation that nobody was ever a poorer cricketer for being physically fitter. It could almost be the motto of young athletes now in his charge.

As for his actual contribution, a few days ago an interesting interview with Gooch by the former Lancashire cricketer Nick Speak, conducted during the Riverside Test, appeared on an Australian sports website. In it, Gooch was anxious to downplay his influence, but there was something arresting about his reduction of batting to four fundamentals: technique, attitude, knowledge and concentration. Simple, accessible, achievable: this is coaching with players in mind, not an invisible scientific-cum-biomechanical gallery.

Technique, Gooch was wont to say, was not all. Prophetically, the Australian player he most liked the look of was Steve Smith, hardly an MCC fashion plate: 'Smith is an interesting player. He is unorthodox and can be difficult to bowl at . . . and I like his attitude.' He reserved his greatest approbation, not surprisingly, for Ian Bell, and as the Englishman guided his team through today's last session it was hard to dispute Gooch's view of him as 'a player in total control of his game'.

Today's *Times* carried an elegant and incisive column by my colleague Simon Barnes about the irresistible rise of the manager in English football – how Premier League clashes are increasingly interpreted as the duels of two suited greybeards. Cricket, Barnes observed, had not gone the same way. Nobody, he noted, thinks of the Ashes in terms of Andy Flower's England versus Darren Lehmann's Australia. The authorial signature on particular cricket policies or tactics is generally illegible. When Michael Clarke stands by the striker's stumps and adjusts his field a foot here and an inch there, he looks like a man in complete and efficient charge – if also a little like a fusspot attending to the feng shui of his living room.

Just occasionally we are reminded of the density of expertise on which the players can now call. When James Anderson dismissed Chris Rogers with a subtle cutter at Trent Bridge, for example, he gestured expansively to his team's balcony where bowling coach David Saker acknowledged the credit. More often, we are guessing. What was Gooch's contribution to England's performance yesterday? Joe Root showed off a pull that's not yet quite fluent, but which will give him attacking options on Australian wickets; Jonathan Trott exhibited some of his old granite-like texture; Alastair Cook nicked off frustratingly early. Four for 247: might have been better, could have been worse.

On the night before this Test match, though, Gooch was among the guest panellists at an evening in honour of the *Guardian*'s peerless nostalgist Frank Keating, one of whose best works, written as Gooch's handpicked literary partner, was *Gooch: The Autobiography*, which manages to be humble and humorous while also bringing out its subject's dignity and integrity.

Gooch reminisced about England's troubled 1981 tour of the West Indies, which Keating also chronicled in moving depth, recounting how his captain Ian Botham forbade running in the mornings because it prevented Gooch from propping up the bar in evenings. He responded with wry humour to the inevitable inquiries about tensions between him and his other great contemporary David Gower.

As Gooch warmed his young men up this morning, of course, both Botham and Gower were aloft in the Sky eyrie – still national favourites. Yet it's arguable that Gooch has left a deeper imprint on modern cricket than either. There are no Bothams or Gowers on the scene today. But there are, in a way, Gooches: batsmen to whom he has imparted his technical acumen, institutional memory and work ethic. They prepare with methodical intent – like Gooch. They stand tall, bats upraised – like Gooch. They . . . well, they like Gooch, and his long and deep relationships, especially with former Essex colleagues Flower and Cook, are fundamental to the England set-up. He'll be out there again tomorrow morning, with his tireless arm and his all-seeing eye, searching for a scoreboard to please him, deserving our salute.

Day Four

SATURDAY 24 AUGUST

Close of play: no play (rain)

Five Test matches is a long time for cricketers to spend in one anoth-er's company, and some tempers in these Ashes have frayed in this last week. How seriously it is hard to tell. The attention has fallen naturally on the public demonstrations, with today's papers herea-bouts busily anatomising Friday's exchanges between Shane Watson, Michael Clarke, Ian Bell and Kevin Pietersen, which are as impressive on the page as the transcript of an 'am-not/are-too' debate between five-year-olds.

Which is fine, actually. The day needed some spice, and here it was, even if the episode may relate more about the desire of Clarke and Watson to present a united front: look at us, shoulder to shoulder, pals again, dishing it out to . . . er . . . the guy who's made 500 runs this sum-mer . . . and is . . . er . . . probably going to be man-of-the-series . . .

Okay, so it's not exactly the golden age of 'how's your wife and my kids?', really, and it may be time to call Warnie in with some *American*

Pie videos to show them how it's done. But like I said, all good fun.

It's the pre-match trash-talking of Stuart Broad and Darren Lehmann that's showing no sign of going away, partly because it's being allowed to hang around. It's difficult to arbitrate on who was the greater tit in the original skirmishings: self-justifying Broad in presenting his failure to walk at Trent Bridge as evidence that 'we're tough', or self-inflating Lehmann in accusing him of 'blatant cheating' when Broad infringed no law or even popularly followed ethical code.

The prize should probably go to Lehmann, not only because he courted the tag of hypocrite by saying in the next breath that he didn't 'advocate walking', but because serious defamation actions have sprung from less. In fact, the radio hosts who gleefully repeated the interview might want to exercise a little more caution. From Clive Lloyd to Imran Khan, cricketers accused of 'cheating' have enjoyed some lucrative days at law – and rightly so.

As for Lehmann exhorting Australians to make Broad's touring life a misery, it was at best a mirthless joke, at worst exactly what the England Cricket Board has called it: an 'incitement'. Should the same fate befall Broad as befell John Crawley in November 1998 – assaulted by thugs as he walked back to a team hotel in Cairns in an incident anxiously hushed up at the time – who would bear responsibility?

But let's be fair to Lehmann, whose candour is usually appealing: he isn't the first commercial radio guest to misspeak in pandering to an audience. What's become oddest about the whole episode is the timorous inaction of Cricket Australia, who have left disciplinary measures entirely to the International Cricket Council. To their credit, the ICC has now levied an appropriate fine. But when you're being out-administered by the ICC, your organisation has a serious credibility problem.

Five days on from Lehmann's remarks, CA have said and done absolutely nothing, effectively condoning an accusation by its coach of 'blatant cheating' against an opposition player. This is the same organisation that leapt to the defence of Joe Root's fuzzy chin three months ago, when chief executive James Sutherland overrode his team's internal management in describing David Warner's actions as 'despicable' – a process which also accelerated the demise of Lehmann's predecessor Mickey Arthur.

The response this time has basically been to pretend that nothing has taken place. On Friday the ABC's Jim Maxwell emailed Sutherland registering his distaste for CA's silence. Maxwell received a blithe response that ignored the comment altogether, referring instead to the weather. CA's website carries no report of Lehmann's fine, simply the ICC press release.

Sutherland has form here. Back in January he responded frivolously to Shane Warne's ugly rumble with Marlon Samuels in a Big Bash League match at the MCG, arguing that it was good for the league's profile, and the outcome of natural 'passion'. He then hemmed and hawed about the suspensions of four key Australian players from the Mohali Test in March, publicly calling himself 'a really firm believer in the fact that those decisions will ultimately stand us in good stead', but privately offering Arthur only equivocal support. Ten years ago, it was Sutherland who pulled up a far mightier Australian team than this, after Steve Waugh failed to intervene in an acrimonious on-field incident involving Glenn McGrath in the West Indies, and committed them to a written 'Spirit of Cricket' manifesto – one of the high points of his tenure as CEO. Commercial KPIs and matrix management aside, it's no longer clear exactly what Sutherland stands for. It seems to depend on the day of the week.

In philosophical moods, Lehmann might also reflect on how times have changed. Ten years ago, he also succumbed to a moment's rage and unprintably offended a Sri Lankan team in an ODI at the Gabba. In the honest and self-critical account he gives of the incident in his autobiography, Lehmann admits to feeling acutely let down by his employer, who offered him no assistance or counsel in the disciplinary process, and who on that occasion *did* publish an article about him on their website, vehemently critical. 'I was disappointed at the lack of support, certainly in the public arena, that I received from Cricket

Australia,' Lehmann writes, recalling having to find his own legal representation through the Australian Cricketers' Association.

So congratulations on joining the establishment, Boof. It always looks after its own . . . until, one day, it doesn't. Because I wouldn't go condemning, say, Virat Kohli for not walking, and calling on Australian fans to 'make him cry' if I were you. Where *some* cricket countries are concerned, diplomacy is of the *utmost* importance.

Day Five
SUNDAY 25 AUGUST

Close of play: England 2nd innings 206/5
(40 overs) – end of match

Whatever one has thought of his team, and whatever he has known to be the case, Michael Clarke has all summer looked like a captain on the field: responsive, purposeful, alive to phases of the games, alert to the susceptibilities of opponents. The man in charge. At around 7 pm tonight at the Oval, that demeanour began to change. He looked anxious, fretful, perhaps even misled.

Clarke had done the daring thing. He had refused to let a sleeping Test lie, had gone out to build a lead and set a target – heartily endorsed by Shane Warne, one of cricket's great sages. And cricket was repaying him how? He was on the brink of losing the unlosable.

The Australians were visibly stalling – as, of course, England had done at Trent Bridge, Old Trafford, and here. And what is sauce for the goose, as they say . . . But that was a Pommy trick – Australians, like James Faulkner the day before, use the phrase 'defensive cricket' with a curl of the lip.

The temptations for Clarke to declare had been historic. Before the Fifth Test of 1972, Ian Chappell made a brisk but telling point to his maturing team. At the time, the Australians trailed 1–2, having to their fury been caught on a suspicious pitch at Headingley seemingly tailored to the wiles of Derek Underwood, and been deprived there-fore of a shot at the Ashes; all they had before them at the Oval a dead rubber. Except, said Chappell, that it wasn't. In years to come, people would not care about the individual games so much as the series margin. What the team were playing for, then, was the differ-ence between 1–3 and two all – and that was all the difference in the world. Australia's victory was a springboard to their great era – not for another five years would they lose a series.

For Clarke, the risk of 0–4 had been worth taking for the chance of 1–3 – at teatime, anyway. There was the chance, too, that England would simply squib any chase, making a farce of the finale, and con-cede to Australia the high ground. Look at us – we tried to make a game. Look at them – they should, as James Faulkner chirped, be 'offering refunds'.

Except that England had gone hard. In fact, while it was a depar-ture from their approach on Friday, it was not a departure from their approach earlier in the day. England's tail had attacked with spirit before lunch, and its bowlers had defended with skill after. It was some of England's best cricket of the series, and there was nothing unex-pected about their pursuing the 227 target with a will, because on this exceedingly flat wicket they could come to little harm.

For his stratagem to succeed, then, Clarke needed England to do something stupid. And grim as they are, cynical as they can be, the team of Alastair Cook and Andy Flower is anything but stupid; on the contrary, they had roped a dope, and Australia's captain looked like paying the ultimate price for underestimating them.

His blushes were saved by cricket's obduracy where light is concerned. There was no possibility that Aleem Dar and Kumar Dharmasena would ignore it, as Nelson famously raised a telescope to his blind eye and ignored a signal to disengage. They are not *those* kind of officials, nor were they overseeing *those* kind of playing conditions; if anything, the umpires indulged England ever so slightly, as Clarke was visibly complaining.

It would have been fun had the old standards applied, for we might then have witnessed the first light appeal by a bowling captain in three-quarters of a century, since Herbert Wade's immortal complaint that Stan McCabe's bravura strokes at Johannesburg were endangering his fielders. But the umpires, as we saw at Old Trafford, have had sole charge in matters of light since October 2010, and the last on-field gesture of Australia's enterprising captain was attempting to look over Dar's shoulder as he consulted his light meter, like a schoolboy stretching to copy from a swot, while the official brushed him away.

It was fatuous, of course – it need hardly be said. This was sport reduced to the level of an occupational health and safety issue, defeat at the hands of the human resources department snatched from the jaws of victory in the name of the spectacular and the memorable. The crowd might have left with a priceless allegiance to Test cricket; what they came away with instead was a better knowledge of ICC playing conditions.

For what we had seen to that stage had been outstanding – certainly, from Kevin Pietersen, the most brilliant batting of the series, a 36-ball half-century, unexampled in Ashes history. It wasn't stand and deliver so much as loom and launch: pressing forward to manufacture half volleys, skittering across the crease to force to leg, driving down the ground, pulling off the front foot – all the while holding the bat with that improbable delicacy, like a posh way to wield a fish knife.

Pietersen had been well set up by Cook and Trott, both of whom hit the ball as cleanly as they had all summer, and was favoured by the backdrop of what has been his favourite English ground since that memorable afternoon eight years ago when he extracted his team from one fire by starting his own. Never mind 360 degrees: his bat was almost orbital, and his bat speed like one of those stockwhips that breaks the speed of sound.

Australia wormed their way back into the game thanks to Faulkner, who bowled a timely and crafty spell from the Vauxhall End just when it was needed, in a scenario for which more than fifty games of T20 had prepared him, even if the pitch may have been drier than he has been used to at his three IPL franchises. His levering out Pietersen and Trott slowed England marginally, and just in time, setting up something really juicy: the possibility, for example, of the two debutants, Faulkner and Chris Woakes, facing off in the final over with, say, eight to win, their countries behind them, careers ahead of them. Although Clarke may not have liked the sound of that much either. The ending bang having threatened to blow up in his face, he was happy to settle for a whimper.

Review
SCOREBOARD PRESSURE

An old joke concerns a chemist, a biologist and a statistician going hunting. The chemist aims at a deer and misses five feet to the right. The biologist aims and misses five feet to the left. 'We got' im,' says the statistician.

That joke has been on Michael Clarke's Australians this summer. In tabulated numerical form, the Ashes of 2013 looks so tight that a statistician might struggle to split the antagonists – if anything, the visitors may even have shaded it.

Of the combination at the Oval, three of Australia's batsmen (Clarke, Watson, Rogers) averaged more than 40, and five of their bowlers paid less than 30 runs per wicket (Harris, Starc, Smith, Lyon and Faulkner). In the same categories for England at the Oval fell only one batsman (Bell) and three bowlers (Anderson, Broad and Swann). Australia's keeper Brad Haddin held a record twenty-nine catches to Prior's eighteen. In four of the five Tests, Australia held first-innings leads; not once did they allow England to make 400, while twice passing it themselves.

In this respect, the series resembled the Ashes of 2009, where Australia had six batsmen with averages over 40 and three bowlers who took 20 wickets, versus two and none, and also lost. But that was a close-run series, which might have tilted the other way but for a coin toss and a selection or two. The 3–0 margin in this rubber implies teams of seriously discrepant qualities. How, then, to explain it?

This was not, as has been widely observed, a series from the top drawer, or what we might think of as the locked drawer occupied by 1902 and 1948 (if you're Australian), or 1981 and 2005 (if you're English). On one reading, it was a kind of battle of the bads, in which England prevailed because its bads were merely lacklustre while Australia's were irredeemably poor.

Under the cosh, England found ways to endure, never prettily, sometimes tediously. They may not always take the most direct route to a win, but they do know how not to lose. When Australia stumbled at Lord's and Riverside, it was from the top of a flight of stairs into a darkened basement with a floor covered in broken glass and crawling with rats.

A statistic widely bandied will be Australia's use of seventeen players in the series versus England's fourteen, although one should be wary here of mistaking cause and effect: losing teams are almost obliged to make changes; winning teams enjoy the luxury of preserving their continuity. Whether Australia's forces were always best disposed is another question. While England altered its top six once, and only after winning the Ashes, Australia had three different opening combinations, and four different number threes, none of whom were Phil Hughes, who had occupied the role in Australia's two preceding series. The captain batted at number four on six occasions, number five on four. Five different batsmen occupied number six. To be sure, rotate a Rubik's cube for long enough and it will eventually solve itself. But you'd better have strong fingers and a high boredom threshold.

Harris, Pattinson, Siddle and Lyon, probably Australia's optimum bowling line-up, never played together. Starc played three Tests and was dropped twice. Australia's man of the series, Ryan Harris, should in hindsight have played at Trent Bridge. This wasn't chemistry, this was alchemy.

As captain, Clarke gave the impression of sedulous preparation, from his leg slip and short mid-wickets for Trott to his deep backward point for Prior. Yet even here was an air of improvisation. No fewer than five fielders stood at short leg for Australia this summer: Cowan, Hughes, Khawaja, Warner and Smith. Yesterday Smith cost Australia a review with his enthusiasm about a pad defection from Trott – his enthusiasm was pardonable, but it was not a mistake an experienced bat-pad catcher would have made.

Of England it was harder to obtain an absolute as distinct from a relative sense, and they tended perhaps to go slightly under-reported, if only because their taciturn leadership, unsentimental proficiency and occasional insouciant gamesmanship made them a less alluring subject than Australia's recent decline and present flux. Their captain, Alastair Cook, seems more like a chief operating officer than a chief executive, implementing prearranged strategies, issuing readymade phrases. He may have been inhibited by his own form, which prevented him placing a personal stamp on his team's performances. But at the centre of a web of tight personal relations, he can take credit for an obviously united dressing room.

Man of the series Bell was both England's best player and their most emblematic member, attaining the kind of everyday excellence that is their hierarchy's overriding objective. Funnily enough, the slow and arid pitches Australia have regarded so dubiously probably ended up doing neither side any particular favours, and may have helped a few of the visitors: how, one wonders, would Steve Smith have fared in a season of green seaming tracks?

In the end, the series will be recalled as having more undulations than actual twists. Predictions of a 3–0 margin were not uncommon in advance – perhaps, if Mickey Arthur's recent comments are to be believed, even at Cricket Australia.

On the credit side of Australia's ledger, they probably outstripped the expectations entertained for them after Lord's. On the debit side, they have now not won a game of international cricket in any form since 10 February 2013 – 196 days – which implies a decline of Spenglerian proportions. And that is a statistic that requires little further elaboration.

FIFTH TEST

The Oval, London 21–25 August 2013
Toss Australia **Match Drawn**

AUSTRALIA	1st Innings			2nd Innings		
CJL Rogers	c Trott	b Swann	23			
DA Warner	c Prior	b Anderson	6	c and	b Anderson	12
SR Watson	c Pietersen	b Broad	176	c Pietersen	b Swann	26
MJ Clarke*		b Anderson	7	not out		28
SPD Smith	not out		138	c Swann	b Broad	7
PM Siddle		b Anderson	23			
BJ Haddin†		b Trott	30	c Prior	b Broad	0
JP Faulkner	c Trott	b Woakes	23	c Prior	b Broad	22
MA Starc		b Swann	13	not out		13
RJ Harris	c and	b Anderson	33		b Broad	1
NM Lyon	not out		0			
EXTRAS	(b 1, lb 12, w 2, nb 5)		20	(lb 2)		2
TOTAL	(9 wkts dec; 128.5 overs; 567 mins)		492	(6 wkts dec; 23 overs; 106 mins)		111

ENGLAND	1st Innings			2nd Innings		
AN Cook*	c Haddin	b Harris	25	lbw	b Faulkner	34
JE Root	c Watson	b Lyon	68	c Haddin	b Harris	11
IJL Trott	lbw	b Starc	40	lbw	b Faulkner	59
KP Pietersen	c Watson	b Starc	50	c Warner	b Harris	62
IR Bell	c Haddin	b Faulkner	45	run out		17
CR Woakes	c Clarke	b Harris	25	not out		17
MJ Prior†	c Starc	b Faulkner	47	not out		0
SCJ Broad		b Starc	9			
GP Swann		b Faulkner	34			
JM Anderson	c Haddin	b Faulkner	4			
SC Kerrigan	not out		1			
EXTRAS	(b 11, lb 10, w 5, nb 3)		29	(lb 4, nb 2)		6
TOTAL	(144.4 overs; 609 mins)		377	(5 wkts; 40 overs; 184 mins)		206

ENGLAND									
1st Innings	O	M	R	W	2nd Innings	O	M	R	W
JM Anderson	29.5	4	95	4		6	1	27	1
SCJ Broad	31	4	128	1		10	2	43	4
GP Swann	33	4	95	2		7	0	39	1
CR Woakes	24	7	96	1					
SC Kerrigan	8	0	53	0					
IJL Trott	3	0	12	1					

AUSTRALIA									
1st Innings	O	M	R	W	2nd Innings	O	M	R	W
MA Starc	33	5	92	3		7	0	48	0
RJ Harris	28	10	64	2		5	0	21	2
JP Faulkner	19.4	3	51	4		8	1	47	2
PM Siddle	28	7	74	0		3	0	16	0
NM Lyon	28	8	59	1		10	0	44	0
SPD Smith	8	3	16	0					
MJ Clarke						2	0	4	0
SR Watson						5	0	22	0

FALL OF WICKETS				
Wicket	Aus - 1st	Eng - 1st	Aus - 2nd	Eng - 2nd
1st	11	68	34	22
2nd	118	118	44	86
3rd	144	176	50	163
4th	289	217	67	170
5th	320	269	83	206
6th	385	299	85	–
7th	422	315	–	–
8th	446	363	–	–
9th	491	368	–	–
10th	–	377	–	–

Umpires: Aleem Dar (Pakistan) and HDPK Dharmasena (Sri Lanka)
Referee: RS Mahanama (Sri Lanka)

TESTS PLAYED IN ENGLAND   July–August 2013

AUSTRALIA - Batting and Fielding

	M	I	NO	HS	Runs	Avge	100	50	Ct/St
MJ Clarke	5	10	2	187	381	47.62	1	1	6
SR Watson	5	10	-	176	418	41.80	1	1	4
CJL Rogers	5	9	-	110	367	40.77	1	2	4
SPD Smith	5	10	1	138	345	38.33	1	2	3
JL Pattinson	2	4	2	35	72	36.00	-	-	1
AC Agar	2	4	-	98	130	32.50	-	1	-
PJ Hughes	2	4	1	81	83	27.66	-	1	3
MA Starc	3	6	2	66	104	26.00	-	1	1
DA Warner	3	6	-	71	138	23.00	-	1	3
BJ Haddin	5	10	1	71	206	22.88	-	2	29
RJ Harris	4	7	2	33	99	19.80	-	-	2
UT Khawaja	3	6	-	54	114	19.00	-	1	2
PM Siddle	5	8	-	23	84	10.50	-	-	-
NM Lyon	3	3	1	8	12	6.00	-	-	1

Also batted (one Test each): **JM Bird 0*, 1*; EJM Cowan 0, 14 (1 ct);**
JP Faulkner 23, 22

AUSTRALIA - Bowling

	O	M	R	W	Avge	Best	5wI	10wM
JP Faulkner	27.4	4	98	6	16.34	4-51	-	-
RJ Harris	162.1	37	470	24	19.58	7-117	2	-
PM Siddle	189.5	52	537	17	31.58	5-50	-	-
MA Starc	120	24	357	11	32.45	3-76	-	-
NM Lyon	118.1	30	303	9	33.66	4-42	-	-
JL Pattinson	91.1	21	307	7	43.85	3-69	-	-

Also bowled: **AC Agar 84-17-248-2; JM Bird 42.3-15-125-2; MJ Clarke 3-0-6-0;**
SPD Smith 31-4-106-4; SR Watson 85.3-38-179-2

ENGLAND - Batting and Fielding									
	M	I	NO	HS	Runs	Avge	100	50	Ct/St
IR Bell	5	10	1	113	562	62.44	3	2	2
KP Pietersen	5	10	-	113	388	38.80	1	3	5
JE Root	5	10	1	180	339	37.66	1	1	2
IJL Trott	5	10	-	59	293	29.30	-	2	6
JM Bairstow	4	7	-	67	203	29.00	-	1	1
AN Cook	5	10	-	62	277	27.70	-	3	7
TT Bresnan	3	5	1	45	103	25.75	-	-	-
SCJ Broad	5	7	-	65	179	25.57	-	1	1
GP Swann	5	7	2	34	126	25.20	-	-	5
MJ Prior	5	9	2	47	133	19.00	-	-	18
JM Anderson	5	7	2	16	36	7.20	-	-	4

Also batted (one Test each): **ST Finn 0, 2*; SC Kerrigan 1*; CR Woakes 25, 17***

ENGLAND - Bowling								
	O	M	R	W	Avge	Best	5wI	10wM
SCJ Broad	185.5	38	604	22	27.45	6-50	2	1
GP Swann	249	41	755	26	29.03	5-44	2	-
JM Anderson	205.4	43	651	22	29.59	5-73	2	-
TT Bresnan	91	20	296	10	29.60	2-25	-	-

Also bowled: **ST Finn 25-3-117-2; SC Kerrigan 8-0-53-0; JE Root 16-5-34-3; IJL Trott 7-0-28-1; CR Woakes 24-7-96-1**

PART II

Australia, November 2013– January 2014

PREAMBLE

England Squad
TALL MEN, LONG SHADOWS

On the eve of the Bodyline series, Australia's Victor Richardson bumped into England's Bill Voce at the races, and the chat turned to cricket. So, asked Richardson, what sort of a team was Voce's? 'Not a bad side,' replied the Notts man, who would shortly be Harold Larwood's partner in crime. 'And if we don't beat you, we'll knock your bloody heads off.' Voce was too modest: his team proved well and truly capable of both.

The same might be said of the team England has selected to defend the Ashes, although its obvious antecedent is not Douglas Jardine's side but Andrew Strauss's. Three years ago, England brought three specimens of fast-bowling megafauna, Stuart Broad, Steve Finn and Chris Tremlett, the last of whom proved a revelation; the strategy proved so successful that the same three have now been reinforced with a fourth, even bigger, in Irish-born Boyd Rankin.

Too many jumbo eggs in the same outsized basket? The plan itself is one thing; about the personnel some doubts must linger. Finn was last seen being thumped around Trent Bridge, and Tremlett bowling some pretty uninspiring stuff on an unused pitch over lunch at the Oval after being excluded from the XI. Rankin is a husky unit to be sure, but so was Steve Harmison, and he had precious little to show for two tours Down Under. England's biggest investment is probably in its coaching expertise, David Saker essentially being entrusted with the task of bringing the three marginal picks into the mainstream of affairs. They will raise statues to him – very tall statues – if he succeeds.

Graham Onions, meanwhile, has paid the penalty for failing to grasp chances on the last couple of English winter tours, despite taking almost 150 wickets in at less than 20 since resuming after injury two years ago. But you could sort of see this coming once England left him out of the XI for the Test at his Durham home ground, then included Chris Woakes and Simon Kerrigan for the Test at the Oval. Either that or England is convinced that Tim Bresnan will have recovered from the stress fractures of the back that ruled him out of the Fifth Test, and will be ready to provide economical wicket-to-wicket variations at grounds like Adelaide Oval and the WACA Ground.

There is more to like about the rest of the squad, all-rounder Ben Stokes just edging out Woakes, and left-handers Michael Carberry and Gary Ballance essentially shadowing Joe Root, depending on whether the young Yorkshireman continues as an opener or returns to the middle order.

Rather like Chris Rogers, the 33-year-old Carberry gets the chance to rebuild an international career he seemed to have forfeited. He has an idiosyncratic technique. His stance is low, slightly open, front toe pointing towards cover; he grips the bat halfway down the handle, held slightly off the ground. As the bowler reaches the halfway point on approach, he cocks his wrists, points the bat toe skywards, and peers down the pitch, as still yet alert as a gun dog ready to retrieve a fallen pheasant. The bat has a way to travel, but the hands not so far. When this tensed mechanism unsprings, it does so decisively, and from a solid base. It is not a method arrived at casually; rather it suggests a thinking through of all its aspects, as Carberry's determination to come back from serious illness suggests reserves of tenacity.

Monty Panesar also earns another chance, personal as well as professional, having struggled to find a cricket role for himself since the advent of Graeme Swann, and to manage his domestic affairs since a marriage bust-up. He proved an asset in India in late 2012, then a liability in New Zealand early in 2013, and did nothing in particular in a solitary outing against the Australians this summer past, but when Kerrigan is the alternative then there frankly isn't one. Back, too, comes Jonny Bairstow, who squeezes into the squad on the basis of his back-up wicketkeeping, with just the possibility that big early runs might lead to his accommodation as a batsman if injury to Matt Prior does not provide an opportunity.

The bowling of Anderson, Broad and Swann is at least a known quantity, and all three will benefit from some R & R in the next few months. None quite sustained their threat all summer in England, and they will badly need stock bowling support to keep their workloads within reasonable bounds Down Under. But they form a reassuring battery for Alastair Cook to experiment around, as England choose between their various vertical options.

Yet what England are really banking on is their top six standing tall after what at all events was a disappointing summer for them – only Ian Bell played to his reputation, and Cook, Prior and Jonathan Trott played well below theirs. Even Kevin Pietersen has a point to prove, his career now almost in parallel with England's fortunes rather than intrinsic to them. He can still touch batting heights reserved for very few, but at other times seem strangely short of motivation, as though Test cricket is now just something he does rather than something he genuinely pursues. England depend on him more than they know, and Pietersen on England perhaps more than he is prepared to acknowledge. When the stars align, as in India, the effect is still powerful.

This is not, then, a top-quality England team, even while full of nous and knowhow, and it will depend as it did at home on seizing opportunities as they come, and also on Australia failing to do the same. They have the advantage of holding the Ashes, and needing only a share of the series in order to retain the urn, the disadvantage of facing a rival on their own turf with nothing to lose. They will leave no stone unturned in their preparation, and clearly none unhurled in their execution. But even Bodyline was closer than it seemed. 'We almost didn't do it, you know,' Jardine confided quietly afterwards. 'The little fellow was damn good.'

Hussey and Ponting v Clarke
LEG-BEFORE WORDS

Nothing in football hurts as much as the truth, says Tony Cascarino in his memoir *Full Time*: 'It is like being caught off side.' The truth hurts in cricket, too, but it is perhaps a bit more like being given out lbw – a matter of interpretation, an invitation of disagreement.

It has been an unhappy few weeks for Michael Clarke, adjudged leg-before by the autobiographies of two players who a year ago were his staunchest teammates, Ricky Ponting and Mike Hussey. As revealed by cherry-picked extracts from Ponting's *At the Close of Play* and Hussey's *Underneath the Southern Cross*, the former nursed doubts about Clarke's attitude to team responsibilities when he was a player, while the latter took a bleak view of a self-protecting Australian team culture under Clarke's leadership. And while Ponting subsequently comes down on the side of the view of Clarke that 'captaincy was the making of him', Hussey airs the misgivings he had from the very beginning, when Clarke acted as locum for Ponting for the ODI series in the West Indies in July 2008.

Hussey recounts how old friends Clarke and Andrew Symonds were estranged during that series by the former's decision to fine the latter for missing a team bus: 'From that moment, they were never the same. If Pup was up one end of the dressing room, Simmo was up the other.' These opposite ends reflected their careers' 'opposite directions', Hussey recounts. 'While Simmo was drifting away from international cricket, Pup was being groomed as the next Australian captain.' The former evidently had a good deal to do with the latter.

To repeat, though, 'truth' is complex. How deep *were* issues around Pup's personality? Ponting's views suggest a keen understanding of

Clarke's 'type', as it were. The emerging Clarke reminded his elder of another unnamed teammate who would be 'chirpy and bubbly if he was going well, but appear a bit grim if things weren't working for him' – and, frankly, I would be surprised had Ponting met only *one* player like this before Clarke. 'The best team-mates are the ones who can keep their moods in check for the sake of the group,' Ponting concludes, and he is surely right, but it does not come naturally to everyone in a team game that nonetheless overtly celebrates and explicitly quantifies individual achievement. And you might say that the best dressing rooms are those that allow for that.

Hussey's allegations about 'insularity' are personally qualified too. 'As a captain,' he notes, 'Pup was a very strong driver and had a clear path that he wanted to take the team on. You were either on it or you were off it.' And Hussey was very much *on* it: he had 'no qualms' about such an approach, and ended up playing 'some of my best cricket under Pup's captaincy'. As he says, 'I don't know quite what the chemistry was but it worked, and in the end that's what matters.' So whatever Hussey's misgivings about the environment, it was one in which he thrived.

Dressing rooms, then, are important places, but also, I suspect, places we are apt to mythologise because they are invested with an aura of cultishness and secrecy, which leads us to overestimate what little we learn about events in them. The books of Ponting and Hussey are instructive in this respect too. Both provide accounts of the one Australian dressing-room story of the last decade that everyone knows: the contretemps between Clarke and Simon Katich in January 2010, whose details require no elaboration. What's interesting is that neither places great weight on the incident itself. Ponting says he saw 'worse arguments' between Australian players – indeed, he confesses to have been involved in one himself.

Of Clarke's prompt exit, Ponting records: 'Michael left immediately after the confrontation, while we just shrugged our shoulders and said, "That's Pup".' In reference to Katich's hasty apology, Hussey quotes the droll response of Test debutant Andrew McDonald: 'Don't worry, mate, this happens all the time in Victoria.' What caused 'massive repercussions', Hussey notes, was not the incident but its disclosure a month later. Hints of friction and disharmony haunt sporting teams as they do political parties, even, and perhaps sometimes especially, when they are exaggerated.

So what can we conclude about Australian cricket's travails from the accounts of these two great players? A key event in the souring of dressing-room mood involved neither Clarke nor Lara Bingle, nor when the team song was sung, nor who went sailing with James Packer, nor whether Watto knew the words to 'True Blue', or any of the other intramural factors people so enjoy speculating about. Instead it was the old-fashioned matter of a player being dropped – the cutting of Katich from the list of Cricket Australia's contracted players in June 2011. Ponting calls this 'as dumb a non-selection as any during my time with the Australian team', one that put everyone 'on notice'. Hussey blames it for entrenching 'the culture of looking after number one'.

This decision was compounded a few months later, Hussey continues, by CA's acceptance of a recommendation in the Argus Review that the Australian captain form part of the national selection panel, which he says caused uneasy players additional angst. As the new captain, argues Hussey, Clarke was invidiously placed. 'I noticed, during that period, that when Michael was around, everyone went a bit quieter, and kept their head down. It's not a comfortable feeling; people aren't being themselves. Overall, I just felt that it drove a wedge between the players and their leader.'

Except that who was perhaps the most spirited voice in the argument for Clarke having these powers? None other than Ponting, who describes responding unambiguously to the question from Don Argus about accountability for the Australian team's performances: 'Until the captain becomes a selector, he can never be truly accountable for what happens in his team.' In the end, principle and practice could be reconciled for only eighteen months. Clarke handed back

Different Strokes, Different Folks: at Trent Bridge, shades of brilliance from an uninhibited Ashton Agar (left) and a studied Ian Bell (above), plus a portrait of insouciance from the unrepentant Stuart Broad (below).

The Whiff of Ashes: collective joy from England as they win the First Test (above), individual dejection from Michael Clarke as Australia lose the Second Test (right).

Hard Graft: two Australian old stagers, Chris Rogers (above left) and Ryan Harris (above), get going in the Third Test at Old Trafford, but rain brings chagrin to Michael Clarke (left).

Triumphal Procession: a gracious handshake from G
Swann for Chris Rogers (above) on his maiden Test
hundred at Riverside; more traditional celebrations f
Tim Bresnan, on dismissing David Warner in the Fou
Test (left); and Mitchell Johnson, on dismissing Jona
Trott (below) in the ODI series. Both were crucial wic
Bresnan's in the short-term, Johnson's in the long-t

Idin Unbound:
tional innings
om Australia's
r Brad Haddin
ift Australia at
ne, with 94 at
Gabba (right)
8 at Adelaide
l, having been
ously dropped
latter at 5 by
hael Carberry
(below).

Don't Look Now: Alastair Cook and Andy Flower can't watch (top) and Stuart Broad can't see as Mitchell Johnson runs amok at Adelaide, although Ben Stokes tries hard not to be staring down (above).

That Winning Feeling: 2013–14 was a summer of Australian euphoria, embodied by centurions David Warner at the Gabba (left) and Steve Smith at the WACA (below). In the latter Test, Cook's first ball fall to Harris completed a session of relentless domination (bottom).

Party Time: Nathan Lyon's 100th Test wicket (above) and another bristling spell from Johnson (right) bring Australia to the brink of a whitewash at the MCG, duly accomplished at the SCG (below).

his selectorial responsibilities in England.

And when it comes time to writing the master narrative of this period in Australian cricket, this is something we will have to come to terms with: that perspectives vary, that men of goodwill will differ, that 'truth' is elusive. Another view is on its way down the pike even as I write: Michael Clarke's *The Ashes Diary* will be published in three weeks. Not that we should expect too much candour from an incumbent Australian captain. He'll be less concerned about lbws than about not hitting his own wicket.

George Bailey
THE COMING MAN?

Not hello. Not what are you working on? The first thing one of Australia's most celebrated novelists said when we met at a literary event last Sunday was: 'What have we got to do to get George Bailey in the Test team?' When I replied not much, and that Bailey seemed to be doing most of the work himself, this seemed to satisfy him. But it was an interesting reflection on the extent of the Baileymania sweeping cricket circles not three weeks from the First Test.

If Australian selection was conducted by phone poll or online vote, Bailey would be a shoo-in for Brisbane; some in the present environment of Clarke-doubt might even plump for him as captain. Last week 'George Bailey' was the popular search on Cricinfo, ahead of 'Sachin Tendulkar' and 'Virat Kohli'. That's like *Kenny* outdoing a Shahrukh Khan blockbuster at the Bollywood box office.

It's not so much the runs, plentiful as these have been. Bailey will have scrabbled far harder in first-class cricket than he's been forced to during the current one-day series in India, where the twin white balls, piebald pitches, and frictionless depopulated outfields have turned 350 into the new 300, and 200 into the new 12 – he has not had to do much running between wickets, for example, which is not the strongest part of his game. Most impressive about Bailey has been the observable serenity of his cricket, as batsman, as partner, as player and as leader. And this has been so since his international beginnings. He smiles unfeignedly. He speaks thoughtfully. He exhibits a mind of his own. He looks like he belongs.

Which is the opposite of the conclusion drawn by Australia's powerful 'not-in-my-day' ex-player lobby after Bailey was tapped to lead the national T20 team in February 2013, having not previously represented his country. In their eyes, Bailey was twice damned. He lacked the blue-collar airs that Australian cricket likes to pride itself on, despite, or maybe also because of, all its modern-day wealth, polish and prestige. Bailey was educated at Launceston Grammar, where his father John finished fifteen years as first XI coach last year. This makes him about as much a private-school product as, for example, the Chappell brothers (Prince Alfred's) and Shane Warne (Mentone Grammar). But it's not untrue to say that Aussie cricket opinion-makers like their favourites a little rougher round the edges, and to have more palpably 'paid their dues'.

Bailey was also already thirty at a stage when it was the common talk of sage judges that international cricket was best started when young – look at Ponting, Tendulkar and Lara, they would say, not to mention the Waughs, Warne and McGrath. I suspect, in fact, that Bailey had already mulled over the idea that he might not make it. Even as he led Tasmania to a Sheffield Shield victory thirty months ago, his career was not obviously going anywhere, and it's an alarming realisation for an ambitious cricketer that his reach might after all exceed his grasp.

Anyway, that may have stood him in good stead. Like his namesake in *It's a Wonderful Life*, Bailey has found grounds for optimism, batting with consistent excellence and leading with deepening aplomb. There's not much a leader can do on the field in the current ODI format, at least in India. The limits on fielders outside the circle have turned captains into occupational health and safety box-tickers. Five in the circle – check. Four outside – check. Bowler and keeper – check.

Okay, let's get ready to retrieve some boundaries. But Bailey has taken to heart the advice of his predecessor Dan Marsh, that a lot about captaincy starts at stumps. And insofar as it is possible to judge from a distance and a remove, the Australians that Bailey is leading in India have been a great deal happier than the last uneasy and riven lot.

The only deficiencies in Bailey's résumé have been the lack of a red-ball hundred for more than eighteen months, including a last Sheffield Shield season through which he could barely buy a first-class run. For a player of his accomplishments, Bailey can look very tentative indeed. In his praise of teammates, too, he occasionally hints at a tincture of insecurity about his own abilities. This, though, matters less than it might in the context of the forthcoming Ashes. The Test role at number six for which Bailey has been auditioning looks to fit him snugly – certainly rather more snugly than the four batsmen Australia rotated through the position in England. Number six is a temperamental rather than chiefly a technical challenge. It is a role like that of a fire warden who does the mustering when the alarm sounds – an especially crucial post in a top order like Australia's prone to spontaneous combustion.

Mike Hussey excelled in the position, bringing to it experience, maturity and a polished all-round game. Bailey's maiden international hundred in February exhibited similar capacities, guiding Australia from the rocky terrain of six for 98 to the sunny uplands of seven for 266: Bailey took 45 steady deliveries over his first 22 runs, then just 65 more deliveries over his last 103.

One other thing. Australia's selectors have copped plenty in the past year – including, last week, from Cricket Australia's chairman. But Bailey's progress has been admirably managed: he was promoted on a hunch, but has not since been advanced ahead of his performances, and when he failed to make a case to be chosen for the England tour did not go. In hindsight, Bailey might have done well on the desiccated Indian takeaway surfaces that England prepared, and his right-handedness would have been a useful counter to Graeme Swann. But John

Inverarity's panel were not to know the conditions that awaited when they picked their party. *Pace* my novelist friend, there will be no reason to sigh 'at last' if and when Bailey progresses to Test cricket. On the contrary, he has emerged as the coming man at a steady, sustainable and altogether reassuring rate.

THE FIRST TEST: Brisbane

THE PEOPLE'S CHOICE

Who needs selectors, eh? Australia today announced a team for the First Test that would probably have been the same as that thrown up by a poll of home viewers. It was also the same twelve I had scribbled down on the back of an envelope a week ago.

In this there is a sense both of vindication and of foreboding, of pleasure in one's own predictive powers and anxiety that everyone has missed something fundamental. But what it is mainly is a reassuring change. During the northern summer, one's impression of their respective selection meetings was that England's took five minutes, and Australia's five Scotches. Australia's best XI seemed to change with the phases of the moon. The batting orders were pure chooklotto.

At least for the moment, there appears a consensus view that might last a fair portion of the summer. The team structure seems easy to pick. David Warner has settled his place with four centuries in eight games in Australia, George Bailey by averaging 80 in half a dozen ODIs in India. The injury Shane Watson sustained during the final game at Nagpur is bad and good news: bad in that it may cost Australia his bowling in the short term, but good inasmuch as it is not so serious as to require the location of another number three, for who on earth would that have been?

The bowling chose itself, really: the four who featured in the Fifth

Test at the Oval, plus Mitchell Johnson, a lock since bowling so swiftly in the limited-overs fixtures at Manchester, Birmingham and Cardiff, unsettling Jonathan Trott among others. Suddenly, then, English and Australian cricket has come a little closer to parity. What can we expect now?

My natural predisposition is to quote A.J.P. Taylor: 'Please don't ask me to predict the future. I have a hard enough job predicting the past.' But my thoughts are pretty much the same as they were six months ago, that Australia probably aren't as bad as we think and England not quite as good as they believe. It turned out that the conduct and conditions of the series in England – grim, attritional cricket played on slow, low pitches – were all in the favour of the hosts' competent proficiency rather than the visitors' mercurial spiritedness.

We can anticipate in Australia, at least, more attractive cricket, with greater scope for flair and imagination; it will be harder for England to restrain and impinge as they did so successfully at home, and as is their wont. That said, the environment should hold few terrors for the visitors: fully eleven of the record-breaking 2010–11 team are here again, with uniformly happy memories of the country, which may be why they have undertaken their tour matches in Perth, Hobart and now Sydney in a fashion rather lower in intensity than three years ago, banking on the skill and nous of their top performers. Kevin Pietersen and Alastair Cook are scheduled to play their hundredth Tests in Brisbane and Perth respectively, and are the kind of players who rise to such occasions.

Nor is it as though England have nothing to prove. Remember the famous lines by the footballer Danny Blanchflower about the game not being about winning? 'It's about glory,' he claimed. 'It's about doing things in style, with a flourish, about going out and beating the other lot, not waiting for them to die of boredom.' Not according to Andy Flower and Alastair Cook, for whom victory is the sole glory, its end justifying almost any means. Rather like the great Australian teams at their peak, who alienated some fans by their visible on-field belligerence, the grimly practical Englishmen leave some of their countrymen cold. When keeper Matt Prior complained after the Oval that it was time for critics to 'show us some respect', *Independent* columnist Michael Calvin diagnosed it as 'the product of an overwrought, self-regarding culture', the players living in 'a vacuum of joylessness and indifference to their wider responsibilities'. Having spent a long time waiting to win, it seems, some fans have raised their sights, and want the winning to make them proud also.

It does not seem at first glance to make much sense to talk of where the teams are in their respective cycles, when it is only months since they last played, and when the likely teams at Brisbane will have roughly the same average age, of a bit over thirty. But there *is* a sense that England's best is behind them, perhaps as much as two years, when they were number one in the world, and that Australia's best lies ahead, glimpsed in the possibilities of David Warner, Steve Smith and James Faulkner. The question is, as my colleague Mike Atherton observed a few months ago, whether the wheel will have turned quite enough between times, and whether it mightn't have suited Australia to play this Ashes when it was originally scheduled, in 2014–15.

What does history say? Victory here would represent a fourth consecutive English Ashes triumph – something England has not accomplished for a century and a quarter, when series were usually of three Tests in duration. That is both a colossal incentive, virtually unique, and a demonstration of how difficult the challenge will be: Australia has historically been much better at sustaining long periods of Ashes supremacy, and even the greatest teams are worn down by time.

History also says that England will find it harder to achieve earlier breaks than at home, because two of the first three Tests are in Brisbane and Perth, where in toto they have won only five times out of thirty-one. Similar preconditions existed three years ago, of course, and Andrew Strauss's team busily made their own history, but England was then surging towards a peak, not coming off one.

Whatever the case, the outset of the series seems crucial – more crucial, actually, than in England, and perhaps especially for Australia. Australian defeat in Brisbane would represent eight losses in ten Tests, from which there would be little bouncing back. Australian victory in Brisbane would not only break a cycle, but connect vindicatingly with memories of Tests at Old Trafford and the Oval, where weather headed Michael Clarke's men off. The toss will therefore matter – in Brisbane it often has. The hosts have made a solid start to this rematch on paper. But they will need some breaks to make them count.

Preview
THE UNCONTROLLABLES

Cricket can be a perverse game. It lies awake at night, tossing and turning in torment at the prospect of minuscule umpiring error. Hey! Get us a Real-time Snicko and New Improved Even Hotter Spot! And make it snappy! Yet at the Gabba this morning, cricket will allow a considerable advantage to accrete on the basis of quaint archaism that should by now probably be called the Two-Sided Preparatory Luck Apportionator, but which we still know as the toss.

Choice of innings won't be the difference between winning and losing in this First Test. And if the forecasts are to be believed then conditions overhead and underfoot will fluctuate throughout the five days. But the toss looms as an opportunity for the lucky winner. England in particular will be drawn to batting, not merely because of the historic Gabba indiscretions of Len Hutton and Nasser Hussain, but because since the start of their summer of 2010 they have lost twice as often when batting second. Runs on the board were also a reliable formula in the 2013 Ashes: England won each time Alastair Cook was able to claim first innings, even without the team compiling a score of 400, and twice being in deficit going into the third innings.

Why? While certainly parched, the pitches did not in the end confer overwhelming favour on Graeme Swann: his fourth-innings wickets still cost 30 runs each. Perhaps it was that the positive cricket Australia endeavoured to play was that little bit harder with half a mind on a pre-existing target, even one seemingly gettable. In a game of tiny margins, the slightest hesitations and faintest second thoughts can be injurious, especially when confidence is brittle.

With the chance to kick proceedings off with the bat at Old Trafford and the Oval, certainly, Michael Clarke's team played as though unburdened, free at last to make the running, to build around handsome hundreds by the captain and Shane Watson. Even at 0–2 in arrears, Australia dominated at Manchester, while England showed all the initiative of pen-pushers stocktaking a stationery cabinet.

That's why Australia's captain will himself lean to batting in the event of winning the toss, although part of him may ponder the alternative, if only because England have faced nobody remotely like Ryan Harris, Mitchell Johnson and even Peter Siddle on the tour so far, and the Gabba's lush outfield and Brisbane's heavy climate should make a pet of the Kookaburra. Cook will also be accompanied by a new opening partner in Michael Carberry, and Test first mornings are like theatrical first nights – unsettling even to the seasoned. Anything can happen in a first hour, even a first over, which got the better of Steve Harmison and Andrew Strauss in Brisbane's last two Ashes Tests. But while bowling first is the innovative option that Shane Warne has virtually trademarked in Clarke's name, there's 'proactivity' and there's 'hyperactivity'. And Clarke hardly needs reminding of the quality of Gabba pitches, having scored 4 hundreds in 11 Test innings here.

The toss, of course, is only one among many random events bound to shape this Test. John Buchanan would probably call them 'uncontrollables', although they're far from inconceivables or insubstantials. Injury has already exerted its influence, impartially as ever, depriving Shane Watson of red-ball preparation coming into the Test, and Tim Bresnan of cricket at all. The former will feel modestly boosted by the latter, Watson having fallen to Bresnan four times for 46 in 88 balls in England. Neutralising Watson will be one of England's stiffest challenges this summer; they will now need to find a new force for doing so. Chris Tremlett dismissed Watson twice in three Tests here four years ago, but the Englishman seems to lack his former kick – a legacy of his own injuries.

It's interesting to contemplate both sides in the event of key absences: Australia without Clarke or Ryan Harris; England without Kevin Pietersen or James Anderson. While well-resourced medical corps stand by ready to render assistance, the 48-day total span of this series offers limited scope for comings and goings. Australia have four splendid pace bowlers in their first-choice twelve, but their reserves thin markedly thereafter. More than half England's squad are thirty-somethings, with some who require careful nursing – including, now, their vice-captain Matt Prior, who injured his calf in Hobart.

Above all the on-field events, let's also remember, will hover sport's superintending deity: luck. In our Occidental rationalism, we tend to discount it. But I suspect every cricketer involved in this series will have it at the back of their minds, expecting cause to bless it, and to remonstrate with it, over the next seven weeks.

Some will take steps. When his team carried all before him in Australia twenty-seven years ago, Mike Gatting went everywhere with a couple of care bears in his coffin. As Steve Waugh approached an Ashes hundred at Headingley twenty years ago, he wiped the sweat away with a red rag, from which, thereafter, he refused to part. There will be all manner of superstitions subtly observed today, from Stuart Broad's lucky green socks to Ryan Harris' tapping of the area of his chest where his mother's star sign is tattooed. Left pads will go on first. Favourite caps will be donned. The Test match is cricket's most comprehensively skilful format, and we onlookers will probably relegate luck to the margins of our thinking in these five. But from the fall of the coin today, no cricketer on either side will wish to be without it.

Summary
ALL THE WAY WITH MITCHELL J

The Gabba Test was a triumph for Australia, and a backhanded vindication for England. Throughout the northern summer, there had been an
undertone of criticism about the approach of Alastair Cook and Andy
Flower to tackling Michael Clarke's men. Why the dusty pitches? Why
the dreary rope-a-dope? The English, some felt, rated the Australians
higher than the Australian rated themselves, and were intent on keeping
them down by any means. The four furious days in Brisbane suggested
that England had been onto something all along. With everything in
their favour for a change, Australia came out swinging, and prostrated
their visitors with a ruthlessness reminiscent of seven years earlier.

It wasn't seven years earlier, of course: this was Australia's first Test
victory since January 2013 and the retirement of Mike Hussey. But it
mattered, clearly, the look of deliverance on Clarke's face at the end a
contrast to his manner and mien in the days before the Test, when he
was terse with the media and taciturn around the public, and to the
first day itself when he succumbed rather tamely to a vehement lifter
from Stuart Broad for 1. By the end, in fact, having peeled off a fine
second-innings hundred, Australia's captain could do no wrong, even a
fine he incurred for verbal abuse of James Anderson being interpreted
as a kind of personal evolution, the metrosexual turning macho.

There was a bit more butchness about the company Clarke was
keeping, too, incarnate in the lucky horseshoe of a moustache that
adorned the bottom lip of man-of-the-match Mitchell Johnson as
he bowled at thrilling speed. 'Bowls like Thomson, looks like Lillee,'
said nostalgia buffs of his nine for 103 – it was a shame they hadn't
restored the dog track to complete the retro-chic tableau. Rather like
the Australians at Chester-le-Street when Stuart Broad slipped himself, the Englishmen seemed taken aback, rather as they were by the

vociferous coverage of the game by the local *Courier-Mail*.

Though they did not make as much of it as they hoped, first innings for Australia turned out to be a useful advantage. It owed everything to Brad Haddin, in his fiftieth Test, and Johnson, after playing just ten Tests in three years, who salvaged a scoreline of six for 132 with a measured alliance of 114 in 231 balls. Until that point only David Warner had batted with conviction, his concentration wavering just as he was about to make it count, against a visiting attack in which Broad was again unflagging. The first-day pitch was tacky, the ball leaving dark indentations, and the outfield slow, the batsmen having to run 10 threes: Johnson thought it a 'par score'. He would do more than anyone else to make it better than that.

The wicket that counted was Clarke's, who looked flinchingly away as a Broad riser zeroed in on the coat of arms on his helmet, and was taken at short leg – the eighth time Broad had done for him in Tests, the majority with short balls, the minority with balls where Clarke was perhaps expecting the short ball. In the afternoon, however, England showed markedly less aggression, Swann being unable to contain with the old ball as he had in England, and the Australian seventh-wicket pair playing strokes with an ever breezier ease. The second new ball did the trick at last, but more runs than expected on the board were a fillip for an Australian team that had of late found them hard to come by.

For an hour or so, Australia's pacemen let their excitement get the better of them, bowling either too short or too full, with Michael Carberry surmounting the early loss of his captain to make a calm impression. Then as lunch approached, the excitement found a productive channel, Johnson bounding in to Jonathan Trott with fielders in formation to leg, then hurrying to squeeze in an additional over before lunch. Trott looked agitated, transfixed, his footwork exaggerated, his head in motion – his nick down the leg side seemed almost foreordained. Lunch in the respective camps would have been a contrasting affair. For an hour afterwards, Carberry and Pietersen held the line, Carberry abjuring his favoured strokes through point in deference to two gullies, Pietersen in one of those moods where it's as if he's trying to impress onlookers with his seriousness. His mid-wicket drive in the first over after drinks was then pure self-indulgence, as though he could contain himself no longer, and the match was at a hinge point with England three for 82.

Actually, Johnson did not so much swing the game as yank it off its hinges altogether. Switching to the Vulture Street End, and to round the wicket, he peppered Carberry's ribs until an edge flew to slip; returning to over the wicket, he pushed across Root who edged obligingly, and into Swann who popped up tamely. Suddenly not just Johnson but his facial growth were the talk of Australia – his moustache would soon be on the point of being offered its own reality TV show. Otherwise there was nothing much visibly different about the bowler who in the corresponding Test in 2010 had been the Barmy Army's favourite butt. This was less a return than a resurrection.

Between times, Nathan Lyon struck with consecutive balls in his fifth over as deliveries to Bell and Prior snagged edges to short leg. The toll – one is nearly tempted to call it the death toll – was six for 9 in 58 balls. The conditions were good for bowling, the pitch having quickened since the first day, the light a little dim, the atmosphere a tad heavy, and the batsmen inhibited by the pressure of measuring off against a total. But it was probably England's most supine hour overseas since the Kingston Test of February 2009 – Andy Flower's first fixture as coach. Only thanks to some bold blows from Broad did England avoid the follow-on, and by the close their arrears was 224, with all Australian second-innings wickets intact, and all eyes on skies, which had shown such exquisite timing at Manchester.

England's bowlers found themselves at work again on the third morning, having barely had time for a shower, shit and shave, and looked understandably weary. Clarke hooked two token short balls from Broad as he settled in to a rehabilitative innings; Warner batted as he had talked in the days before the Test, directly, buoyantly and not a little brashly. It was the perfect partnership in the ideal setting, the biggest and second-swiftest of the game, defying England's routine restraining efforts of deep-set fields and slowpoke over rates. As Cook tried not to overwork Anderson and Broad this early in the series, Swann, never allowed to settle, again was singled out for manhandling. The break came luckily when Warner, shortly after lofting Broad for six down the ground, nicked awkwardly. Although Swann at last collected some consolation wickets, looking theatrically relieved, Haddin and Johnson reprised their first-innings alliance by adding 90 at better than a run a ball, extending Australia's advantage beyond half a thousand.

By now all eyes were trained on the players' enclosure, where Clarke was standing rather more relaxedly than he had on the first morning, and he called a halt in time for fifteen overs. It was essential England not lose a wicket in this time: they lost two, and almost a third. After Carberry had nicked on unluckily, Trott's battle with Johnson, and with himself, was briefly resumed, with England's number three the loser again. No sooner had Clarke posted his leg side sentries than Trott, off balance and on edge, shovelled a nondescript delivery down long leg's throat. It was baffling – not least to Trott himself, who departed holding the bat by the blade, as though this was the way it now felt in his hands.

Full of the joys of spring, Warner swaggered into the evening press conference to pronounce the dismissal 'pretty poor and pretty weak' – a breach of the omerta observed by most cricketers about one another's performances, but only expressing what many were thinking. The garrulous Australian might have said the same about the single with which Pietersen got off the mark, although it was Warner's failure to hit the stumps direct from point that saved Cook from being run out without scoring. This was cricket at its most crassly selfish, and every bit as culpable as Trott's self-immolation.

Pietersen played more soberly on the fourth morning, as Harris and Siddle sustained marauding pace. The first ball after drinks, however, Pietersen addressed as though trying to demonstrate how Trott had been out the night before, hazily holing out to long leg. Cook went on playing with utter deliberation, as though he had nothing else planned until Christmas, and Bell settled in alongside him – but really, Pietersen's was a frivolous dismissal, and the sort of stuff to tip a dressing room over if it was already tilting.

Bell nicked off after lunch as the weather closed in, the eventual electrified hailstorm obscuring the view from one side of the ground to the other. But neither it nor the England captain would last long enough to have a significant impact: two balls after the resumption of play, Cook edged a cramped cut from Lyon, who promptly cleaned Prior up again in the leg trap. Clarke then recalled Johnson to, as Francis Urquhart used to phrase it, 'put a bit of stick about', and the Australians, after a mainly barren year, enjoyed their moment volubly, causing some observers to worry about the effect on impressionable pitch microphones. As ever, what was heard by viewers amounted to barely a fragment of the dialogue: Clarke telling James Anderson to 'get ready for a broken fuckin' arm', put to air apparently by mistake. But that entailed a week of breast beating and garment rending about sledging's perceived resurgence – where would the modern Ashes be without it?

If the Australians were excited, even a little euphoric, who really could blame them after a year like theirs? It was a victory in which each man could feel a stake, not least man-of-the-match Johnson and man-of-the-team-song Lyon, who led Australia in it for the first time since he had been entrusted with the task in January. For Clarke and Warner, first seen during this Ashes cycle at a sackcloth press conference, it was also a bonding experience. For England, it was a short, sharp, salutary shock, a fulfilment perhaps of their worst forebodings. Ian Chappell pronounced Australia's lead 'rather more than one–nil' and in this he was surely right.

Day One
THURSDAY 21 NOVEMBER

Close of play: Australia 1st innings 273/8
(BJ Haddin 78*, RJ Harris 4*, 90 overs)

'None of us like it,' said the stalwart Yorkshireman Maurice Leyland of short-pitched fast bowling. 'It's just that some of us show it more than others.' And Michael Clarke is starting to become one of those showing it.

When he took guard to his *bête noire* Stuart Broad after lunch at the Gabba today, it was the kind of scenario about which both would have been wargaming for months, perspiring in the nets, poring over video. In his new book, Clarke describes a mental technique he applies before Test matches where he visualises how each bowler will attack him, and pictures himself counterattacking.

What, though, does Clarke see when he tries to imagine Broad? Presumably not something like he saw today, which he barely saw at all: recoiling from a lifter that seamed back and homed in, he ducked his head and raised his gloves self-protectively. That, however, is the recurring vision for others, and Australia's captain headed to the dressing room with such chagrined resignation that you half expected him to break into a weary jog. As the rebound came to rest in his hands at short leg, meanwhile, Ian Bell pumped his fists for a full second and a half before rolling the ball to the umpire. You don't get much animation from this England side – more micturation. But nothing, you fancy, pleases them so much as the satisfactory execution of a plan, and this is now officially an oldie but a goodie.

It was in Brisbane four years ago that England first demonstrated an interest in Clarke's back-foot technique. Clarke had batted against England with creamy smoothness in the preceding two Ashes series, all eagle eye and nimble feet. On a pitch that wasn't the quickest,

Stuart Broad and James Anderson both set out to jam him up, sensing that the Australian was not quite comfortable either pulling or evading. The effect was immediate. Broad hit Clarke's helmet on the coat of arms once, the splice of his bat twice, and thought he had an edge that Hot Spot could not detect, someone perhaps exhaling at the wrong instant. After an uncomfortable hour and a quarter, Clarke nicked off to Steve Finn playing an awkward stiff-armed pull, and never quite recovered his savoir faire.

At that stage the short ball appeared merely a chink in Clarke's armour; since then it has spread into a bad case of rust, beyond the WD-40 potential of coaching, at least at the moment. When Clarke was not falling to the actual short ball in England, he seemed to be falling in looking for it, either hanging back out of the line, or trying to manufacture shots to get off strike – succumbing, as it were, not to the bullet but to the ricochet.

In one respect, Clarke is fortunate. The world does not abound in top-class fast bowling at present. Against most countries, a susceptibility to the searing short-pitched lifter is like being vulnerable to the one that pitches leg and hits off – yes, it's a weakness, but it's one you can live with. But this is its own perplexity. Its makes Broad – tall, slippery, razor-edged – an out-of-the-ordinary opponent. And Clarke has grown so grooved and honed with the years as to make difficult that step up to another level, especially with a bad back of which he is conscious if not actively protective.

Clarke executed the first part of his captain's skill set correctly at least, by winning the toss, and taking first innings with alacrity. With Australia one for 71 on the brink of lunch, he would have felt it a job relatively well done. The pitch was blameless, the microclimate congenial, the crowd in good humour. Yet it was noticeable throughout this period that whenever Clarke appeared in the players' enclosure, he was upright or leaning, grim-faced, a little strained. The smiles are for the public appearances now. The sunny celebrity cricketer of a year ago, who made back-to-back double-hundreds with the ease of an experienced guest on a talk show, now seems an age away – he has cut an irritable figure this week, rationing his remarks by the syllable, promoting a diary that seems to have been a strangely solitary endeavour.

Clarke would have been entitled to his frustrations today. Watson, Smith and Bailey succumbed to deliveries on a fifth-stump line – shots neither completely defensive nor wholeheartedly offensive. Warner holed out with the hard work done but the important work still to do. By midafternoon, the best time to bat at the Gabba, Australia had no specialist batsmen remaining, and England held the match on a taut rein.

From then, the rein rather slackened. It was almost as though the game had proceeded in advance of England's plans, and in the choice between game and plans Cook can generally be relied on to adhere to the plans. Swann came on, and bowled tidily enough, but no more, and Clarke's vice-captain applied a clear head and a straight bat to the Australian predicament. Brad Haddin's 114-run partnership with Mitchell Johnson showed purpose without haste – something their nominal betters would do well to emulate.

Haddin batted as trenchantly, in fact, as he had spoken the day before, living out his conviction that Australia were a 'more settled' team, playing to a 'clear message' and enjoying 'a great game' – a contrast to the anxious ensemble 'jumping at shadows' and experiencing 'insecurity around everything' that Haddin encountered on rejoining teammates in Mohali six months ago. Overtly directed at former coach Mickey Arthur, Haddin's criticisms offered other inferences for the drawing – for that bitterly unhappy team in India was led, of course, by Clarke, and with a freer hand than ever, following the retirements of Ricky Ponting and Mike Hussey. Perhaps Clarke's problems do not begin and end with the short-pitched riser.

Day Two
FRIDAY 22 NOVEMBER

Close of play: Australia 2nd innings 65/0
(CJL Rogers 15*, DA Warner 45*, 22 overs)

'Which Mitch?' It is a wonder some savvy marketing man has not
secured a copyright over this phrase, as they have 'baggy green' and
'Bradman', for the Mitchell Johnson who turns up on any given day is
a riddle wrapped in a mystery inside an enigma.

Actually, they normally both do, in some degree. Even on his most
errant days, Johnson will bowl a ball within the capabilities of nobody
else in international cricket – absurdly fast, brutally short. He may then
lapse into overs of dross, with the memory of the potential remaining,
a tad confoundingly.

Today was the jubilant reverse. The dross was on display early, in
three preliminary overs of straining round-arm that aroused the speed
gun's interest, but also kept fine leg busy. His four wickets in the afternoon were then all about his unique method and physical prowess.

At the press conference the night before, funnily enough, Johnson
had prophesied as much. 'Tomorrow will definitely be a little bit
quicker, the ball will move a little more sideways,' he said, after discussing his fine first-day innings. 'We've got a great bowling unit, I'm
really looking forward to bowling on this Gabba wicket again.' In that
quiet, faltering voice of his that sounds like somebody lost and asking
directions, of course, it had hardly seemed a prediction – more a gentle back-patting for his fellows. But runs seem to foretell wickets from
Johnson, as showers bring flowers.

The day actually began well for the visitors, England making
short, good work of the last two Australian wickets. Michael Carberry
homed in swiftly when he sensed that Brad Haddin would return for a
second run, the 33-year-old arm getting the better of 36-year-old legs.

Carberry then dug himself a comfortable ditch, sun glinting off the streamlined helmet that gives him the look of a futuristic policeman.

With memory of the trouble Johnson had given Jonathan Trott during the ODI series in England, however, Michael Clarke went about implementing a plan as obvious as it was alluring. Trott's elaborate movements across the crease have created a kind of back alley of bemusement for him down the leg side. Fielders were elaborately reconfigured; noisy chat was exchanged. Watching the clock as vigilantly as a low-level public servant, Australia squeezed in an extra over before lunch, and made it count. Feathering to Haddin, Trott was on his way regretfully, but almost resignedly. The Australians' gleeful mobbing of Johnson suggested a cheerfully noisy gathering round the bain-marie to come.

This was a classic Johnson wicket, in the sense that he is not your man if you want your outswingers classical and your seams exquisitely vertical. Johnson is frustrating and formidable for the same reasons – the sheer unpredictability of his variations from that sidewinding arm, the inconstancy of the seam's influence as the ball saucers through the air. Even his bounce is unlike that obtained by other fast bowlers. Not for him the vertical take-off of a delivery from, say, Glenn McGrath; more the rise up a steep ramp, where the ball keeps coming and coming, so that sternum height becomes clavicle height becomes mandible height, as your hands struggle to adjust.

Again, when Johnson resumed to Carberry an hour later, round the wicket with a short leg, it hardly took a mind-reader to penetrate anyone's thoughts. Carberry had left the ball composedly all day, but slipped subtly into a rut, unable to add to his total in twenty-five deliveries. Recoiling after a blow to the chest, he offered a haphazard hook, then neither quite played nor quite left the ball as it crossed his airspace. At the point of release, the ball was probably outside the return crease; at the end of its flight, it was in the hands of a wide-standing slip. Carberry would not have seen a lot of that in county cricket.

By now, the game was well and truly afoot. When Pietersen played a slightly casual mid-wicket drive at Harris, the scoreboard's electronic exultation of 'Pietersen OUT!' was thoroughly justified. Pretty soon, there was a danger the board might run short of exclamation marks. The greatest rejoicing was occasioned by 'Bell OUT!', when the man of the series in England failed to ride Nathan Lyon's overspin and bounce, followed by 'Prior OUT!', when England's vice-captain succumbed in identical fashion. Johnson completed his comeback mission when Joe Root played for in-curve and failed to cover out-curve, and Swann played mainly for self-defence.

Perhaps the most remarkable statistic amid all this mayhem was that England scored only 39 runs between lunch and tea in 25 overs – here was not merely rout but drought. In this precise encirclement, Johnson was abetted by Harris, Siddle and Lyon, and Johnson's point about the 'bowling unit' proved to have been quietly well made. Johnson plus Pattinson and Starc, for example, lacks the same stable core. As it was, Michael Clarke was able to maintain attacking formations through a period when he might otherwise have fallen back on the modern gambit of 'bowling dry'.

After tea, what had been Australia's problem in the northern summer was England's. England's innings was briefer than Australia's humiliating capitulation at Lord's, barely giving its bowlers time for a rub-down, let alone a decent rest. They toiled staunchly but stiffly. Australia's bowlers, meanwhile, enjoyed extra time to drain their isotonic drinks, chew their energy bars, consult their gurus, complete their wellness reports, etc. And over the course of a full-fledged five-Test series, these remissions are going to matter.

The Australian selectors' decision to rest their fast-bowling threesome in the week before the Test also stood vindicated. When enough of the right Mitch is seen, of course, selectors deserve their satisfaction – if partly as consolation for those opposite occasions.

Day Three
SATURDAY 23 NOVEMBER

Close of play: England 2nd innings 24/2
(AN Cook 11*, KP Pietersen 3*, 15 overs)

When Neville Cardus once accurately foretold a big Donald Bradman hundred after a slightly thin run of scores, he described it as 'not prophetic, merely deductive'. Similar sentiments were tempting to reach for as Michael Clarke achieved three figures this afternoon, two days after a nadir of sorts.

Tempting but deceptive: there is nothing inevitable about a hundred, even for a batsman who has now made 25 of them in 98 Tests. One lapse, one misfortune, one wrinkle in time, and all can come to nought. Australia's captain avoided them all today, including the voodoo of Stuart Broad's bouncer. There was hardly a false note in his 113, or in David Warner's 124 for that matter, and the ritual roasting of the pom proved its abiding popularity during their partnership of 158 in 175 balls.

They came together at a slightly delicate juncture for Australia, after the loss of Chris Rogers and Shane Watson in the day's first eight overs, although the scenario was rather more congenial than Clarke had faced on Thursday. Broad was now bowling his thirty-fourth over of the match, England's innings having barely afforded him a breather, and the pitch was a third-day belter, not a first-day bruiser. The short balls Broad produced were lethargic, run-of-the-mill. Clarke made solid connection with the first, pulling in front of square, and slighter with the second, which flew finer. Both sped to the boundary. Broad was able to propel only seven other deliveries to his nemesis before requiring respite.

It was not, perhaps, sufficient evidence to quell doubts about Clarke's technique against the short ball – no sooner had Broad finished than Clarke was signalling for new gloves, as he tends to when nervous. But soon after, Australia's skipper played a delectable shot, a broad-batted defensive block from Anderson that somehow penetrated the leg side for three, attesting the soundness of the underlying game. Warner punched the next ball straight, which Pietersen's languid chase turned into another three, and raised the openers' half-century. Rain then sprinkled, but Australia was back on track.

There could, in fact, hardly be a more complementary technical and temperamental batting combination for Australia than Clarke and Warner at the moment: Clarke the fluent right-handed driver, Warner the rasping left-handed cutter, both fleet-footed runners who feed off one another's confidence. They were also the ideal conjunction for the challenge of quick runs with an eye on a late-afternoon declaration. The difference conditions can make was clearly seen. On the low, dry wickets of the northern summer, the hosts were always able to slow the visitors' progress on the occasions the latter held the upper hand. On this pitch, flat but consistent in bounce and carry, two instinctively aggressive batsmen already with a comfortable lead were simply too hot to hold.

One over when Swann resumed after lunch showed them in exquisite harmony. To the first and third deliveries, Clarke went deep in the crease to work the ball backward of point for two and three; to the second he took advantage of a little bit of extra loop and hit a six into the vicinity of the players' enclosure. For good measure, Warner bounced the last ball over long off, and two overs from Swann ended up costing 28.

While this was not the best day to judge England's attack, because it was in the role of a defence, there were some disturbing signs for Andy Flower and David Saker. Four years ago, Tremlett's inexpression somehow enlarged his threat – then he was an impassive automaton with the sculpted cheekbones, programmed to deliver balls at 140 kmh at opposition breastbones. Now this inexpression has the effect of making him look like a duck in a shooting gallery, running in one way, walking back the other, having let the ball go at a set-and-forget 130 kmh. His short balls today sat up invitingly; when he overpitched he was driven greedily. Although his figures ended up bordering on the respectable, his mentor and advocate Saker will have worked a miracle if Tremlett plays a significant role in this series.

Tremlett was always, of course, a selectorial speculation, having played so little international cricket in the last two years. Swann's day provided richer food for thought. Without a rough to bowl into, without much of a purpose to bowl at, he leaked 113 runs in 21 overs with only two belated wickets to show for it. This deals a blow to England's plans that goes beyond this match. Swann is one of three world-class bowlers the visitors have brought with them, with a proven capacity for incisive wicket taking and long containing spells. Here he proved capable of neither, posing threat not even to the left-handers he has traditionally troubled: like Johnson on the first day, Warner today played him with ease, if not a little contempt, which may have been the message. In his recent autobiography, Ricky Ponting describes Swann as a bowler 'excellent when things are going well for him', but who 'loses his rhythm when the pressure's on'. Word may have got around.

Theories will abound in the next week about Swann's missing mojo. Is his elbow troubling him? Is he bowling too fast? Is he bowling too much from round the wicket? Is he unsettled by Australia's rotation of the strike? Actually, probably everything is connected, and it goes as much to mood. The perkiest thing about Swann today was his shirt, buttoned characteristically to the throat, so that its vertical collars looked like a uniform from a science-fiction series. Otherwise he rubbed his bowling hand in the dirt after each ball and accepted his hat back at the end of each over with a long-suffering air that may have communicated itself to others.

If ever a cricketer was long-suffering at the moment, it is Swann's teammate Jonathan Trott, whose bubble of habit has now been well and truly punctured. His woebegone Hilditchian hook to backward square leg off Johnson in late evening reeked of defeat. Michael Clarke might have exemplified the darkest hour coming just before the dawn today. But sometimes the darkest hour just stays dark.

Day Four
SUNDAY 24 NOVEMBER

Close of play: England 2nd innings 179
(81.1 overs) – end of match

What a difference a mere twelve thousand miles can make. On the evidence of the First Test, the polarities of the Ashes have been reversed, with mainly the same cricketers featuring in opposite roles, Australia the implacable pursuer, England the panting pursued.

Well, that and the uncommon denominator of man-of-the-match Mitchell Johnson – and here, what a difference *three years* has made. In the corresponding Test of the last Ashes down under, Johnson gave up 170 runs without taking a wicket, made a demoralised duck and dropped a crucial catch. At least he turned up on time and in correct attire.

In *this* Brisbane Test, with the visible addition of only a moustache, Johnson was about as thrilling as it possible for a fast bowler to be: raw, relentless, hard to pick up, impossible to predict, and, actually, just the kind of cricketer bound to unsettle a team such as England, which controls the controllables, achieves the achievables and eats the edibles, down to the last haloumi kebab. Johnson can hardly be planned for, because he destroys either everything in his path or himself. If you happen to appear in his proximity in the former event, just console yourself that it has happened to others. Actually, it's only eleven months since Johnson last happened, to Sri Lanka at the MCG: he dismissed six batsmen cheaply, lamed two others painfully and belted an unbeaten 92. On the evidence of only two further Tests, however, he made it to England solely for the one-day internationals. Did Australia miss a trick by excluding him from the northern leg of these XL Ashes? In hindsight, it is strange that he was not considered one of Australia's best six pacemen six months ago, but now looms so large.

Strange and not, because it was the concurrence of Johnson and the Gabba that was so formidable. Late in the day, in a fourth spell on a fourth-day pitch, Johnson was still obtaining carry through to Brad Haddin at head height. Against English batsmen who hardly experienced a ball above waist height in their home series, it was a fierce initiation, and one half-century among them reflected their disorientation and diffidence.

Alastair Cook alone looked likely to detain Australia. He was batting when I passed the Gabba nets at 9 am, taking his daily ration of throwdowns from coach Graham Gooch, as much part of his ritual as a gentleman's morning constitutional. Mentally, perhaps, he was already batting. As Kevin Pietersen chatted relaxedly in the players' enclosure, awaiting the commencement of play, Cook could be seen studiously modelling his stance.

In the middle it was seriously sticky, humidity at 80 per cent. After a few overs, Harris looked like he'd walked through a car wash; when Bell removed his helmet on being dismissed, he was the same shade as a lightly basted Christmas turkey fresh from the oven; longitudinal fissures edged with green on the first morning were now darkly outlined. As ever, the palms of Cook's gloves stayed white, and his hair remained unmussed. He ran circumspectly, usually rejecting second and third runs he might have sprinted for; often he jogged; every so often he walked. It was like a man pacing himself as he ascended a hill – a giant, steep, uneven, uninviting hill. He is no stranger to gradients: a year ago he batted nine and a quarter hours at Ahmedabad in what turned out to be a losing match, although it preluded a series win.

The lurking threat of Johnson, remained: when he wasn't bowling in this Test, it was almost like you were waiting for him to bowl, and you sensed that England somehow felt the same. When he came on at last after forty-five minutes, it wasn't altogether surprising that Pietersen helped him down long leg's throat. In the presence of aggression, some will always hanker to aggress, as it were. England didn't do much of it in this game, and when they did it went increasingly wrong.

Johnson wasn't the only natural force on display during the day. A storm in these parts is a Storm, and as the players evacuated ahead of the weather at 2 pm, the big screen flashed an official warning, urging patrons in the event of rain to 'follow instructions from GABBA staff and seek shelter from exposed areas of the venue'; there was no request to assume the brace position or offer of an oxygen mask, although perhaps this was understood. In fact, the crowd rather relished it, roaring approval at the first sign of hail, and enjoying the veritable blizzard as though it were part of the in-game entertainment.

They relished even more that the ground was bathed in sunshine within twenty-five minutes, and that Cook was out no sooner had play been resumed, the first of four English wickets for 19, to complement their first-innings subsidence of six for 9. Johnson, of course, hardly wrested Australia their 1–0 lead on his own. Haddin had a superlative fiftieth Test; the partnership of David Warner and Michael Clarke featured probably the best Australian Test batting in nearly a year; Nathan Lyon convincingly outspun his opposite number. Yet one also sensed that the addition of Johnson went beyond his statistical contribution of nine wickets and 103 runs – that his impact was also a catalyst in the volatility of the final day. There is something about having velocity and lethality in your corner to make cricketers walk a little taller, talk a little louder. England were pretty voluble on the first day as Stuart Broad made early inroads on Australia's order; they were eventually drowned out. What a difference, too, only a few days can make.

Jonathan Trott
WHEN THE BUBBLE BURSTS

Mental disintegration, anyone? After a defeat on the scale of England's at the Gabba, psychological speculation is almost mandatory. But in one crucial case, it was scarcely necessary – there was the evidence of our own eyes.

In Brisbane, Jonathan Trott was more at sea than Thor Heyerdahl.

David Warner notoriously called it 'backing away', but more properly it was fronting away, toppling towards the off as Mitchell Johnson homed in on leg, swishing and shovelling at passing lifters to which he could have realistically abjured a stroke, and perishing on the brinks of lunch and of stumps as though he almost could not bear to go on.

This was more than usually noteworthy, for Trott's career has actually been characterised by the opposite, an earthbound phlegmatism accentuated by his slightly bottom-heavy physique. Trott has faced nearly 8000 Test deliveries without hitting a six – an extraordinary statistic in our big-hitting modern age. So the sight of him deliberately hitting in the air while fielders were lurking back suggested a problem between the ears, rather than with the feet, the hands, or even the 'scared eyes'. Now Trott is on his way home with a 'stress-related' disorder that his coach Andy Flower says he has 'managed . . . very successfully' for 'several years'. He is accompanied, hopefully, by the good wishes of all in cricket.

Was he the susceptible type? The suspicion lingers. Trott is famous for his fussiness at the crease, a series of pedantic, guard-checking rituals over which he will not be hurried, driving bowler and fielders quietly crazy. In his autobiography earlier this year, Matt Prior described Trott as 'the most sledged player in county cricket', and this proven capacity to soak abuse up is actually one of the reasons England have relied on him as a boundary fielder in Australia. To use a bit of modern jargon, then, Trott is a player who thrives in his 'bubble' – a secure area in which he can cordon off his own game and leave what is happening elsewhere to sort itself out. As Johnson steadily insinuated himself into this bubble, Trott could not expel him without bursting it.

The process was gradual. Johnson was, of course, one of the bowlers who went round the park at the Oval in 2009 when Trott made his Test debut, looking like someone who had already been around for a decade. Trott and Johnson then had an interesting if low-key contest three years ago. Although Trott had a splendiferous series overall, Johnson was the most successful Australian against him, dismissing him thrice for 105 runs from 170 balls.

In the one-day series at the end of the northern summer, their meetings took on particular significance. Trott faced only twenty-two deliveries from Johnson, but these included a fierce lifter that had him caught behind, another that hit him in the helmet grille, and two very fast deliveries shown on replay to be hitting the stumps, for which the DRS issued lbw reprieves.

Trott will always be somewhat vulnerable to extreme pace at shorter lengths because of unusual trigger movements that involve his back foot moving forward – he is lucky, rather like Michael Clarke, that there isn't more 150-clicks stuff flying round in modern cricket. Trott had apparently been submitting himself to hour after hour on bowling machines primed to drop short at high speeds in an attempt to find his way back technically. But what Johnson really did, one fancies, was undermine something even more fundamental to Trott's sense of self. Trott prides himself on his cast-iron concentration, which more than once he has defined as 'the absence of irrelevant thoughts'. He was not hemmed in so much by irrelevant thoughts here as by thoughts both relevant *and* irrelevant, between which he can apparently no longer distinguish.

Trott's ordeal becomes the latest to be publicly lived out in a time of greater candour about cricket's mental toll, including but also going beyond the travails Marcus Trescothick famously outlined in *Coming Back to Me* in 2008. Just in the last two months, for example, both the captains in the last Ashes series in Australia have gone into detail about mental battles they endured during their careers.

In *Driving Ambition,* Andrew Strauss makes an acute observation about his anguish on England's tour of New Zealand five years ago, writing that his predicament was worsened by the need to conform to a stoical stereotype while feeling 'tired beyond measure, under pressure, searching for form and feeling very alone'. 'Although I never felt I was depressed,' Strauss recalled, 'I found myself desperately trying to show everyone, the management and my teammates, that I was fine, fully in control of myself and relaxed about the prospect of going out to bat, when I was actually in a state of near panic.'

The concluding chapters of Ricky Ponting's *At the Close of Play*, meanwhile, articulate thought processes into which he slipped towards the end of his career, feeling always one innings from oblivion, struggling to hold doubt at bay. As he says, 'I had heard sports psychologists talk about the "little voice" that sits on athletes' shoulders as they compete. It's a negative voice, one that says you're no good, that you can't win, that's it not worth it, that you should give up. The great athletes are able to ignore that little voice, or tell it to go away . . . I couldn't get rid of the little bastard at the end.' At last Ponting told his wife: 'I'm not sure I can do this anymore. I don't think I can keep putting myself through it.' It's easy to imagine the same sentiments echoing in the mind of Jonathan Trott.

Darren Lehmann
EL BOOFO

In all the atmosphere of mutual congratulation and international recrimination after the Gabba Test match, one notable milestone went almost completely unnoticed: Darren Lehmann's first Test win as Australia's coach at the sixth attempt.

It was an oversight and a tribute, testament to the naturalness with which the mantle of coach sits on Lehmann's shoulders even after the suddenness of his appointment barely five months ago, and the relative scarcity of success since. When Lehmann arrived at his embargoed media conference after the game, the air was of here-we-go-again, all-in-a-day's-work: nobody even ribbed him about the disreputable smudge beneath his nose currently impersonating a moustache. Were he a South American football manager, he would already have a semititular nickname, like El Boofo.

There remains something a tad shabby about the way Lehmann's predecessor, Mickey Arthur, was summarily despatched in July, enabling everyone else in proximity to exonerate themselves – let's not forget how Cricket Australia's board and executive rushed to give Arthur, and by implication Michael Clarke, full public support for their controversial Mohali suspensions. But there was also something vaguely distasteful about the axing of England's Peter Moores four years ago, and Andy Flower has amply filled the breach since. From unpromising beginnings, then, can emerge noteworthy careers.

The leitmotiv of Lehmann's coaching has been 'enjoyment' – an idea that always sounds appealing, but a quality that can be elusive in a professional sporting environment. Frankly, no experience is quite so enjoyable as winning. So it may be that Lehmann's outstanding achievement as coach has not been winning in Australia so much as preserving the team's confidence and morale in England when they did not.

The Australians lost disastrously at Lord's and at Riverside, but regrouped after each setback to play good cricket at Old Trafford and the Oval respectively – demonstrating thereby that while defeat can be chastening it need not become self-reinforcing. Lehmann then showed sufficient faith in his set-up to leave the coaching of the Australian team in India to his deputy, Steve Rixon.

That said, Lehmann has not been reluctant to exert influence on that same set-up. Space has been made to reintroduce Craig McDermott as bowling coach and Mike Young as fielding coach, and to bring in Lehmann's strength and conditioning coach with Queensland, Damien Mednis; don't be surprised if Queensland's highly regarded physiotherapist Martin Love takes on a role too.

Lehmann's tenure has also reinforced a respect for cricket knowledge and heritage around the Australian team, which does not always reconcile readily with the bulging, clipboard managerialism of high-performance manager Pat Howard, but for the moment they appear to be coexisting. It signals a modest but not insignificant shift in Australian cricket thinking. When Cricket Australia created the role of national coach in 1986, it appointed a former Test cricketer

(Bob Simpson) and succeeded him with another former Test cricketer (Geoff Marsh). That mould was broken fourteen years ago by the appointment of a former first-class cricketer turned professional coach (John Buchanan), who was succeeded by another (Tim Nielsen), who was succeeded by another (Arthur).

No rule says that a Test coach must have been a Test cricketer, or even that the better the latter, the better the former: none of Viv Richards, Kapil Dev, Javed Miandad or Glenn Turner made hugely successful off-field leaders. But especially these days, having done it oneself, preferably in the recent past, and being able to talk from experience, about bad moments as well as good, are useful attributes. Knowledge is depreciating fast in this fast-changing game, while 'empathy' is the most fashionable of modern qualities. It's only a decade since Lehmann was arguably the best player of slow bowling in the world – incurably inventive, innately aggressive. The verve and initiative with which Clarke and David Warner took down Graeme Swann on the third day in Brisbane was a plan with Lehmann's fingerprints all over it. Lehmann even played a couple of games in the Indian Premier League, for the Rajasthan Royals, before spending four years in the league as a coach. His connections with certain of his charges, therefore, are strong and deep. Ryan Harris, for example, has played under Lehmann for South Australia, Queensland, the Deccan Chargers and the Kings XI Punjab, and I dare say remains among the first Australians that Lehmann picks wherever they are playing.

This joint role of coach and selector remains a potentially sensitive one. Though the arrangement was a recommendation of the Argus Review, hybrid functions don't always make for easy peace. They remind me a bit of Tobias in *Arrested Development* crowing that his qualifications as an analyst and a therapist have made him 'the world's first analrapist'. In his recent autobiography, Mike Hussey expresses the traditional misgivings about such blurring of management responsibilities. 'If I was a player and was really struggling,' he says, 'I would like to feel confident in going to the coach and baring my heart.' Certainly you cannot help but wonder about the dynamic around a coach-selector when a team is altering its make-up as often as Australia was in England. Lehmann is adamant that the team's current top six will have a 'good go at it', but selectors can legitimately differ on how good 'good' is.

Nor is everyone as yet entirely enamoured of Lehmann, even if the allegiances are not perhaps as you might expect them. One night in Brisbane, an Australian and an English journalist were overheard in vehement disagreement about the Australian coach, although it was the Australian expressing ambivalence, harking back to that infamous verbal detonation against Sri Lanka in January 2003, and the Englishman who was praising Lehmann to the skies, in light of the esteem in which he's held in the broadacres – Lehmann is married to the sister of Craig White (Victoria, Yorkshire and England). As to the abrasive edge on Australia's cricket this season, it will be interesting to see how long it keeps up, for our visitors this time next year, India, may not be quite such an easy mark as love-to-hate-'em poms. In the meantime, though, El Boofo goes on living the dream.

FIRST TEST Woolloongabba, Brisbane 21–24 November 2013
Toss Australia   **Australia won by 381 runs**

AUSTRALIA	1st Innings			2nd Innings		
CJL Rogers	c Bell	b Broad	1	c Carberry	b Broad	16
DA Warner	c Pietersen	b Broad	49	c Prior	b Broad	124
SR Watson	c Swann	b Broad	22	c Broad	b Tremlett	6
MJ Clarke*	c Bell	b Broad	1		b Swann	113
SPD Smith	c Cook	b Tremlett	31	c Prior	b Tremlett	0
GJ Bailey	c Cook	b Anderson	3		b Swann	34
BJ Haddin†	run out		94	c Anderson	b Tremlett	53
MG Johnson		b Broad	64	not out		39
PM Siddle	c Cook	b Anderson	7	not out		4
RJ Harris	c Prior	b Broad	9			
NM Lyon	not out		1			
EXTRAS	(lb 11, w 1, nb 1)		13	(b 4, lb 8)		12
TOTAL	(97.1 overs; 416 mins)		295	(7 wkts dec; 94 overs; 420 mins)		401

ENGLAND	1st Innings			2nd Innings		
AN Cook*	c Haddin	b Harris	13	c Haddin	b Lyon	65
MA Carberry	c Watson	b Johnson	40		b Harris	0
IJL Trott	c Haddin	b Johnson	10	c Lyon	b Johnson	9
KP Pietersen	c Bailey	b Harris	18	c sub (CJM Sabburg)	b Johnson	26
IR Bell	c Smith	b Lyon	5	c Haddin	b Siddle	32
JE Root	c Smith	b Johnson	2	not out		26
MJ Prior†	c Smith	b Lyon	0	c Warner	b Lyon	4
SCJ Broad	c Rogers	b Siddle	32	c Haddin	b Johnson	4
GP Swann	c Bailey	b Johnson	0	c Smith	b Johnson	0
CT Tremlett	c Lyon	b Harris	8	c Bailey	b Harris	7
JM Anderson	not out		2	c and	b Johnson	2
EXTRAS	(b 4, lb 2)		6	(lb 2, w 1, nb 1)		4
TOTAL	(52.4 overs; 246 mins)		136	(81.1 overs; 326 mins)		179

ENGLAND

1st Innings	O	M	R	W	2nd Innings	O	M	R	W
JM Anderson	25.1	5	67	2		19	2	73	0
SCJ Broad	24	3	81	6		16	4	55	2
CT Tremlett	19	3	51	1		17	2	69	3
GP Swann	26	4	80	0		27	2	135	2
JE Root	3	1	5	0		15	2	57	0

AUSTRALIA

1st Innings	O	M	R	W	2nd Innings	O	M	R	W
RJ Harris	15	5	28	3		19	4	49	2
MG Johnson	17	2	61	4		21.1	7	42	5
PM Siddle	11.4	3	24	1		15	3	25	1
NM Lyon	9	4	17	2		20	6	46	2
SPD Smith						4	1	15	0
SR Watson						2	2	0	0

FALL OF WICKETS

Wicket	Aus - 1st	Eng - 1st	Aus - 2nd	Eng - 2nd
1st	12	28	67	1
2nd	71	55	75	10
3rd	73	82	233	72
4th	83	87	242	130
5th	100	87	294	142
6th	132	87	305	146
7th	246	89	395	151
8th	265	91	–	151
9th	282	110	–	172
10th	295	136	–	179

Umpires: Aleem Dar (Pakistan) and HDPK Dharmasena (Sri Lanka)
Referee: JJ Crowe (New Zealand)

THE SECOND TEST: Adelaide

BEARING UP UNDER THE STRAIN

There was one rousing moment amid England's otherwise grim and unavailing retreat on the fourth and final day of the First Test at the Gabba, as Mitchell Johnson worked up a fierce heat from the Vulture Street End.

The third ball of Johnson's ninth over was just about the perfect lifter, ascending from not that short a length, and seeming to follow Ian Bell as he limboed further and further backwards, until it looked like he was involved in a form of cricket yoga. It was, nonetheless, textbook stuff: at no stage did Bell take his eye off the ball. When he conferred afterwards with Alastair Cook they exchanged a ritual glove touch with the vigour of a high five.

It was a glimpse of both the thrill of fast bowling and also the exhilaration of counteracting it. Bell was not to benefit much by his survival, falling soon afterward to a Siddle sizzler. But it's this spirit, a relish of the contest and a pleasure in unity, which England must tap into at Adelaide Oval if they're not to fall by the wayside in these Ashes. The whistling in the dark from the England camp since Brisbane has emphasised the team's resilience – that a year ago Cook's men found themselves in the self-same predicament against M.S. Dhoni's team in India, and surged back to wrest the rubber. The circumstances of that series, however, rather suited England in their discipline and system – so much so, in fact, that they rolled similar conditions out for the Ashes at home.

A year on and the observable reality is that England are perhaps two years beyond their peak, that they now rely at least partly on what a boxing afficionado would call 'ringcraft' – preparation, experience, strategy, sagacity. This is fine, except that it has a tendency to make them a stationary target. And when England's well-laid plans go astray, they find it as pleasant as the prospect of colorectal surgery. While Australia confidently named its XI at Adelaide Oval today, England remained visibly sunk in deliberations. Which explains, perhaps, batting coach Graham Gooch's quirky choice of words a few days ago, when he referred not to the time-honoured 'executing of skill sets', or even the jargon du jour of playing 'with intent', but to 'will', with the inference that it had been lacking in Brisbane.

Why might that have been? This is an England team heavy with battle honours: not quite the MBEs pinned eagerly on their immediate forebears, but awards, medals, ribbons and riches aplenty. Three of them featured in the ICC Test team of the year named this week; no fewer than nine of them were involved in all of England's three consecutive Ashes victories, in 2009, 2010–11 and 2013. A fourth consecutive Ashes triumph? Well, it's a fine thing and worth fighting for, having not been accomplished since the reign of Queen Victoria, but it's a secular grail at best. And as football coaches and managers will tell you, back-to-back premierships and pennants are hardest of all to achieve.

Which is why, you sense, that the critical player for England this summer will turn out to be not Bell or Cook, resilient as they are, or Anderson and Broad, robust as they are, but Kevin Pietersen. Pietersen is the player whose dander rises at the contest, whose ego thrives on gratification, but whose will seems to come and go. If not the most conspicuous failure at Brisbane, he was perhaps the most confounding. In the first innings, he seemed simply to lose interest, as though he had something better to do or somewhere better to be; in the second, he holed idly out in the deep, leaving his champions to reach for the standard rationalisations about this being 'the way that he plays'.

Interestingly Pietersen did not make the ICC Test or ODI teams of the year, unlike the two others here, Cook and Michael Clarke, approaching 8000 Test runs; Cheteshwar Pujara, A.B. de Villiers and Mike Hussey were also rated ahead of him. These fruit-salad teams are always of variable quality, but in excluding Pietersen the selectors *did* express something of his unclassifiability. Is he is a genuinely great batsman? Or is it merely that he is capable of great innings?

Adelaide Oval is one of the venues where he has looked the former, with a commanding 158 in 2006 and a downright intimidating 227 in 2010. That he's been out on the lash with Stuart Broad in Adelaide, which the local tabloid thinks so scandalous, may be the best news England has had since they arrived in Australia. Australia prize his wicket highly – sometimes perhaps more highly than Pietersen does. But this is the series he needs to seize for the sake of both England and his own reputation, regardless of which matters more to him.

Individual performances, however, will take this England team only part of the way. The stepping-up might even need to be literal. Earlier this year, Matt Prior revealed a piquant, almost allegorical, back story to England's last Test in Adelaide three years ago, which began at such a breakneck pace with the run-out of Simon Katich.

At the Gabba, England had rued the lifelessness of the pitch. Hussey had edged his first ball just short of second slip, and gone on to make a sumptuous 195. Sensing after a few minutes that the same might apply at Adelaide Oval, Prior suggested that his cordon come forward a yard. 'Let's want this,' he said. And like a fairytale, Ricky Ponting edged the very next delivery low to slip; Clarke was shortly to follow. Over five Tests, such little steps, little gestures and little touches, expressing ambition, avidity and belief, mark the difference between really wanting and merely wishing.

Summary

WELCOME TO THE PLEASUREDOME

England's 218-run defeat in the Second Test at Adelaide Oval flattered them. It was about the only thing that did. Perhaps no team holding the Ashes has ever been written off as completely after a loss, following on as it did from their capitulation at the Gabba. They flattered again to deceive with early wickets, but it took only a day for spirit and ambition to overhaul and overwhelm professional proficiency and preparation. After the match, Michael Clarke was low-key, but you could sense his excitement; Alastair Cook was dignified, but you could detect his horror. More than four years after regaining the Ashes, England appeared within days of giving them up.

It wasn't unforeseeable. The teams alighted in Adelaide in very different shapes, Australia cheerfully selecting the same XI, and England trying to squeeze together something like a XV, seeing the need for more spin, more speed and more batting. At last they went with Monty Panesar's left-arm slows rather than Chris Tremlett's right-arm talls, and replaced the departed Trott with up-and-coming but uncapped all-rounder Ben Stokes – something of a surprise when Tim Bresnan was available to them again and reverse swing was predicted on the ground's new drop-in pitch.

Also on debut, effectively, was the new stadium – for that's what Adelaide Oval now is, rather than a cricket ground, albeit conceived on lines less brutal than the Gabba and less monumental than the MCG. The home of South Australian cricket has gained tens of thousands of seats in return for losing some of its connection with the city, now invisible from within, and accessibility, its picturesque gates having been replaced by cavernous vaults of ingress; the Cathedral End has become so in name only, St Peter's now being completely obscured, and the long straight boundaries, which were the

distinguishing characteristics of the playing surface, have been truncated. What they say isn't true, by the way: you *can* stand in the way
of progress. What you can't stand in the way of is football.

Australia again won the right to first innings, and again did not
make the best of the first day, which dawned dimly and remained so
until lunch, there being three rain interruptions in the opening session. After David Warner had flared briefly, Chris Rogers and Shane
Watson dealt with the fluctuations, Rogers at one stage pulling away
just as a cloud passed to flood the ground with sunlight, only for the
players to be running off minutes later seeking shelter from a down-
pour. It was hard going, with both Swann and Panesar obtaining
surprising turn. At times, Rogers had three fielders close in on the leg
side, close enough to be sharing a table with him in a café.

There was a sense of imminent major happenings not quite occurring. Rogers (27) should by rights have been lbw to Panesar, but the
DRS, as it is inclined to out of a false politeness, upheld a poor decision by Dharmasena. In the next two overs Rogers cover drove Swann
and cut Panesar for four, his first assertive shots; on other occasions,
wandering world-wearily to leg between deliveries, he almost looked
sick of his own struggles. Watson, meanwhile, played soberly if not
sombrely in the 'V', in search of his timing, and his entitlement to
the number three berth. For all their application, the Test was nicely
balanced when Australia lost three for 19 in 39 balls just before tea.
Advantage only tilted in their direction after the break, when George
Bailey took the initiative against the spinners, using his feet and hitting down the ground towards a newly inviting perimeter, while
Michael Clarke settled in, already with an eye for the morrow. Clarke
contributed barely a third of their 87-run partnership, but it was only a
deposit on his planned purchase.

If they had but known it, England were already in the process of
losing the match. Panesar muffed a caught-and-bowled chance when
Bailey was 10, Root missed a mid-wicket clip when Clarke was 18, and
Carberry a loose cut when Haddin was 5, after England had broken

through with the second new ball: acceptance of that last chance would have reduced Australia to six for 265, with their tail exposed. As it was, England returned for the second day with a faint sense of dread – it proved well founded.

To the first delivery of day two, Michael Clarke came down the wicket to Panesar, did not quite get to the pitch of the ball, and miscued just over extra cover's head. It wasn't quite the Ashes, but it was one of those moments when fate considers its options. Having come down against Australia on a semi-regular basis in England, it now nodded Clarke's way, and he, perhaps sensing same, continued to attack, the ball being at its hardest and the pitch at its flattest after a rolling. Australia would dictate or be damned, and Cook reacted unpredictably with some novel fields, including a short cover, a leg gully and two men back for the hook. The problem with the last was that one of the men was Panesar, who never looked likely to get under a top edge from Haddin (30) off Anderson.

Anderson actually bowled probably his best spell of the series, obscuring his bowling hand as he sought reverse swing, but Australia were now surging. England had one last opportunity to retard them, when Stokes, zippy but generally too short, drew Haddin (51) into a drive and celebrated what should have been his first Test wicket. Third umpire Tony Hill, however, detected a no ball that Ray Erasmus had somehow missed, prolonging the partnership into the afternoon. Fate had decided it was payback time.

By now Clarke was in superb touch, turning length into a thing for the batsman, not the bowler, with twinkling feet and brimming confidence. The short stuff that had troubled him in Brisbane was here hardly an option, and Broad and Anderson barely tried it; in fact, Cook used his fastest bowler for only eleven overs in the day, seemingly resigned to containing the damage for England rather than inflicting further on Australia. Clarke (91) gave another chance, straight into and straight out of Bell's hands at short leg, before reaching his twenty-sixth Test century, and his sixth at the venue. He must feel like rolling the pitch up and taking it with him. Now that it's a drop-in, he probably can.

Captain and vice-captain had added 200 in 304 balls by the time they were separated, and the ball could not have been deeper in Australia's court had the game been taking place next door at Memorial Drive. Haddin donned the baggy green that seems perfectly contoured for his head and swept three sixes off Swann, who ran exasperated fingers through his newly short-cropped hair. Australia's vice-captain then made short work of the 90s with a drive through mid-on, a nick through a vacant slip and a pull shot off Stokes, celebrating with another six swept from Panesar. At last Harris, with a full body swing but a minimal backlift, then hit a hearty half-century, sweeping Swann for consecutive sixes to raise Australia's 500 and expedite a declaration.

Twenty-one overs of the second day remained, and Johnson was given the first of them, proceeding to bowl the seven fastest balls of the match. They were also some of the fullest, the Australians having observed the pitch's muted bounce and the tendency of the odd delivery to stay down. The effect was electrifying. Cook's defence soon yielded like a flimsy door under a pounding; Carberry and Root held on, nervously strokeless. Harris and Siddle steamed in as well, before Johnson resumed for a final thrust, hitting Root resoundingly in the chest. When Root soon after sought a single to get off strike, Carberry responded with a seeming reluctance that almost cost him his wicket. One for 35 at the close, England were lucky it was no worse – although that was not far away.

It was Lyon who achieved the breakthrough for Australia early on the third morning, when Root swept imprudently at a ball that bounced more than he expected. A fretful Pietersen then picked out the finer of two mid-wicket catchers as he came impetuously down the wicket at Siddle – the kind of shot to silence a dressing room that would already have been subdued. At length a phase of five maidens got under Carberry's skin, and he wasted a commendable half-century, his first in a Test, by pulling to the left of Warner in the ring, who took a brilliant catch in an outstretched hand. There was no longer much point in talking about England's arrears in terms of runs – it was measurable in parsecs.

The afternoon became The Johnson Show, with a bill of passing guests, all pausing briefly, none looking comfortable, amid a general air of chaos. Stokes was thought to have nicked a delivery into his pads and awarded four for overthrows, then given out lbw on referral; Prior, peppered with short stuff, nicked the first ball pitched up to him; Broad and Anderson were bowled by the first balls they received. Broad prolonged the agony nearly seven minutes by asking that shining bolts on the sightscreen be obscured – as if, as Robertson-Glasgow once said of a batsman holding up Larwood, 'seized with that last love of life which must have urged victims of old to address some trivial and delaying remark to the executioner'. Worst of all, perhaps, was Swann throwing his bat at a wide one, making a mockery of Bell's efforts to keep the innings alive at his end. Panesar put the conditions in perspective with an hour's blocking while Bell played some superb strokes, including a six over cover from Harris, and some lofted drives from the spinners, thereby dissuading Clarke from enforcing the follow-on. But that was England's only accomplishment. Johnson's seven for 40 was virile fast bowling meeting impotent batting, with the stumps, demolished four times, bearing the brunt.

Though Anderson briefly checked Australia by removing Rogers and Watson cheaply, and Panesar bowled Clarke with a lovely delivery, Warner's free-flowing strokes maintained the home team's momentum towards victory. In the evening press conferences, Johnson predicted more of the same, although his captain sprang a surprise the following morning by declaring at the overnight score. It transpired that Clarke merely had an eye on the weather, but at the time it seemed marvellously Macchiavellian, for it left Cook with barely fifteen minutes to compose himself before taking up arms against Johnson again, and the bowler found the perfect response to a batsman anxious about the fuller ball: a hissing bouncer along the left-armer's alleyway of anxiety, at which Cook top-edged a pull. Harris hovering on the newly near fence had time to make ground and take a tumbling catch.

With two days to bat, and their best long-distance batsman gone, England had never looked more forlorn. Carberry got a bigger piece of his pull shot but picked out Lyon at backward square leg, and another four-day Test was in prospect. In the event, Root took root and Pietersen took note as they had not the day before. For an hour either side of lunch, the pair toiled honourably against hostile bowling and fielding. If it wasn't too little, however, it was too late. Pietersen's staid half-century was ended by a skimmer from Siddle, who thereby claimed the wicket of England's number four for the ninth time – not quite McGrath v. Atherton, but on the way. After giving up some inviting dross earlier, Steve Smith then conned Bell into shovelling a low full-toss to mid-on – a third Smith win over England's best player, forming a third of his Test wickets.

Root carried on studiously, justifying his selection as successor to Trott with a visible relish for the contest, while Stokes hung in roughly, absorbing and turning back some Australian aggression. A brush of shoulders with Johnson as they passed in mid-wicket briefly detained umpires Dharmasena and Erasmus, who reported both, perhaps to give them something to do – otherwise, with their recourse to video for virtually everything, including a check on the front line after each wicket, they seemed almost completely redundant. ICC referee Jeff Crowe dismissed the reports anyway.

Prior's first half-century in nine Tests, which began diffidently before opening out, extended the Test into the final day, but not for long or with much conviction. He and Broad became the third and fourth batsmen to succumb to pull shots; Swann and Panesar fell wildly and timidly, so that even if the rain that ended up skirting the ground had fallen then, it would have been irrelevant. The flattery was now all for the Australians.

Day One
THURSDAY 5 DECEMBER

Close of play: Australia 1st innings 273/5
(MJ Clarke 48*, BJ Haddin 7*, 91 overs)

Pitches produce unpredictable effects. Batsmen shrink from a shade of green. Bowlers tend to see the world through straw-coloured glasses. But the opposite can also apply.

Michael Clarke just refrained from dancing a jig when he won the toss at Adelaide Oval this morning, allowing his batsmen first use of a new surface – dropped in, of course, but looking worthy to follow in the local tradition of pitches as perishable as granite. And so it has played. First-day pitches are inclined to scuff, the sun having yet to harden their upper crust, but this one is still wearing its few blemishes lightly, like marks on linoleum removable with just a bit of Ajax.

The game became, therefore, not just a battle between bat and ball, but also between batsmen and themselves. Wasting a start on a pitch ripe with runs can be far more frustrating than failing on a dicey deck, where chance and luck are your dearest frenemies. Likewise can an unexpected breakthrough feel doubly availing to a fielding side. That was certainly the sense you got as England celebrated the wicket of David Warner, who struck the ball peachily for half an hour then poked softly to point. Adelaide's new big screen is only just out of a striking batsman's eyeline at the Cathedral End, so that just before his dismissal Warner had found himself gazing up at a replay sequence of his four clinking boundaries. The stroke by which he perished was that of a batsman in a mild reverie already contemplating the carnage of the afternoon.

No such allegation could be aimed at Shane Watson and Chris Rogers, two batsmen for whom this series means more than most, who pursued their batting with utmost seriousness, intent on realising prior investments in it. Watson, whose technique over the years has passed through more hands than a boxed set of *Breaking Bad*, has spent much of the last few months recalibrating the front-foot stride that kept tripping him up in England, consulting Darren Lehmann and Michael Di Venuto in Australia, the Rajasthan Royals' Zubin Bharucha and New South Wales' Mark O'Neill, Uncle Tom Cobley being otherwise engaged. Their influence is palpable: Watson is now playing so relentlessly straight that Alastair Cook feels he can dispense with a fine leg; when the Australian finally glanced one after lunch, the nearest English player was in the dressing room.

On a pitch more congenial to Swann and Panesar than perhaps either of them expected, Watson toiled hard. He has never been a natural at using his feet to slow bowling, moving as daintily as an elephant in a tutu. Occasionally his weight of shot made you quail for the ball. The bat speed when he straight drove Swann for four before lunch would have created a breeze at the bowler's end. When he lofted Panesar down the ground for six after the break, the ball travelled almost as far high as it did long. Otherwise he was solemn, straight-batted, straitlaced.

In the hiatus between Ashes series, Rogers took counsel from Dean Jones about counteracting Graeme Swann, who dismissed him six times in England, and has adjusted his stance so as to free himself to move down the wicket. First on the dance floor at Prahran CC functions and never missing an episode of *Dancing with the Stars*, Rogers is naturally quick on his feet. He hinted at benefiting from the tuition in the Shield game at the MCG a month ago, looking fluent against Nathan Lyon and Steve O'Keefe. Since then, though, he has played four indeterminate innings without passing 15 – not cause for alarm so much as for introspection, run-making being a habit out of which you don't want to slip for too long. So here at Adelaide he stuck to what he knew and felt safe.

The score mounted, but without threatening to engulf England. This was not Australia 'moving the game on', as Michael Clarke likes to put it, but endeavouring to set the game down, and it did not come quite so naturally as blasting, blazing, effing and blinding did in Brisbane. There was an air throughout the partnership of two batsmen thinking hard: Here is a pitch on which I will only get out through my own follies, so if I banish all error I can theoretically bat indefinitely. The near-inevitable occurred when Watson and Rogers both fell within six balls of one another, guilty of slight misjudgements, shots neither aggressive nor defensive in character. They had batted ably but not decisively: 28 scoring shots in 167 balls conveys the degree of Rogers' restraint.

Only after tea did Australia really begin addressing the ball rather than premeditating the situation. Still following the impulses he channelled so successfully in India, George Bailey approached the game as breezily as a Sheffield Shield fixture. He has made three hundreds for Tasmania at Adelaide Oval, including a scintillating 101 in a Ryobi Cup final in March last year, and when he attacked today held nothing back: in three Test innings he has hit as many sixes as fours. He too, though, should have gone further, pulling a short ball a little too lightheartedly.

For England, this was one of a number of things to go right on a day they really needed to, including some external variables: the climate was mild, the atmosphere a good deal more welcoming than the Gabba, and the rub of the green roughly even. The toll of what went amiss, however, was at the close unclear. Joe Root should really have held Clarke (18) at mid-wicket off Swann, and Michael Carberry should definitely have held Haddin (5) at backward point – as drops go, it bordered on the flippant. Every run the pair make tomorrow will be gall and wormwood. Both players already boast three-figure averages at Adelaide Oval: they, at least, will feel no compunction about capitalising on their good fortune.

Day Two
FRIDAY 6 DECEMBER

Close of play: England 1st innings 35/1
(MA Carberry 20*, JE Root 9*, 21 overs)

In the range of cricket events guaranteed to sap morale, the needless and avoidable rank highly. There's the misfield and the overthrow;
there's the loss of a wicket to a run-out, or to a part-time bowler.

Yet among vexations nothing quite rivals taking a wicket with a
no ball, thereby forfeiting it. It is the loss of an advantage to the most
minuscule of transgressions, a bitter curdling of the milk of success.
And should it eventuate in the vicinity again of any member of this
England team, they will hark back to today – especially Ben Stokes.

Just after noon, 24-year-old Stokes was in the middle of a positive spell from the Cathedral End. Working up a brisk pace, he had
beaten the edges of both overnight batsmen, Michael Clarke and
Brad Haddin. The fourth ball of his eleventh over landed on a testing
length, drew a telling edge, and Haddin had no objection when sent
on his way by umpire Ray Erasmus. Few maiden Test wickets could
have seemed so timely: Australia, six for 367, momentarily held up in
the nick of time as they threatened to streak away. Just then, however, Erasmus had a second thought, detaining the departing Haddin
while a review was undertaken of the landing position of Stokes'
front foot . . . and, as the seconds passed, a murmuring in the crowd
grew towards a thunderclap of exultation. Haddin turned back with a
delighted toss of the head.

The no ball was actually a clear one; that Erasmus missed it really
beggars belief. Stokes in relation to the front line for the preceding few
overs would, in fact, have made an interesting study: had the umpire
overlooked previous no balls that, were they called, might have made
the bowler warier of the front line? But that was academic, even if the

ensuing debate between Stokes and Haddin at the over's end was conducted in more layman's terms. Press-box lip-readers pored over the
replays, it being hard to know exactly what one could say under the
circumstances. 'I'll get you next time I comply with Law 24'? 'You've
just overstepped the Ashes'?

A jibe about the urn would not have been out of place. Haddin's
partnership with Clarke, born the previous evening, had only just
passed three figures; it was to double, and thereby cube England's
woes, by wending and blending its way past the second day's mid-
point. In doing so it turned Australia's in-between scoreline of the first
day into a total that, to paraphrase the famous Bodyline telegram sent
from here eighty years ago, assumed proportions to menace the best
interests of Alastair Cook.

Australia's captain and vice-captain both toted century averages at
Adelaide Oval into the Test, and in maintaining them showed how
those records had been earned. The equivocation of the first day was at
once consigned to the past. Two experienced cricketers took the game
on against a still relatively new ball and prospered.

In the first innings at Brisbane, of course, Clarke had provided
evidence of a weakness to the short ball. On reflection, it might better have been deemed a non-strength: rare today are the bowlers
and pitches that seriously jolt a batsman. When Stuart Broad came
round the wicket and dropped short today, the ball barely rose ster-
num-high, and Clarke glided it laconically behind point for one of
his 17 fours.

Clarke was more measured here than in his euphoric assault on
the Proteas on the same ground a year ago. In defence he struck poses
of guard-dog watchfulness; in attack he ran full pelt between wickets,
head down, arms pumping. His twenty-sixth Test hundred was a triumph of assiduous discipline and drilling, rehearsed seemingly down
to the last gesture: he had probably kissed his wife that morning pre-
tending she was the coat of arms on his helmet.

Haddin lived a little more dangerously, even before his video reprieve. On 18, he might have been run out from backward point, but Michael Carberry's aim was awry. On 30, he top-edged Anderson to fine leg, where Monty Panesar did everything possible to ensure he arrived at the ball on the first bounce, being slow to move, indirect to the ball, and disinclined to dive. What Ian Chappell once said of Phil Tufnell can be applied to Panesar: England look better when he is bowling because at least then he is not fielding. A related question for Cook was what Panesar was doing at fine leg in the first place.

Haddin's in due course proved the truly dismaying shots for England, making the field seem simultaneously small enough to clear but too large to patrol. Showing the confidence with which he hit through the line, almost half his runs came in the vector from mid-wicket to mid-on; five times he swept, effortlessly, for six. Haddin paused to let his captain walk off first at lunch; otherwise he stood back for nobody.

When it was England's turn, Clarke and Haddin threw down another gauntlet by allotting first over to Mitchell Johnson, scourge of Brisbane, rather than to Ryan Harris. While the pitch here is slower, air is the same everywhere, and the ball from Johnson split it at velocities in excess of 150 kmh on its way to splitting Cook's stumps. Erasmus again needed advice from the crease video monitor, although Johnson was as comfortably in as Stokes had been obviously over.

Johnson was so appreciably pacey that Harris and Siddle in their turn resembled slow traffic in a fast lane. His impacts were percussive. Hit in the chest in Johnson's second spell, Joe Root bore the blow with Woodfullesque stoicism, only to play and miss a little hazily at the follow-up. He would have felt a long way from Sheffield Collegiate CC.

It was appropriate that Root and Carberry should have been in possession in the last hour, for it was the reprieves they granted Clarke and Haddin respectively on the first day that England were also rueing today, dropped catches forming their own genre of cricket calamities. England's only consolation was that it might have been worse. Called by Root for a single off the penultimate ball, Carberry started slowly, ran diagonally, and would have been well short had Chris Rogers hit the stumps direct from cover – what might have been another self-inflicted wound ended up merely as a narrow squeak. Arguably England were due a stroke of fortune, although today they rather made their own luck.

Day Three
SATURDAY 7 DECEMBER

Close of play: Australia 2nd innings 132/3
(DA Warner 83*, SPD Smith 23*, 39 overs)

'To bowl fast,' wrote the Englishman Frank Tyson, in perhaps the best-known passages on the subject, 'is to revel in the glad animal action, to thrill in physical power and to enjoy a sneaking feeling of superiority over the mortals who play the game.'

For much of Mitchell Johnson's career, it is a passage you might have struggled to explain to him. He seems a gentle soul – easygoing, soft-spoken, too polite for a 'feeling of superiority', let alone thrills and revelry. Even last night, as he kicked back with the media after taking five for 16 in five overs, surging into Australia's ten greatest Test wicket takers, he sounded like he couldn't get out of the room quickly enough.

That demeanour has coloured views of him somewhat. He has been both heavily vaunted – it's fifteen years since Dennis Lillee described him as a 'once-in-a-lifetime prospect' – and hastily discounted. Only ten months ago, Shane Warne in his much-publicised critique of Australian cricket excluded Johnson from his eighteen-man Test squad to 'help us get back to Number 1 in the world'.

Yet here we are a few weeks from Christmas, and Johnson is providing Australian cricket with its most thrilling theatre since Warne himself. Today on an Adelaide Oval pitch just a little up and down in bounce but otherwise excellent, his reverse swing and straight-ahead speed dissolved England's middle and lower order like a wave washing over a sand castle.

Normally reticent Johnson rather revelled in it too. He loosened up with expansive shoulder rolls. He celebrated wickets with jubilant leaps. Twice he was on a hat trick, and his responses to demolishing the poorly protected stumps of Stuart Broad and James Anderson with the first deliveries they received even had a touch of schaden-freude. He admitted feeling 'a little bit emotional'; some English batsmen might now be feeling the same.

What has turned the butt of the Barmy Army's long-running joke into the Jeff Thomson *de nos jours*? The only visible change to Johnson's physiognomy is the moustache, now almost bushy enough to infringe Campbell Newman's anti-bikie laws. You can take your pick of other factors: switching states, becoming a parent, going on Twitter. To his technique there have been quiet adjustments: he now runs in straighter and more economically, and delivers in the main with a higher arm. He has never looked fitter, and by now probably puts smiley faces on his wellness forms.

But just as notable, perhaps, is what has not changed. Johnson is *still* quick – comfortably, now, quicker than anybody in the world. The Englishmen who subdued him in 2009 and 2010–11, meanwhile, are that little bit older, slower and tireder. Their mask of professional calm, in fact, seems to be slipping with each over of this series: Matt Prior and Graeme Swann, worldly cricketers with more than 130 Tests between them, have together eked out four scoring shots in six innings.

Johnson proved too much for the young'uns today as well, of course: Ben Stokes was struck on the pads before he could so much as twitch. But this is an England team built on seniority, and Johnson is making it look senescent. He has, then, renovated not just himself, but fast bowl-ing more generally, emphasising its special relevance to a seam-bowling world grooved at 135 kmh. He is 100 per cent shock value.

It was not a one-note, one-name day: Test cricket never is. And the turning point arguably involved not Johnson and the shock of the new, but Siddle and a subtle but significant ongoing battle. As ever, Clarke greeted Pietersen with the two mid-wicket catchers who are now his permanent shadow: when Pietersen sits down in restaurants these days, two waiting staff probably take up positions in relation to him where mid-wicket would stand. Some might have taken this as a caution, or at least under consideration; England's mercurial number four viewed it as a mixture of invitation and bluff. The premeditated pick-up shot he played to Siddle was either a riposte to the fielders' presence or a pretence of their non-existence. Perhaps not even Pietersen knows.

It was a reminder that for all Johnson's sudden impact, many of these Ashes antagonists have been hard at it since July, and are deep in one another's heads. Siddle has not enjoyed the encomiums that Ryan Harris or James Anderson have, but he has carried out a task where England's most dangerous batsman is concerned. So far, Siddle has effectively bowled a total of 32 badgering and boring overs to his rival in six and a half Tests for an analysis of four for 76; in all he has dismissed Pietersen eight times in Test cricket, more than any other bowler.

Above all, the shot was heedless of England's position, two wickets down, 500 in arrears, with a partner playing just his third Test, and the batsman next in playing his first. It was wanton cricket executed with an air of indifference, and, frankly, Pietersen's third example of same in this series – all exhibits in the case that England's fortunes do not rank uppermost among his priorities.

Thereafter, only Ian Bell barred Australia's path, and he could be manoeuvred round. As finely as he batted for his undefeated 72, he became not so much a partner as an eyewitness, while accident piled on accident 22 yards away. When the last wicket fell, he patted Panesar's back solicitously and walked off very nearly unrecognised. The limelight, naturally, fell on Johnson. As he walked down the players' race at Adelaide Oval, his face was lit up by flashbulbs, like a catwalk model. Assuming Australian success here, he will have been the decisive factor in his country's last three Ashes victories (having been man of the

match in Australia's win in Perth three years ago). If that doesn't justify
sensations of superiority to ordinary mortals, not much does.

Day Four
SUNDAY 8 DECEMBER

Close of play: England 2nd innings 247/6
(MJ Prior 31*, SCJ Broad 22*, 90 overs)

'Wretched, weak, timid, gormless.' The morning's headline on Cricinfo
left out only 'scared eyes'. England's position in the Second Test as the
fourth day dawned was not merely untenable but indefensible. Their
fight was for scraps of dignity, and scrappy scraps at that.

They endured long enough for Joe Root to burnish his reputation somewhat, but when he departed after four and a quarter hours it
was with head bowed, and the merest acknowledgement of generous
applause. Rightly so: if anyone in the England brains trust talks about
'taking away positives' from this Test, they should be not just scoffed
at, but sectioned.

The day before the Test, that trust could be seen in earnest convoca-
tion around the Adelaide Oval pitch, permutating draft combinations
in light of its dryness and colouration. Really, they could have picked
anyone. This hard-driven Australian team would tell W. G. Grace: 'Get
ready for a broken fuckin' beard.'

It looked like ending very quickly indeed when Michael Clarke
declared as late as possible before play, pitching his opposite number
Alastair Cook into action against Mitchell Johnson rather earlier than
he, or anyone, expected.

Johnson belongs to a category of bowlers it is signally difficult to
prepare against. The Australians once readied for Lasith Malinga's
slingers by taking the legs off a bowling machine; a year ago, I watched
Australians preparing for lofty Morne Morkel by taking throwdowns
from Stuart Law standing on a box. But to build your own Johnson

would require the services of Victor Frankenstein.

The English were actually aware of Johnson's threat before this tour, going to the trouble of bringing quick left-handers Tymal Mills and Harry Gurney to bowl in their nets before the Tests: Mills, genuinely pacey, left a vivid bruise on Cook's bicep a month ago, an image of which circulated freely on social media. But in the context of a 530-run deficit in a Test match, a wicked riser hugging you as uncomfortably as a badly cut suit, from a bowler who has cleaned you up in the first innings with something full and very fast, is just about the worst delivery to receive in starting.

Cook's hook was a confused, almost involuntary shot, jammed up by the angle, hemmed in by the situation. Regret would have set in about halfway through the stroke, and lasted all the day. England's captain survived only sixteen deliveries in this match, on an excellent batting surface at a ground where he batted for more than seven hours three years ago: it is the most telling of eclipses.

Australia's captain, meanwhile, was on something of a roll. He relieved Johnson after only four maiden overs, the first of more than twenty bowling changes for the day – a sharing of the workload made with half an eye on the Perth Test in which the teams will be involved as soon as Friday. Clarke deployed all six of his full- and part-time bowlers before lunch, probing for breakthroughs, although there was urgency rather than haste to the Australian effort, and the fielding remained rivetingly tight. As Root and Pietersen held them up for more than two hours either side of lunch, they lost neither patience nor purpose.

Pietersen approached his task as carefully as he should have the day before, playing with exaggerated correctness, conspicuous discretion, and princess-and-the-pea particularity about inactivity in all areas of his batting panorama, despite the ends of the new Adelaide Oval having been turned into icebergs of whiteness with canvas sheeting. He could probably detect the wing-beat of one of those tsunami-causing Japanese butterflies.

In midafternoon, Johnson bowled searchingly to Root with two

fielders on the leg-side boundary and another at leg gully for the short
ball, beating edges every so often with reverse swing, burning ears
with his own version of a Sergio Leone monologue whenever he did.
Root responded with soundness on the back foot, a straight bat and a
seraphic smile – England's best batting thus far for the series, or at any
rate their least worst.

The conditions held no real terrors. Clarke's formations suggested
only a pitch on which the odd delivery was staying down or not coming through: Siddle bowled to Root with a screen of three short
fielders and to Bell with two short covers, a deeper cover two-thirds
of the way to the boundary, and a backward point halfway. If they did
not generate wickets directly, they added to the sense of pressure without remission. There was always something for batsmen to think about,
adjust to, factor in. Having Steve Smith bowl without an outfield to
Bell just before tea turned into another coup: England's standard-
bearer for the last five months seized too greedily on a low full-toss,
and miscued to mid-on where the predatory Johnson swooped.

Root and Ben Stokes hung about by their fingernails after the
break – formative experiences for both, one fancies, as they mature
into the inheritors of this England team. If it is any consolation, some
fine careers have started at the bottom, and these two were surrounded
but did not surrender. Both fell playing defensively in the vain hope of
enduring into the following morning. It is their seniors on this expedi-
tion who have fallen short.

Further obsequies will follow at this match's conclusion today.
In the meantime, it needs remarking that Ray Erasmus and Kumar
Dharmasena have officiated here as actively as two people who won
a contest to stand in for the umpires, with the stipulation that every
so often they make the sign of a square with their hands. Supervision
of the front line they seem to have abandoned altogether, standing
well back: virtually every decision has needed ratification by the third
umpire checking for a 'foot fault'. It hasn't been 'wretched, weak, timid,
gormless', but nor has it been far short of that.

Day Five
MONDAY 9 DECEMBER

Close of play: England 2nd innings 312
(101.4 overs) – end of match

With moments to elapse of this one-sided Adelaide Test today, James Anderson made surprisingly solid contact with a ball from Peter Siddle, sending it back down a depopulated ground towards the straight boundary – what turned out to be the game's final scoring shot.

Onlookers immediately earmarked it four – something to be retrieved rather than chased. Yet three Australians set off in pursuit: Chris Rogers from short cover, Mitchell Johnson from forward square leg, George Bailey from short leg, still under his helmet. And although the last two peeled off, Rogers kept going full pelt all the way, just failing to make it. This proved the difference between Australia winning by 218 runs and 220 runs.

It was a trivial and a telling moment. From winning the toss to winning the match, Australia conceded their opponents nothing. And in this now clearly funicular Ashes affair, the home team's fielding has been an index of their progress and cohesion – as indeed it was England's three years ago. Back then at this venue, if you recall, England played what their coach Andy Flower described as a 'perfect Test': a first-day rout of Australia, a relentless two-day drive towards a declaration, a steady last-innings asphyxiation. And it all started with Jonathan Trott's direct hit to run Simon Katich out in the first over, executed with a sniper's clinical efficiency – the kind of fielding that lifts your own team and leaves your rivals reeling.

On *this* occasion in Adelaide, the equivalent effort was Australian: David Warner's diving one-handed catch at square leg to dismiss Michael Carberry, ending England's best partnership and precipitating their worst subsidence. For with that catch, Mitchell Johnson could commence his next spell to the debutant Ben Stokes, and England's innings ended up being not so much completed as abandoned.

For Australia, this represents a considerable improvement in the last six months. In England, Michael Clarke's team fielded adequately, but no better. They executed a single run-out at the last possible moment – the final delivery of the series – and dropped several crucial catches. Had Australia accepted chances offered by Joe Root at Lord's and Old Trafford, in fact, there's actually no guarantee the youthful Yorkshireman would have been playing, and excelling, here. After putting down the second of these, Michael Clarke wrote self-critically in his recently published *Ashes Diary*: 'As captain I have to lead by example in catching as much as in batting.'

In Adelaide, that is what Clarke did, accepting three smart slip catches as part of a near-flawless effort. Australia's errors condensed to a rough total of one catch: one half-chance at the wicket, two quarter-chances at bat-pad. Some standouts in the fielding enterprise are obvious. Not only has Warner scored more runs in this series than anyone, but I suspect he has saved more, both directly and indirectly. He patrols the ring and the outfield with the jubilation of a little boy on a bouncy castle. Yet what's most impressive is that Australia's outcricket reveals no obvious weak links – a tribute to long-time assistant coach Steve Rixon and recently rehired fielding consultant Mike Young. Elders Rogers and Harris, who took crucial boundary catches here, lose little by comparison with younger peers. Brad Haddin's limber 200th Test catch likewise belied his years.

England is not an altogether shabby fielding unit, but its standards have slipped, and in Adelaide it had a bad match in the air, dropping three catches in the last session of the first day. Carberry at point alone spared Haddin twice, with a hard-handed pratfall and a slowpoke pick-up when the Australian keeper was 5 and 18 respectively. Seven years ago, England left Monty Panesar out of a Test team here because of his poor fielding; here he was included in spite of it. He did not touch the first ball hit to him, diving over it like a soldier jumping into a foxhole; batsmen routinely took extra runs on his weak arm, spectators cheered him patronisingly.

Worst of all, posted to fine leg on the second morning when Anderson was dropping short to Haddin, he funked a top-edge catch – poor fielding *and* field placing. Had it been possible to read Anderson's mind at the time, he would probably have been in breach of about ten clauses of the ICC code of conduct. I compared Panesar to Phil Tufnell a few days ago, but that may have been harsh, on Tufnell. Tuffers caught a Michael Slater top edge at third man here nineteen years ago – one of the most uplifting acts of fielding I have ever seen, for its sheer miraculousness. There was never the slightest possibility of Panesar doing likewise.

The other dimension of fielding, of course, is what it expresses about your team. It is the set of cricket skills that involves the least, and least meaningful, statistical recognition. Unlike baseball, which faithfully records its 'errors', cricket has no individual measures for runs prevented, or runs conceded, or proportions of catches accepted successfully. That being so, fielding becomes a qualitative rather than a quantitative factor – a reflection of how team members are pulling for one another. And in this series it is faithfully mirroring the balance of power on the field, with Australia forming a kind of electrified fence, and England an unkempt herbaceous border.

The huddle Clarke's team formed at the end of the Adelaide Test was a happy portrait of mutual reinforcement, the Indian file of variously dressed Englishmen that formed for the post-match handshakes a sorry troop. That will not change readily. Fielding is about confidence and enjoyment as much as technique, and England's cricket at the moment has a generally hurt and demoralised air. Yet they need to start somewhere. Rogers did not quite reach the rope in time today. But if you don't chase, you won't catch anything.

A Comparison
1958–59 AND ALL THAT

In my hallway at home hangs a fading framed document, an auto-graphed team sheet of England's Ashes team of 1958–59, replete with storied names: May, Cowdrey, Graveney, Dexter, Bailey, Evans, Tyson, Trueman, Statham, Laker, Lock. I'm fond of it for several reasons, one being that it was a kind gift of the daughter of Sir Robert Menzies when I was researching her father's life. But I appreciate above all its tinge of doom, for perhaps no cricket team visiting Australia has travelled so hopefully, performed so haplessly and departed so help-lessly – well, perhaps till now.

Then, as today, England arrived in search of a fourth consecutive victory against Australia, with a team full of heroes from the preced-ing wins. The casting today is almost a remake of the original. Graeme Swann plays the part of the famous finger spinner Laker. James Anderson fits the bill as the Lancastrian paceman Statham. Chris Tremlett is the horses-for-courses-pick-on-the-basis-of-prior-success Tyson.

Above all, Alastair Cook makes an interesting update of the serene, superbly groomed son of the establishment Peter May. Alan Ross called the parting of Peter May's hair 'a symbolic representation of single-mindedness and innocence'. There is something similar about the square set of Cook's sculpted jaw. Like May, Cook is twenty-eight, in his batting prime after a career of more-or-less unleavened success, and struggling with pressures he has not previously known.

You can read accounts of May's mission and drop Cook's name in without too much of a stretch. Jack Fingleton's classic *Four Chukkas to Australia* concluded: 'Peter May is the most defensively minded cap-tain I have seen . . . May attacks the batsman when he first comes in. Should he get a start, however, May switches his attack to defence in depth.' Sounds like Shane Warne on Cook. There are differences aplenty, too, of course – the bowling is more legal now, and the atmosphere less polite. But as Mark Twain contended, while history does not repeat, it does rhyme, and the shortcomings of these England teams separated by fifty-five years might be felt to form a heroic couplet.

The weaknesses of May's team proved to be what had initially been taken as strengths: experience, maturity, prior success. 'Australian cricket . . . [is] a young man's game and we had too many players on their last tour,' May later reflected. 'If you have lost the keen edge, Australia finds it out.' And there was no resharpening that edge once the team had arrived. The Englishman Ian Peebles, correspondent for the *Sunday Times*, put it decorously: 'Most members of the side have played a great deal of cricket . . . and the wear and tear on the joints must eventually tell.' The sports science jargon is now more high-falutin', but the phenomenon is just as recognisable. No two bowlers have bowled more international deliveries in the last three years than Anderson and Swann. More than their joints have been worn and torn.

The contrast between the teams fifty-five years ago was especially pronounced in the field. 'The [England] team moved around ever so slowly,' reported Fingleton, 'as if walking on the bones of interred cricketers.' Australia's fielding, by contrast, was 'superb to watch', featuring lots of close catchers, who because of England's general caution with the bat were seldom endangered. Again, it all sounds very familiar.

Because fielding is such an expression of the personality of a team, attitude came to be thought of as being as much a factor as athleticism. Fingleton thought that the cricket treadmill had 'destroyed something vital in the average English players' enjoyment of the game', that the team was a 'sad one', lacking 'fun, gaiety and spontaneity'. Keith Miller said that he had 'never known an England side more spiritless'. Peebles wondered whether it wasn't a team surfeited with success who had taken the challenge too lightly after victories in 1953, 1954–55 and 1956. 'Whether or not they were too confident is difficult to say,' he ventured. 'The side certainly had had a fine run, but . . . such victories did not fit players for the severe struggle under Australian conditions.'

Asked on Monday if the same might apply to his team, Cook acknowledged the perception: 'It's a good question. Sometimes, when you haven't been playing well, that's one thing you start looking at — whether we do have that hunger.' The England captain's further remarks involved lines wide enough to be read between. He said first that he felt 'from speaking to the guys, and watching them' that England still had the will to resist; then he added that 'the only way we can drag it out is by getting that hunger, that desperation, back into our game', from which comment the absence of same could be inferred.

The 1958–59 Ashes also has parallels with the present from the winners' perspective. Richie Benaud and Michael Clarke may not be body doubles as captain, but their teams have in common a core of players with shared experience of Ashes defeat: for Neil Harvey, Alan Davidson, Colin McDonald and Ken Mackay, read Brad Haddin, Ryan Harris, Peter Siddle and Mitchell Johnson. In his autobiography, May recalled Benaud's comments in 'something like bewilderment' after the final Test at Sydney: 'I've played three series against England over nearly six years and I've never known what it's like to win one before.' Clarke does, but only once out of five. Hungry? Desperate? My word.

And while the Australian nations of 1958 and 2013 might appear to share little, common to both is a perception of cricket as under social and cultural threat, in need of victory to re-enchant the country's public. The great grandee of London's *Daily Telegraph*, E. W. Swanton, wrote a wonderfully eccentric column on the eve of the 1958–59 Ashes about the attractions rivalling cricket Down Under. 'The average young Australian,' he opined, 'is inclined to spend most of his weekends under water, studying the varieties of marine nature, spearing fish, and caring for his lady friend.' By Swanton's lights, then, Richie Benaud's team beat not only England, but scuba and sex. That's probably something not even Michael Clarke can accomplish.

SECOND TEST Adelaide Oval 5–9 December 2013

Toss Australia   **Australia won by 218 runs**

AUSTRALIA	1st Innings			2nd Innings		
CJL Rogers	c Prior	b Swann	72	c Prior	b Anderson	2
DA Warner	c Carberry	b Broad	29	not out		83
SR Watson	c and	b Anderson	51	c Carberry	b Anderson	0
MJ Clarke*	c Anderson	b Stokes	148		b Panesar	22
SPD Smith		b Panesar	6	not out		23
GJ Bailey	c Swann	b Broad	53			
BJ Haddin†	c Prior	b Broad	118			
MG Johnson	c Broad	b Swann	5			
PM Siddle	c Prior	b Stokes	2			
RJ Harris	not out		55			
NM Lyon	not out		17			
EXTRAS	(b 8, lb 1, w 1, nb 4)		14	(b 1, lb 1)		2
TOTAL	(9 wkts dec; 158 overs; 634 mins)		570	(3 wkts dec; 39 overs; 163 mins)		132

ENGLAND	1st Innings			2nd Innings		
AN Cook*		b Johnson	3	c Harris	b Johnson	1
MA Carberry	c Warner	b Watson	60	c Lyon	b Siddle	14
JE Root	c Rogers	b Lyon	15	c Haddin	b Lyon	87
KP Pietersen	c Bailey	b Siddle	4		b Siddle	53
IR Bell	not out		72	c Johnson	b Smith	6
BA Stokes	lbw	b Johnson	1	c Clarke	b Harris	28
MJ Prior†	c Haddin	b Johnson	0	c Harris	b Siddle	69
SCJ Broad		b Johnson	0	c Lyon	b Siddle	29
GP Swann	c Clarke	b Johnson	7	c Clarke	b Harris	6
JM Anderson		b Johnson	0	not out		13
MS Panesar		b Johnson	2	c Rogers	b Harris	0
EXTRAS	(lb 3, w 2, nb 3)		8	(lb 1, w 4, nb 1)		6
TOTAL	(68.2 overs; 308 mins)		172	(101.4 overs; 439 mins)		312

ENGLAND 1st Innings	O	M	R	W	2nd Innings	O	M	R	W
JM Anderson	30	10	85	1		7	1	19	2
SCJ Broad	30	3	98	3		6	0	19	0
GP Swann	36	4	151	2		9	3	31	0
MS Panesar	44	7	157	1		10	0	41	1
BA Stokes	18	2	70	2		7	3	20	0

AUSTRALIA 1st Innings	O	M	R	W	2nd Innings	O	M	R	W
MG Johnson	17.2	8	40	7		24	8	73	1
RJ Harris	14	8	31	0		19.4	3	54	3
NM Lyon	20	5	64	1		26	7	78	1
PM Siddle	14	4	34	1		19	4	57	4
SR Watson	3	3	0	1		6	3	6	0
SPD Smith						7	0	43	1

FALL OF WICKETS Wicket	Aus - 1st	Eng - 1st	Aus - 2nd	Eng - 2nd
1st	34	9	4	1
2nd	155	57	4	20
3rd	155	66	65	131
4th	174	111	–	143
5th	257	117	–	171
6th	457	117	–	210
7th	474	117	–	255
8th	483	135	–	293
9th	529	135	–	301
10th	–	172	–	312

Umpires: HDPK Dharmasena (Sri Lanka) and M Erasmus (South Africa)
Referee: JJ Crowe (New Zealand)

THE THIRD TEST: Perth

LIFE IN THE FAST LANE

Google 'fast WACA pitch' and the search engine retrieves 1.9 million hits. It feels like there should be more. 'Fast WACA pitch' is one of those cricket memes that comes trippingly off the tongue, like the 'ego of Kevin Pietersen', the 'enigma of Shane Watson' and now the 'moustache of Mitchell Johnson'.

As a foundation myth of Australian cricket, 'fast WACA pitch' also has the advantage of being true. It is a tremendous place to bowl at pace; it is also, after a while, a tremendous place to bat. The first innings of Australia and South Africa a year ago were wound up in less than five sessions; South Africa then romped along at better than five an over for 500 minutes on the way to winning by more than 300 runs.

Even the practice pitches are fast at the WACA. In his autobiography, Stuart Broad's father Chris recalls arriving here twenty-seven years ago and being knocked over in the nets so often that he was afraid to go back again. He then went out and blasted 162 as England made nearly 600. Western Australia, a state of extremes, hosts cricket to match. To this now comes Australia's most extreme cricketer, in the hottest and hairiest form of his career. In prospect is the cricket equivalent of watching Donald Campbell drive the *Bluebird* on Lake Eyre.

Yet here's a curious thing. With seventeen wickets at a pin's fee

in this series, Johnson is clearly the difference between the teams. At
Adelaide Oval, word of his return to the bowling crease was apparently enticing spectators back to their seats from the hospitality
areas – something hardly known since Shane Warne was in his pomp.
But only six of Johnson's wickets have been in England's top five, and
Jonathan Trott, representing two of those, is no longer here. Johnson
has dismissed Kevin Pietersen just once, with one of his worst balls,
and Ian Bell not at all. His superlative first-over bouncer to unseat
Alastair Cook in Adelaide was his only second-innings scalp.

What we have is a study both of fast bowling's direct effects, in
terms of eclipsing specialist batsmen, and also its indirect effects, in
destabilising a whole order. The fact is that England's upper echelons
have been punching under their weights for the last two years, averaging below their career averages, having lost the 'daddy hundred' habit
they picked up at their peak. The most reliable component of their batting has been the redoubtable Bell, abetted by numbers seven to ten.

Every bit as valuable as Johnson's early breaks, then, has been the
dismay he has spread in his second, third and fourth spells among batsmen used to a softer ball and cushier conditions. Johnson has used his
bouncer well, and the threat of his bouncer even better: Stuart Broad's
startled jump and Graeme Swann's retreating flails at Adelaide were
the shots of batsmen playing at its ghost. As Johnson's bowling coach
Craig McDermott noted on Tuesday: 'There's not too many tailenders around the place who bat below seven that enjoy playing a lot of
balls around their helmet, so, so be it.' And McDermott can personally
attest the cumulative effects of intimidatory fast bowling, having been
reduced over the course of his own career from an accomplished junior
all-rounder to a quavering number eleven.

Some other outcomes of Johnson are less measurable, but no less
tangible. His presence has made for a more abrasive Ashes than in
England. There's something about being in the presence of really fast
bowling that sets not only pulses racing but mouths, both among the
targeters, determined to amplify its threat, and the targeted, resolved to

drown them out, with broken fuckin' relations the result.

Adrenalin trips switches of aggression. Needing to bat two days at Adelaide, England lost four wickets to pull shots, none of which they could control, three of which were contingent on finding open space or carrying out of the park. They were fight-fire-with-fire shots. What one normally fights fire with, of course, is water.

So Johnson is a phenomenon not simply in the poles he takes or the bones he breaks, but in all the things he makes you think about apart from the only one of importance – the ball he is bowling to you. All of it is coupled to a quiet, almost withdrawn off-field nature. His moustache is so popular it is probably about to be franchised, but Johnson finds the fuss bemusing. His front arm is encased in vivid tattoos, but in discussing them he sounds like Sidd Finch reciting a Zen koan. Something about that is confounding too.

So how do England counter the conjunction of Johnson and the 'fast WACA pitch', which overwhelmed them even when they were playing well three years ago? What they badly need is a batsman to push on. Every member of their top five in Adelaide has 'been in the contest' in this series, as they say, and made a half-century. The best they have done thereafter is the 87 that Joe Root compiled in Adelaide.

It did not do, and certainly will not do here. Perth is no stranger to batting collapses, of course, and they are somehow starker for the brilliant light and sapping heat. Australia lost eight for 19 here against the West Indies twenty years ago to cough up the Worrell Trophy. But, to reiterate, it's with good reason that a decade ago this was the venue where Matthew Hayden set the world Test record score, against Zimbabwe, on a pitch lightening towards white beneath a blazing sun – much as this one looked today.

Conveying something of the sense of impunity a good batsman can enjoy once set, the average of the 19 hundreds at the WACA in the dozen Tests of this century is 224. Balls race to the boundary across a smooth, slightly convex outfield. Only the fittest bowlers maintain their pace in later spells. The most culpable misdemeanour a batsman can commit at the WACA, then, is not to get out for 0 but to get out for 30. Google 'big WACA hundreds' and you also get 1.9 million hits. It's not a meme, but it's not meaningless either.

Summary
THE CRACK-UP

At 1.44 pm on Tuesday 17 December 2013, Australia reclaimed the Ashes after more than four years and three consecutive series defeats, having utterly incinerated their opponents. The circumstances were entirely fitting. The day was hot. The margin was emphatic. James Anderson and Stuart Broad, who had irritated and lorded it over the Australians in England, were at the wicket. As the last wicket fell to Mitchell Johnson, his 23rd of the series, his former scourge, the Barmy Army, were silent, having spent much of the previous two days singing 'The Hokey-Pokey', after three days of loyally chanting 'We're Gonna Win 3–2.' The scenes of Australian triumph after George Bailey accepted the catch at short leg from Anderson's fend were unabashedly emotional, full of joy and affirmation, and also relief on a Mafeking scale.

It had taken fourteen days of cricket to turn the Ashes topsy-turvy. Michael Clarke cautiously would not agree that it was his career highlight; Alastair Cook had no doubt about it being his career lowlight; indeed it can have been seldom in history that a captain has gone from being cock of the roost to feather duster so quickly. It was only 124 days since England had been setting off fireworks at the Oval, where seventeen of the same cricketers had been involved.

Although the rambling, sun-blasted WACA offered a contrast to the stark newness of Adelaide Oval, the only change in the teams from the Second Test was Tim Bresnan replacing Monty Panesar. The conduct of the game was similar also, Australia winning the toss, recovering from an indifferent start, defending a total, charging to a declaration, then setting to prise England out in the fourth innings. The stakes being so great, the Australians began nervously, losing Rogers to a misunderstanding, Watson to a misjudgement, and Clarke and Warner to mistimings of Swann, whose opening spell of 5-0-18-2 was his best of the tour. When Bailey top-edged an ungainly one-handed pull shot, the hosts were four for 134 – a good day's work for England on an excellent pitch. It was Steve Smith who now ratified his achievements in the away Ashes, opening his account by hitting Swann into the Lillee-Marsh Stand, and continuing in the same bouncy vein, as cheerful and cheeky as a telegram boy on a bicycle. England had no more plan for bowling to him than they'd had in the northern summer. When they dropped short, as they did too often, Smith pulled avidly in front of square; off the hip and the toes, he also made merry. The heat was intense – the kind that generates mirages. But the only illusions were England's, and Haddin helped Smith dispel them in a partnership of 124 in 218 balls. Busy as ever, Haddin hit through and across the line without fear, Anderson and Broad achieving little sideways movement, and Swann minimal purchase.

Australia's innings survived another eighty minutes on the second morning, each tailender pitching in usefully against some inconsistent bowling and less than urgent captaincy, but Cook and Carberry survived an awkward spell before lunch and some time after in growing comfort. It was their best and most convincing opening partnership, despite the second-day pitch being slightly quicker than the first, Cook playing as fluently as he had for six months, Carberry as proficiently as he had in his brief Test career. Their stand had swelled to 85 in 105 minutes by the time Shane Watson broke it with the game's first smidgen of swing, and Joe Root fell victim to the DRS's eccentricities: given out caught behind in the absence of compelling evidence by umpire Erasmus, his referral was rejected in the absence of compelling counterevidence, to form a perfect non-decision decision.

As at Brisbane, Lyon preyed successfully on Cook's cut, and Siddle on Pietersen's ego, and England at four for 180 by the close had squandered its careful start, a state that soon worsened the next day. Erasmus seemed to get his lbw call in Bell's favour right in the third over after resumption, only to have it overturned by an improbable black-box projection, which the Australians sought only because they had a referral up their sleeves on the eve of the 80-over reset. With a new ball at their beck and widening fissures at which to aim, Australia's pace attack again made short work of England's tail, Stokes and Prior perishing wildly, the rest mutedly. The full pitch that struck Broad's boot not only gained an lbw verdict, but sent the victim to hospital for the inevitable 'scans'. A more superficial scan of his teammates in the field as they came out 134 runs in arrears suggested some deep psychic wounds.

Warner set the stump mics humming as he set the old scoreboard spinning, storming to 50 in 56 balls with 42 in boundaries, dragging Rogers along in his slipstream. This was batting as dismaying in its way as Johnson's bowling, complete with soundtrack, and England's outcricket plumbed harrowing depths, Prior setting an abject example. Warner's fifth Test century was not as spectacular as his second, at the same venue two years earlier, but in its way it was both more assured and more devastating, England's celebration when he succumbed trying to repeat a six down the ground looked more like a wake.

Still more destructive hitting was to come, before lunch on the fourth day from Watson, who resumed on 29 from 66 balls and reached three figures in another 40. Watson took chances with both hands: he should have been run out by Root from mid-off on 51; on 87, he swung wantonly at Stokes and visibly remonstrated with himself; on 90, he was missed off Anderson by Bresnan at long off, who took the catch only to topple over the line; on 103, he was missed at cover by Bell, a childishly simple chance, although Bresnan at last had the presence of mind to throw down the stumps as Watson exhibited an absence of mind in merely jogging a run. Between times, his bat detonated like cannonfire. He hit two fours and a six from Swann's first over of the day, a four and three sixes in his next; all were in the 'V', in the vague direction of Gloucester Park. He reached his hundred, rather deftly, with a boundary from a leg glance, signifying his booming confidence with a full Freddie – the Christ pose, face on to the dressing room.

Having administered the requisite man-love, George Bailey took Australia to a declaration and Anderson to the cleaners, pillaging 28 from the exhausted paceman's final over. In fact, if you wanted to administer the Ludovico technique to an English cricket fan, footage of this session would be just the job. It culminated with Cook's castling from the first ball of England's second innings; as he went back to a ball from Harris that seamed away to snip the off bail.

In fact, Australia made less even progress through the afternoon, being slowed by Pietersen, Bell, and most impressively Stokes. Pietersen, as usual, looked in no trouble until he tried to repeat a straight six off Lyon that the breeze dropped into Harris's hands at long on. Bell proceeded with utmost control to another half-century only to touch an upper cut from Siddle, and Stokes advanced with growing command on a maiden Test century, defending straight, standing tall. There was something to be said for the scenario: everything to gain, nothing to lose, the minimum of expectation, the opportunity to do what came naturally. And as time at the crease rubbed off a few of the 22-year-old's rough edges, attacking fields opened up scoring options, while Australia reciprocated his generosity in donating half-trackers – after tea on the fourth day was probably the hosts' loosest session of the series, as their contrite bowlers later confessed. Prior helped Stokes carry the game into a final day.

It was at last a matter of waiting. On a pitch scored with sunspots of rough and cracks darker than David Warner's moustache, both batsmen struggled not just with the sideways movement, but simply to keep their footing; the crevasse at the Prindiville Stand end looked deeper than the Marianas Trench. A dozen deliveries seared past the edge in the first hour, jagging both ways, drawing philosophical smiles. Although Prior finally fell to an improvident waft, Stokes was not to be denied, reaching his century off 159 deliveries with 16 boundaries and dragging England to lunch at six for 332. Lopping off England's tail, however, required only 38 more balls, despite Broad's dispensing with his moonboot for seven of them, being branded a 'pea heart' by Haddin for his trouble. The Australians had had the courtesy to clap Stokes's hundred at least, as England had scorned to do for Warner the previous day. They could afford a little belated generosity.

Day One
FRIDAY 13 DECEMBER

Close of play: Australia 1st innings 326/6
(SPD Smith 103*, MG Johnson 39*, 87 overs)

So deep are we in the Ashes present, that the Ashes future is hard to contemplate. And with more than half the players in the series on the far side of thirty, it is almost easier to predict who will be attending the Lord's Test of 2015 than who will play in it.

About the presence of one player, however, you can already make an educated assumption. At twenty-four, Steve Smith is the youngest member of his team. Yet each day he seems to tick another box, today being one of the boxier ones: a maiden Test century in Australia. Funnily enough, Smith's record at the WACA Ground had previously been poor: just one first-class fifty in half a dozen games, and an average of 17. Yet he tackled the task and the conditions with typical jauntiness, and with cross bat shots that made him look as Western Australian as Swan Lager and secessionism.

Including lunch, Smith was an hour getting off the mark – never a pleasant sensation. With the wicket of Michael Clarke, Graeme Swann was bowling a teasing loop, inviting Smith down the track – an invitation that seldom needs reissuing. To his sixteenth ball, Smith advanced again, and drove straight for six. It was an impudent shot, though not an imprudent one: barely 150 metres from sightscreen to sightscreen, 30 metres shorter than the MCG, the WACA rewards hitters in the

'V'. It was with a similar shot, too, that Smith registered his maiden Test century at the Oval three months ago – it was like he was taking up the thread of an old conversation.

To Swann, Smith kept on coming, springing down the pitch two or three times an over, even if it was to play defensively. Most modern batsmen use their feet to spinners reluctantly, as though fearful of trip-wires and booby traps, preferring the security of the crease and the comfort of their thick-edged cudgels. Smith is so relaxed he might almost be humming a tune as he progresses down the track. For all the time he spends out of his ground, he has been stumped only once in twenty-nine Test innings.

The exciting additional element to Smith's batting this afternoon was his pull shot, which he played to balls only slightly short, trusting his eye and the bounce. Like many a visiting bowling attack, England's grew excited by the lift on offer, and Smith took toll. Seven of his thirteen boundaries accrued to mid-wicket, including the shot to reach his hundred, and 81 of his 103 runs were accumulated to leg – not so much a bias as a cause.

Smith's technique, of course, is all tics and twitches, quirks and quiddities – but then, so is that of Shivnarine Chanderpaul, whom you could hardly say was doing it wrong. And if Smith's experience is not yet especially deep it is already exceptionally wide. His cricket CV reads like the Who's Who entry of a clubbable man about town: Sutherland, NSW, Sydney Sixers, Kent, Worcestershire, Kochi Tuskers Kerala, Pune Warriors, Royal Challengers Bangalore, plus several others I may have missed, and a few he may not even remember.

If Smith is a near-certain starter for Lord's in 2015, Brad Haddin, who will by then be in his thirty-eighth year, is probably not – and it's in that take-everything, leave-nothing spirit that he has tackled his cricket this summer. Australia's scoreline of five for 143 when he came to the wicket today was potentially alarming, but his familiar presence made it less so, and his virile strokes steadily helped Smith restore Australia's equilibrium. When Haddin took a step or two down the wicket to hit Bresnan into the terraces beyond mid-off, it was another 'V' for victory sign.

No less than at Brisbane and Adelaide, the toss had been a valuable one for Michael Clarke to win, giving his bowlers additional recovery time after the demands of three consecutive days in the field at Adelaide Oval, with the further possibility of the sun opening the WACA's traditional cracks. England were buoyed early by a misunderstanding between Warner and Rogers which a Royal Commission could probably not get to the bottom of. The call was Rogers', but a call is not the only material influence on a run; batsmen also respond to one another's physical cues. For a fatal fraction of a second, each partner mirrored the hesitation of the other, and James Anderson took advantage of the breakdown in negotiations, summing the situation up nicely by throwing at the end to which the 36-year-old rather than the 27-year-old was running.

That left Warner to carry Australia's cause forward, which he did with typical brio. You can't say you aren't warned with Warner. His helmet and gloves feature patches of hazard orange and racing-flag chequer, as if to remind you that danger is never far away, and even in serious phases of play his antic spirit will assert itself. To Broad he played one horrid swipe that would have endangered spider-cam had he connected. To Bresnan he attempted a baseball slug that the bowler following through could just not grasp with his outstretched right hand. In the same over, however, Warner mowed a pull shot for six over mid-on, a right-field homer from this left-field competitor. The report of the bat sounded like a Purdey 12-bore echoing over a grouse moor.

Strangely, the one shot in Warner's locker that has not been in the finest fettle lately is a stroke that has customarily been a strength of his – the cut, by which he fell for the third time in four outs in this series. Michael Carberry would have been forgiven had his life flashed before his eyes at backward point, for he had dropped an identical chance in Adelaide to spare Haddin, but he made no mistake this time. As is often the case at the WACA, the batting microclimate was at its best after tea, Mitchell Johnson hitting crisply through the line, and putting his arm round Smith's shoulders as the pair sauntered in at stumps. It's true that there remains much about Lord's 2015 we do not know. But which team will go into the match with custody of the Ashes seems ever more obvious.

Day Two
SATURDAY 14 DECEMBER

Close of play: England 1st innings 180/4
(IR Bell 9*, BA Stokes 14*, 68 overs)

An odd wrinkle of Alastair Cook's career is that the WACA is where he watched the only Test match he saw live before he played one. That was ten years ago, when he was a teenage visitor playing club cricket for Willetton, in southern Perth, and Australia were hosting, and roasting, Pakistan, by the small matter of nearly 500 runs.

What did Cook derive from the experience, apart from a sense of Australia's formidable prowess in their own environs? Interestingly, Australia's three most successful batsmen were all West Australians: Justin Langer, Damien Martyn and Adam Gilchrist. Langer alone made 191 and 97. Something of their local knowledge must have seeped in: three years later, Perth would be where Cook made his first Test hundred in Australia. Alternatively, as England's captain illustrated today, perhaps the WACA offers conditions that he finds welcoming, including pace that suits his repertoire of nudges and bounce that suits his back-foot game. Whatever the case, Cook, who has spent a lot of this tour looking like a cowboy whose horse has been shot from under him, sat a bit taller in the saddle, only to fall at the last to an unforseen misfire – the Test at the close was keenly poised.

The tricks of batting at the WACA have been set down so often that they should almost have been carved into tablets. You play with a

vertical bat, a horizontal bat or nothing: it was Bob Simpson's conviction that 90 per cent of deliveries bowled here could be safely left, such
was the pitch's lift and carry. It happens that few players in the modern game do the nothing thing with as much willingness, or even quiet
enthusiasm, as Cook. Bowl a fifth-stump line to the visiting skipper all day and you fancy he would go to stumps 0 not out. Winston
Churchill once said that nothing was quite so exhilarating as being
shot at with no result. Cook has a somewhat similar relationship with
the cricket ball.

Every part of those defensive arts was needed as England began
their reply to Australia's 385 in an awkward half-hour before lunch,
and Mitchell Johnson took the new ball from the Members' End to
an expectant roar: on a pitch where James Anderson could reach 146
kmh, Johnson could surely reach warp factor five. In fact, Australia's
only glimmer of a wicket before lunch was from Harris's seventh delivery, which turned Cook (3) inside out, and flew fast and low to third
slip's right, where Smith just failed to accept the chance. A lot of key
inches have gone Australia's way in these Ashes – deservedly so. This
went England's, and you could hardly begrudge it them.

After lunch, as Johnson threatened then broke the 150 kmh bar-
rier, batting life grew a tad more hectic. In Johnson's second over,
Cook essayed an ambitious hook to a bouncer well wide of off stump,
fended two from his Adam's apple, withdrew with a wave of his hand
as Johnson approached – a fly, at that stage quite possibly, as a raucous
spectator once advised Douglas Jardine, the only friend he had. In the
next over, Carberry (18) hooked Siddle wildly, and was blessed that the
ball fell equidistant between square leg and fine leg, just beyond the
reach of a chasing Haddin. He punched gloves with his captain afterwards, although Cook must have wanted to clip him round the ears.

Gradually, threat abated. The sun blazed, the air was still, and the
40-degree atmosphere grew vaguely soporific. Even the Barmy Army
were subdued, the crowd having perhaps worked out who they were
and where they came from, and there being no need to tell them

who they were and where they came from – they being, of course, the Barmy Barmy Army, Barmy Army, Barmy Army, etc. (repeat until hoarse, bored, or you forget the words).

Carberry took a step down the pitch and lofted Lyon's second ball straight with a decided flourish, followed by a pregnant look as it dropped into the crowd beside the sightscreen. Cook took no such liberties, severely straight and rigidly upright when not abstaining altogether. But just when England could congratulate themselves on having had more than a share of the day, Carberry illustrated that the leave is something requiring as much conviction as a stroke: in a couple of minds, he neither quite played nor quite left Harris and dragged on. Root then played a ball from Watson he could also conceivably have left, and may conceivably not have hit, but was convicted of a catch at the wicket by the DRS because there was insufficient doubt to eliminate the original doubt.

One wondered if it brought some amusement to the BCCI's Naryanaswami Srinivasan, who at tea took a look around the venue where India won't play a Test next summer, accompanied by his counterparts, CA's Wally Edwards and the ECB's Giles Clarke. 'So how is that system working out for you?' you could imagine Srini asking, in between carving the cricket world up like an ancestral fortune.

As the Fremantle Doctor cooled the ground after tea, Australia steadily took the Test back, asserting the home-ground advantage they have exercised so ably this summer. Clarke's bowlers hit their naggingest lengths – the lengths that had largely eluded England the day before – and his fielders threw themselves around the ring with a will and a purpose. Even Watson at extra cover went to ground a couple of times, deliberately rather than as a result of injury. It turned into one of the best sessions of the series: a clear sky, a key moment, a crowd contriving to sound bigger than the 20 000 registered by the turnstiles, each ball loaded, each over a little ordeal, runs accumulating at 2.6 an over. This was too much like hard graft for Pietersen, who succumbed as soon as his nemesis Siddle was reintroduced, pulling carelessly off the front foot to mid-on, where the wicketless Johnson found a way to place the mark of his mo on the day with another athletic catch.

The crucial moment, however, was when Cook, seeking to break the siege, cut Lyon with a bat at the diagonal and sliced to backward point. It ended a fine innings. It emphasised, too, that Cook, for all his poise, pluck and finely grooved game, will only ever be a visitor here.

Day Three
SUNDAY 15 DECEMBER

Close of play: Australia 2nd innings 235/3
(SR Watson 29*, SPD Smith 5*, 70 overs)

Keith Moon famously boasted of being the best Keith Moon-style drummer in the world. Something similar has come to be true of David Warner, who in this Ashes series has formed his own little batting genre of one.

The early stages of Warner's career were about likenesses. Virender Sehwag. Sanath Jayasuriya. Mark McGwire, even. Yet the batsman who surged to 112 from 140 balls at the WACA today was an original rather than a version, as much action waiting to happen as not so long ago he looked an accident in the making.

Shortly before tea, Graeme Swann curled a ball to Warner well wide of off stump, nearly unreachable. Then another. Then another. Four in a row, in fact. Swann has more than 250 Test wickets, and once had a reputation for lethality to left-handers that matched David Beckham's for free kicks. Yet this was the best Swann could do: get Warner to leave him outside off. And weirdly, it did not seem such a bad plan, momentarily and in the absence of anything else. Warner was in *that* kind of form, a blur of bat speed and bravado, yet not so insensible to the needs of the occasion, as Pietersen had been on Saturday, that he needed to assert his virility at every event.

In the first innings, Warner had used what looked an old favourite bat, bound with four strips of tape, a contrast to the pristine blades of his teammates; today he took up a blade new and gleaming, although, as evidenced when he drove Anderson down the ground with merely a flex of the wrist and a tensing of the forearm, clearly just as vorpal. Likewise unchanged was Warner's little tic between deliveries. In the fashion of M.S. Dhoni, he undoes the Velcro wristbands of his gloves and waits in this state of partial undress as the bowler walks back to his mark, a little like a boxer in his corner awaiting the bell. His last regathering act before resuming his crouch is to reglove, which he does with deliberation and delicacy.

Then the pugilistic strokes start to flow. These today included a cut of delirious precision. The second ball of Swann's fifth over was neither really short nor really wide, but Warner positioned himself with room to slash backward of point from just inches outside off stump, trusting the bounce and his talent. When Swann dropped legitimately short a few balls later, it was no challenge to do the same. And when Swann's length deserted him again half an hour after tea, Warner's sixteenth boundary in less than three hours brought up his fifth century in his twenty-fifth Test.

The WACA ground announcer was taking hospitality to a fault as the bowlers were rotated: 'At the members end, please welcome Ben Stokes'; 'From the Prindiville Stand end, please welcome Graeme Swann.' Warner welcomed them all, as the spider made welcome the fly. For example, he knew he was guaranteed at least one short ball an over from the callow Stokes, waited patiently, and blasted it unerringly. And he treated Tim Bresnan like a bowling machine, disposing of him almost lightheartedly as he overpitched and underpitched.

England's day started as it was destined to continue. In the third over, Ian Bell came a long way forward, was hit above the knee roll by Harris and rightly spared by umpire Erasmus. The Australians sought a review, probably chiefly because the 80-over reset impended, and looked as surprised as anyone when the technology suggested that the ball, after hitting the pad, would have stayed down and hit the top of middle, which would make it the first ball in the history of the WACA Ground to so behave. It was treated, of course, with utmost credulity, because none must question the machine.

With this second DRS misadventure in their innings, England seemed to be overcome with fatalism. When a short ball from Johnson veered crazily off a crack, something similar appeared to form in the minds of the batsmen. Two deliveries later, Stokes was caught at the wicket attempting to cover drive on the up. You could not have asked for a more exact template for how not to bat at the WACA. It was as brainless as a starfish – as brainless, actually, as Stokes's overs of short-pitched dross to Smith on the first day.

England's shortcomings on this tour, however, cannot be laid at the feet of its next generation. It has been Alastair Cook's trustiest liegemen who have let him down worst. Matt Prior's hook shot to Peter Siddle was as feckless as any played on this tour – such a cop-out it was hardly even worth the effort of booing. England's vice-captain is the player who after the Ashes in England huffily demanded that critics 'show us some respect' – here he was as disrespectful of his teammates as any critic could be.

Prior failed his captain when England resumed, too, twice failing to stump Warner (13 and 89) off Swann, and standing stock-still as an edge from Rogers (26) flew past him, forcing Cook to make a late and forlorn dive. In his stationary crouch looking on, Prior briefly resembled a garden gnome done up as a wicketkeeper, and to England's cause these last five months he has increasingly looked as much use.

Swann whirled on, not a little bravely into the wind, and finally got the better of Warner, who could not resist trying for a second six down the ground. The batsman departed amid a grateful tumult, having turned what might have been a rather procedural afternoon into something fans might take away as a memory – with two years to wait until their next Test, they needed something.

As Chris Gayle's interest in Test cricket has faded, Warner's fireplug figure has become about as box office as the five-day game gets – coincidentally or not, as his short-form runs have rather dried up. *Who* would have thought it?

Day Four
MONDAY 16 DECEMBER

Close of play: England 2nd innings 251/5
(BA Stokes 72*, MJ Prior 7*, 67 overs)

Sixes have become so profuse in modern cricket that it is tempting to regard them as a kind of everyday natural phenomenon – regulation overhead hazard, or standard leather precipitation. Yet their inundation of the Ashes of 2013–14 has grown so pronounced as to constitute not just an imminent record, but a leading indicator of Australian advantage.

The rain of big hits before lunch at the WACA today took to 35 the number of sixes struck by Australians this series, in 6 innings: the record is England's, with 36 in 10 innings in the summer of 2005. A couple more muscular blows in Melbourne and a statistical vestige of former English glories will be erased.

Rationally, how you come by your runs hardly matters – what matters is that they come. But the Australian smiting this summer has had qualities both strategic and symbolic. A score of sixes have been struck off Graeme Swann, on whom Alastair Cook had been relying to lay down a containing barrage in overs 40 to 80. Deprived of Swann's capacities for containment, Cook has had to ride his seamers harder, negating their attacking threat.

There's been a jubilation about Australia's strokeplay too, binding the team in the joy of six. John Arlott once called the big hit 'the most companionable of cricket acts', turning the game into a carnival, casting the bowler 'in the part of clown'. You can project yourself into Australia's dressing room, imagine the shared jollity, the jokey competition: size *is* important where sixes are concerned. As George Bailey hit three of them in the last over of the Australian innings from James Anderson today, part of a record 28 runs from a Test over, you could almost hear the side-splitting and back-patting.

Not that Australia's ascendancy has been solely aerial. It has had solid foundations. At 6.30 pm on Friday evening, when most of his teammates would have been thinking of their evening plans, Shane Watson was to be found in the nets at the WACA Ground, receiving throwdowns from Australia's batting coach Michael Di Venuto – a form of penance as well as practice, for his dismissal six hours earlier had been of the unnecessary kind, not quite soft but not exactly flint-hard either.

Watson made a cautious start on Sunday night, compiling 29 in 66 deliveries, as if restrained by gossamer bonds like those of the Lilliputians on Gulliver. With one bound today he was free, coming down the pitch to Swann and hitting with such precision into the Prindiville Stand that he might have been offering catches to a specific spectator. He needed only a further 40 balls to overhaul three figures. When he swipes his sweet willow, Watson makes grounds look impossibly small. And as the WACA's straight boundaries are comparatively short, he seemed to shrink its dimensions to something like those of a Subbuteo table.

Yet although his bat has previously been muted in the series, Watson has not been an irrelevant figure, achieving useful breaks with the ball, fielding well at slip and in the ring, and maybe looking just a little visibly happier than usual – a reflection of his dressing room, and perhaps above all his coach. Watson was even happy to participate in a boundaryside Q & A with Channel 9 about two minutes after his dismissal, sponsor's cap on his head, positive vibe on his lips.

In this otherwise earnest series, Watson's run-out actually had a comic value worth preserving, bowler Bresnan throwing the non-striker's stumps down after collecting a catch that had spilled from Bell's hands at short cover. Mind you, any English laughter should have been rueful. An inch or two awry and Bresnan's hurl would have been a four-overthrow addition to a now bulging catalogue of outcricket error, ranging today from Root's earlier failure to run Watson (51) out from mid-off to the later fall of a mishit from Bailey (9) between Bell and Anderson at cover.

A fun story between Tests concerned the withdrawal from sale of the official Ashes electronic cricket game, due to glitches that resulted in what was reported as 'fielders moving in an apparent state of confusion, diving on the ground randomly and either throwing the ball in the wrong direction or just standing and looking at it as if the idea of picking it up never occurs to them'. Thanks to England, life is now imitating art.

Watson, of course, made it sting; so did Bailey, one of whose sixes was a miscue that summed up both the puniness of the WACA's dimensions and the turn of the wheel. Australia began this Ashes cycle barely able to lay a bat on Anderson – now its misfires are flying out of the ground and Anderson's figures are resembling those he clocked up here seven years ago.

As at Adelaide Oval, Michael Clarke's declaration yielded the wicket of his counterpart immediately if not sooner. Harris's first delivery, zeroing in on the top of off as though along an invisible wire, was, to a batsman predisposed to play back, unimprovable. Cook's hundredth Test has become like that of his predecessor, a nightmare from which there is no awaking, but unlike Andrew Strauss, Cook still has the torments of two Tests to come.

Root took some minutes to make it to the middle, and two hours to make 19, for neither of which he can really be blamed, except that the contrast in activity from earlier could hardly have been more acute. By losing three consecutive tosses this summer, England have effectively started each Test a little behind, and been forced to bat under accumulating pressure – part of it, of course, self-accumulating. The contrast was complete when Pietersen, having successfully cleared long on once to register England's eighth six of the series, tried to repeat the effort by hitting Lyon into the Swan River. Ryan Harris had a while to wait as the ball held up in the breeze but hardly needed to move as it fell a good way short – rather like England in this series.

Day Five
TUESDAY 17 DECEMBER

Close of play: England 2nd innings 353
(103.2 overs) – end of match

'How good is this?' Ricky Ponting asked Michael Clarke in the aftermath of Australia's last Ashes series victory, nearly seven years ago. 'This is the way we're going to finish every series against England, right?'

Wrong. That whitewash then was about as comprehensive as the win Australia secured today at 1.45 pm, with England similarly blanked on the scoreboard. But between times a superiority once regarded as inevitable had been rendered decidedly evitable by eight English Test victories to two.

Only Clarke among his team could advise on how to celebrate winning the Ashes: the rest, even senior players such as Brad Haddin and Peter Siddle, had never savoured the sensations before, even if I dare say they have since found a way.

The circumstances, in fact, make this a better victory than even that high summer of 2006–07, which was won by Ponting's once-in-a-lifetime team of talents, against opponents in a mess and a captain in his cups. It was that Australian team's last efflorescence; it was this Australian team's first, after a year in which they had won none and lost seven of their preceding nine Tests. In less than a month, the group of Clarke and coach Darren Lehmann have transformed an *annus horribilis* into an *aestas mirabilis*.

They have done it, moreover, against a formidable force of seasoned cricketers, who had just defeated them comfortably at home and brought with them to Australia their full hyper-professional kit and caboodle, fuelled by superfood, rich in supernumeraries – pre-play meetings of the England squad sometimes seem designed to intimidate opponents by sheer numbers.

After England's 3–0 win in England, which he thought a 'fair reflection of the series', Ponting himself had predicted that 'the whole Australian team is going to have to improve an awful lot to win back the Ashes'. That they have done so is assuredly the zenith of Clarke's career, and testament to a coach, selectors and support unit who have forborne some thin times, and not so long ago.

Mitchell Johnson has been *a* difference between the series, if not perhaps *the only* difference. This Ashes cycle has been a compelling illustration of the differences between home and away, even in this globalised modern cricket world. Players who flourished on the slow, low and desiccated pitches of the northern summer have been neutralised if not cowed by Australian surfaces and the particular predicaments they pose. Others who found the English conditions frustrating have thrived on pace and bounce, and the licence to attack afforded by cumulative advantage. Johnson, meanwhile, has been allowed to stretch for extra velocity and vehemence by the sheer reliability of his comrades Siddle, Harris and Lyon, and fielding tighter than a Hollywood celebrity's face.

What's been interesting about talking to members of the Australian camp over the last few days has been their realism. We do well here, they point out. We did well here last season, almost inflicting defeat on the world's number one, South Africa, in Adelaide, then obliterating Sri Lanka. How would this team, in its present mood, fare in India now? Perhaps a little better than Clarke's party did in March and April, comes the response, but they would still be challenged; they will be challenged again when they visit South Africa in a few months' time.

How to sum Australia's advance up, then? Perhaps that an always fairly good team has counteracted a tendency at times to play really badly. Don't forget that on the first day of each Test this summer, the

Australians found themselves vulnerably placed. Even after the fillip of winning the toss, they were six for 132 in Brisbane and five for 143 in Perth, and, had England held three chances in Adelaide, might have been bowled out for less than 300.

But where in England such positions became routs, this summer they have been turned into defensible fortifications. Wins have been instigated in the first instance by not losing. So as manifestly critical as Johnson has been, as great a contributor has been the indefatigable Haddin, who a year ago seemed to have played his last Test, and would probably not have been involved in this series had Matthew Wade maintained any semblance of form. His 325 runs at an average of 65 have included two decisive first innings, not to mention missing only one half-chance while accepting fifteen others.

The selection policy in general, in fact, has involved not so much new opportunities as second chances – in the case of David Warner after one night's disgrace, in the case of Chris Rogers after more than five years' unfashionability. Second chances are rejuvenating, especially when they might well be last chances. The key members of this Australian team have experienced a lot of setbacks and sorrows, and a determination not to add to them has been a powerful motivation.

England? They have had, by contrast, a long period of above-average success, including a spell as the world's number one team. Alastair Cook, James Anderson, Kevin Pietersen and Ian Bell were here for the whitewash of 2006–07, after which the England Cricket Board strove mightily to put its house in order. When they wore their caps in the field, they were noticeably weathered; Pietersen's might even be described as distressed felt. But what in other circumstances might have conveyed sagacity instead came to symbolise miles on the clock, and, frankly, the lack of anything much else to give.

Two other splendid competitors in Graeme Swann and Matt Prior appear to have come on a tour too far, as well: memories of video diaries and sprinkler dancing seem many more than three years old. Swann and Prior now know what it felt like to be on the receiving end seven years ago. What goes around comes around – sometimes more than once.

Alastair Cook

A GOOD MAN IN DARK TIMES

In his autobiography, Andrew Strauss describes an encounter after the Perth Test of 2006, and a feeling his successor Alastair Cook can now probably identify with.

Strauss found himself in a lift at the team hotel with a group of England supporters, still wearing their face paint, streaked with sweat, smouldering with indignation. One of them at last broke the uncomfortable silence. '"You know, you should be ashamed of yourself," he said. "You and your teammates are a disgrace. I was embarrassed watching an England team play with so little fight."' Strauss recoiled. 'Each word hit home like a dagger to my heart . . . There was nothing I could really say in my defence, other than "We are trying our best, you know." The words sounded hollow.'

The media pack around Cook on Tuesday was more tactful, but their questions would have felt just as dagger-like, and his replies every bit as inadequate. For cricketers, having to speak about failure is every bit as tough as failure itself, perhaps more so, because words are a language that comes less naturally to them than deeds.

Actually, Cook spoke well, mingling candour, humility and dignity. He dealt effectively with the lingering questions about England's 'hunger' by paying tribute to Australia's superior skills, he was admirably loyal to his coach and his team, he was entirely frank about his batting, and declined to use the strain of captaincy as an excuse. 'There's always a strain, but the challenge of being a captain is trying to deal with it,' Cook said. 'I can honestly say that when I go out there as a batter, I'm thinking as a batter. My mind is not thinking about what's going on elsewhere.' Yet because the relationship between batting and captaincy is a two-way street, another question arises around Cook: whether his batting is affecting his captaincy. It's a question with two dimensions.

The first dimension is this: Cook is a very typical modern captain, in the sense that he has been an outstanding player since his junior years, and promoted on the basis of his on-field performances rather than a natural tactical acumen. Players singled out early tend to go on being the youngest member of the teams they play in, and in so doing accumulate little direct leadership experience – see also Ricky Ponting.

Like Ponting, Cook's strongest suit as captain has been his capacity to inspire by professional example. In India earlier this year, he looked the more authoritative for making mountains of runs. Against Australia over the last five months, his statistics and stature have been roughly parallel. This is the hardest place of all for a captain to be in: to be calling for improved collective performance when his own individual performance is under pressure, to be requesting something he cannot guarantee delivering himself. I suspect that Cook, a thoroughly decent man, finds it especially awkward, even a little crass.

The second dimension to the question is necessarily more speculative. Cook insists that he is not thinking about his captaincy when he is batting. But is he thinking about batting while captaining? There was first a hint of this at Trent Bridge in July. On the second morning, England smashed their way through the tail down to number eleven, whom Cook then trusted to get himself out. The number eleven was, of course, Ashton Agar, who, batting under negligible pressure, took startling toll.

In all three Tests this summer, England have found themselves fielding on the first day. In all three they have done pretty well, penetrating successfully into Australia's lower middle order, to the point that they might have anticipated commencing their own innings within an hour or so. In all three they have let advantage slip and been repulsed, with Brad Haddin acting as Australia's counterpuncher-in-chief.

Opening the batting requires mental readiness and willpower. If you're in the field, you'll start your preparations subtly ahead of time, attuned for the sprint to the dressing room as the last wicket falls. That need for ordered thinking does not reconcile readily with the need for initiative and flexibility in captaincy. On four occasions this summer, too, Cook has had to bat after declarations, basically at ten minutes' notice.

My guess – and it is purely a guess – is that Cook has at critical stages at the crease and in the field not been quite *there*, or, as they say, 'in the moment', with examples ranging from his impulsive hook shot on the fourth morning at Adelaide Oval to his reticent ring fields with a nearly new ball on the second morning at the WACA. He could have done with more help from his senior players.

A last question about Cook's captaincy concerns his relations with those senior players, and his own emotional register. Strauss, who probably knows him as well as anyone, is arguing that Cook needs to 'stand above and a bit away from some of those players who are very good friends of his', the better to objectively analyse their approach and contribution. In some senses, Cook is in a similar situation to Ponting in 2005. His previously successful team is being overrun, their successful formula having been decoded. Does he stick? Does he twist? Does he pat backs or get on them?

To revert to his story from seven years ago, Strauss recalled that his first response to the bait from the disgruntled English fan was a flash of anger. Strauss was hurting. Couldn't his antagonist understand that? Then Strauss got to thinking: 'They had saved up their money and travelled twelve thousand miles to see a famous English victory on Australian soil. They got the opposite. They were entitled to feel short changed. I realised that my anger did not lie with them; it lay with myself and the rest of the team. We had let ourselves down. I made a vow that if I ever came back to Australia on a cricket tour, it would be different.' Strauss kept that vow. Can Cook?

Darren Lehmann
THE CULT OF BOOF

Boof, eh? Everyone likes him. Even, I learned yesterday, my mum, who cares little and knows less about sport. 'I'm just glad to see Darren Lehmann getting the credit he deserves,' she said, a propos of nothing. 'He just seems like a nice bloke.'

In this, Lehmann joins a very small pantheon of sporting personages about whom my mum has expressed any view at all, previously restricted, frankly, to various Geelong footballers, such as Buddha Hocking and Dasher Milburn, and, just lately, Ange Postecoglou – 'nice blokes' to a man.

Well, yes. In his geniality, laconicism and utter everydayness, Lehmann is a character of immense demotic appeal, unmistakably 'one of us'. So what might this say about his success as a coach of the Australian team, and, indeed, the failure of his predecessor, South African Mickey Arthur?

I say 'failure', but that should be qualified. Under Arthur, Australia lost two series in six, one narrowly to South Africa, one overwhelmingly in India. Coaches have survived with inferior records. Taking his countryman's part, the respected South African journalist Neil Manthorp argues in the first edition of the new journal *Between Wickets* that Arthur fell because of his closeness to Clarke during the Australians' 'homeworkgate' fiasco in Mohali. Clarke, observes Manthorp, was determined to discipline the disaffected Shane Watson, and in doing so was obligated to discipline others. Arthur, believing that he had no choice but to support something about which the captain was so adamant, was required to defend the position, in doing so became identified with it, and thus was readily made a scapegoat.

For outsiders not privy to the team environment – and that includes basically all of us – the Mohali suspensions are a difficult judgement call to fathom. It seemed, and still seems, ridiculous that grown men paid enormous sums of money should have found it so hard to comply with such a trivial request. But what we can say, I think with some conviction, is that under Lehmann the situation would not have deteriorated so badly, and the tensions would have been addressed earlier. Nor would an executive general manager of Cricket Australia have publicly criticised Watson as 'a team player – sometimes'. Strange days indeed, and not that long ago.

Lehmann has advantages Arthur never had, notably the authority that comes with a substantial playing record, and significant history with both Clarke and Watson as teammates. To Lehmann can be credited that Clarke and Watson made their relationship workable, and victory has now done the rest. Teammates' foibles become so much less irritating with the help of a celebratory beer or six.

Those seeking to define Lehmann's coaching contribution these last few months have tended to concentrate on the feel-goodness of his regime, his jokes of the day, his commitment to enjoyment, etc. But Australia has also played cricket in ways we fondly and not fancifully perceive as 'Australian': excellent fast bowling, enterprising batting, splendid fielding, and a bit of verbal abrasion. The only thing missing from the classic Australian formula has been wrist spin, although Nathan Lyon's finger spin has adequately filled the breach. And without wanting to sound too essentialist about it, is there an argument waiting to be made here that Australian cricketers should only ever be coached by other Australians?

When some made this case at around the time of Arthur's appointment not much more than two years ago, it sounded suspiciously parochial. What was so special about Australia when a South African and a Zimbabwean could coach India, and an Australian and an Englishman coach Pakistan? Surely our cricket culture was more cosmopolitan and inclusive? Shane Warne, for example, did not seem to think a foreigner was a problem. Earlier this year he named as his preferred coach for Australia the New Zealander Stephen Fleming, although perhaps Fleming could have been rendered Australian on the Phar Lap principle ('Australian Horse Wins'; 'New Zealand Horse Loses').

I'm bound to say, nonetheless, that Lehmann's success has made a case, if not an overwhelming or definitive one, that Australian players do better when urged to do what arguably comes naturally and nationally. Not that Mickey Arthur tried to instill wholly alien ways, or indeed that his set-up was not amply Australian, in management, in selection and in support – simply that the necessary cues and intuitions may be more readily accessible to a coach who is a countryman.

By the same token, Australianness is not a static concept. And at the risk of a bit more cod sociology, one other aspect of Lehmann's vernacular credibility is kind of topical at present. His blue collar is not painted on. He springs from a semi-professional past where sportsmen worked, and worked with their hands at that. His first job, aged sixteen, on the Holden assembly line in Elizabeth is something he talks of as being a formative influence. 'The people out there were sensational, salt of the earth and . . . they really took me under their wing,' he has recalled. 'I thought I was the luckiest kid alive . . . Sport is definitely important in life, but working alongside men in their fifties who have to work every day putting axles together to feed their wife and three kids and pay the mortgage will definitely keep your feet glued to the ground.'

In the last few months, this world described by Lehmann has taken a few steps closer to becoming not just history, but archaeology. The social implications of the transformation of Australia's economy can only be guessed at. So while celebrating Darren Lehmann makes us feel good – even my mum – we have ever less connection to the work, communities and values that made him. Our way of life is changing. So is our sport. What we will make of them is anyone's guess.

Graeme Swann

BLACK SWANN EVENT

Graeme Swann has a habit unusual among cricketers. Regardless of how he has gone, he unfailingly watches the highlights of the day's cricket in his hotel room in the evening. It is, he has said, 'cathartic if you've done badly and an ego massage if you've done well'.

Maintaining the habit this summer must have pushed his catharsis into primal-scream territory. He has been involved in highlights aplenty, but as the butt of batsmen who have smashed him hither and yon. His wickets in the series have cost him nearly 80 runs each and his overs 4 each, while his six cameos at the batting crease have lasted a frantic fifty-seven deliveries. Troubled by a long-term injury that locks his elbow up at crazy angles from time to time, he has looked a man fighting wars on all fronts.

In this context, the logic of his retirement announcement today is flawless – flawless for himself anyway. 'When I came out on this trip, I half expected it to be my last tour for England,' Swann admitted. 'It was probably halfway through the Perth game [that I made the decision].

'My body doesn't like playing long forms of cricket. My arm doesn't cope very well with bowling 30–40 overs in the first innings and then repeating it in the second innings a day later. I could feel my performances tapering off towards the back end of games and I wasn't happy with that. I'm not willing just to hang on and get by being a bit-part player. I want to be a guy who wants to win matches for England and I don't feel I was doing that in the second innings any more. As a result, it is time to go.'

Actually, he's mistaken. The time to go, as could be inferred from other remarks Swann made, was after the Oval Test, when he *did* consider giving it away. As so often, the first instinct was right; his mistake was being talked around. In a way his retirement here is an admission of, and attempt to remedy, that first error. But is what's happened now a second error?

A couple of weeks ago, I cast Swann as Jim Laker in my re-run of the 1958–59 Ashes, and he now completes the parallel, for Laker also retired while the tour was in progress – actually foreshadowing his exit while the team was en route. Laker even did it in a newspaper column, just as Swann has now – rather controversial in its time, though nowadays we are strangely inured to such practices. In so doing, his captain Peter May later complained, Laker caused his team some consternation, in effectively acknowledging to his opponents that he was past his best. And we might well ask: Which is worse, making the admission of decline publicly and sticking round, or coming to the private realisation and not?

Actually, Swann's retirement shows more clearly the tension between personal pride and collective loyalty. Laker did at least face the consequences of his decision; England face the consequences of Swann's without him. Inter alia his choice means that England will have to replace by far their best catcher with by far their worst fielder, the joke of Panesar's inabilities having thinned to nothingness at Adelaide. Nil–3 is a tough predicament in which to leave colleagues with whom one has shared so much: when Damien Martyn quit while he was behind seven years ago, at least his team was ahead. If anything, Swann's last act as an international cricketer was to boost the morale of his opponents.

Swann has also created two further headaches for his camp. The first is a public-relations misstep: an *en passant* comment about unnamed players who have 'no idea how far up their own backsides they are' but who might in future be 'embarrassed about how they carry on'. It's all very well to say 'no names', but it's not like there aren't a few possible subjects for such remark on both sides. Assumptions today ranged from Kevin Pietersen to David Warner, although I suspect it applies more generally, and expresses a belief longer held – Swann combined a light heart with a knowing head. But if social media since has been anything to go by, today was not the day to throw out another negative storyline.

The second headache is a selection challenge: a forced change to a team that already faces voluntary ones. England has been looking set to pick Jonny Bairstow for Melbourne, ahead of their out-of-form vice-captain Matt Prior. Now they also face including Panesar, hardly bowling so well anyway. They may hold back from a third alteration because of these two. Whatever the case, Swann has effectively gazumped the selectors, and all because of a desire to retire 'near at being at the top', which makes less sense than it seems to, because who, really, does? Retirement and decline are inseparable. If we did not decline, in terms of output achieved and satisfaction derived, we would never retire. Are two Tests *so* hard to get through?

Let's be kind, though: at his best, Swann reminded me of Cardus's line about no long innings ever being played against Wilfred Rhodes without the batsman being left 'intellectually worn and weary'. Left-handers groped at him down the line. Which would turn? Which would skid? Which would bounce? To right-handers he gave more scoring opportunities because of his preparedness to bowl a line wide of off in search of what he joyously called 'the cheese ball': the top-of-off delivery puncturing bat and pad that undid, for instance, Ricky Ponting at Edgbaston in 2009.

Yet Swann, I always felt, bowled at his best when there wasn't much encouragement, or at least *too much* expectation. It would have been good to see him at the MCG again, for I hardly saw him bowl better than during 2010's Boxing Day Test: 27-11-59-2, including five consecutive maidens to Michael Clarke from round the wicket, whom he at last had caught at second slip. There wasn't a micron of turn on offer; Swann did it all in the air, like he was pulling a kite on a string, against one of Australia's nimblest players of slow bowling.

Meanwhile, at the other end, the ball was reverse-swinging drunkenly for Anderson, Bresnan and Tremlett, and England surging to Ashes supremacy. It was the very definition of a 'bowling unit' in action. Swann would have watched the highlights that night with a huge smile on his dial, little aware of the far tougher times to come. What a shame he could not in the end get through them.

Sledging
WHY BOTHER?

There's been a lot of sledging about this Ashes summer. There's also been a lot of sledging, as it were, of sledging. Can it be right? Can it be fair?

There's even been sledging of the sledging of sledging, by my newspaper colleague Janet Albrechtsen, who waxed nostalgic about no-nonsense '70s cricket and '70s parenthood – and get ready for some broken fuckin' prose: 'Today, the stifling PC prism is overlaid on the cricket field the moment a bit of verbal biff pushes the envelope.'

And yet Albrechtsen has a point. Cricket is game replete with aggressive acts – hard hitting, fast bowling – that nonetheless pro-scribes physical contact. If some excess of belligerence is decanted verbally, should we be in the least surprised? In fact, it's probably the non-contact team sports that are naturally the lippiest. Baseball, for example, has a long tradition of 'trash talk', which Jim Bouton brought to life in his classic diary of the 1960s major leagues, *Ball Four*: 'Gee your wife was great last night' – 'Oh she wasn't that great' – 'You should have been there earlier. She was terrific.'

Even more time is spent in repose in cricket than in baseball, especially with England's funereal over rates. Maybe we should be thankful for a bit of additional banter: by giving the television some-thing else to study between deliveries, it may stand in the way of more advertisements.

Yet there's a question that is almost never asked about sledging, and to coaches and players, who leave the moral arbitrations to others and regard all as fair in love and Waugh, it's the only one that matters: does it work? That is, does it undermine your opponent and enlarge your own threat?

And nobody really knows. Not even Steve Waugh was sure. If

anything, he downplayed its effectiveness, arguing aphoristically that sledging didn't affect good players, and that you were going to get bad players out anyway. His Steveness himself, of course, thrived on the verbal giving and the receiving, so visibly that England players once decided in a Test that they would simply say nothing to him. When Waugh came out to bat and a few of his verbal baits were not taken, he quickly worked out what was up. 'So nobody's talking to me, eh?' he said. 'All right, I'll talk to myself, then.'

What we *can* say is that players hear it, and *are* conscious of it. That at least was the conclusion of a recent academic case study, 'Sledging in Cricket: Elite English Batsmen's Experiences of Verbal Gamesship', published two years ago in the *Journal of Clinical Sport Psychology*. Ten young players on the cusp of first-class cricket told researchers Samuele Joseph and Duncan Cramer at Loughborough University that they 'did consider sledging to be effective, both when the fielding team was winning and when the game was close', noting that its intensity was greatest when their innings began or at signs of their vulnerability (playing and missing, difficulty getting the ball away, etc).

Although only three of them had directly consulted sports psychologists, all had devised coping mechanisms involving 'self-talk', rituals of preparation between deliveries, talking with partners between overs, controlled breathing, and even smiling. 'Unless you're deaf, you do hear it,' said one respondent. 'So whatever you hear, you process and try and turn it around . . . the positive way.'

Interestingly, none of them objected to sledging and, rather like Waugh, acknowledged that the response to it was a skill to harness. 'Sledging' switched them 'on'. The trick was not to get too 'on'. The authors noted: 'It is generally believed that people need some arousal to perform at their best, and those who are too laid-back often perform at substandard levels. In the current study, this was supported by some participants who commented that they need the confrontation that sledging produces to become engaged in the match . . . On the other hand, too much arousal can make performers tense and prone to

errors. Herein, some participants reported that over-arousal often leads
to poor technique and overly aggressive shot selection.'

What we know far less of, and I suspect it is relevant to Michael
Clarke's Australian team, is the effect of sledging on the sledgor, as
distinct from the sledgee. One of the most fascinating studies related
to sledging, a look at 'trash talk' in a high-school basketball team, was
published fifteen years ago by its former coach with a researcher from
Temple University. The boys of Philadelphia's Hardwick High, mainly
African-American, were notoriously verbal on court, as the authors
noted:

> We observed players deriding an opponents' skills, often by empha-
> sizing his weakness: "Your sorry ass can't stop me!". . . Some of the
> comments were misogynist: "Raped you" (after a steal); or "Used
> you like a bitch" (after going one-on-one to the basket); some were
> aggressive: "J in your eye" (for a jump shot taken over an opponent)
> or "Dunked on your head". Many comments staked claims to turf:
> "*My* Ball!" or "*My* Board!" (Backboard) (after grabbing a rebound);
> others were simply mildly humorous put-downs: "Call 911, there's
> been a robbery" or "Buckets, it's all about buckets."

This was not, however, simply a 'game face'. Their coach noted
that the 'trash talk' was mainly a continuation of that in which they
indulged around each other, particularly on the team bus in preparation for games. And this preparatory banter, while it sounded at first
wild and indiscriminate, was actually highly ritualised, and occurred
within mutually agreed rules and taboos. 'One player, Chad, was very
close to his mother who was significantly overweight and everyone avoided using her size as a topic for insults,' noted the authors.
'Midway through the season, Lewis . . . experienced the loss of a
brother who died of a massive heart attack while shooting hoops at a
community center . . . Upon his return, Lewis was never the target of
even the mildest put-down.'

When the boys got on court, the coach realised, they were also performing for each other, as well as dealing with stresses concerning their own masculinity, self-image and self-worth. The control in the experiment, as it were, was the team's best player, Khalil. He said little; he would occasionally glare. Secure in his abilities, he had no need to put on an additional performance.

So a view of sledging as merely the expression of contempt or hatred for opponents is simplistic. It neglects, among other things, sledging's performative dimension – its expression of a team's cohesion and common purpose. Personally, I doubt that sledging has made England play any the worse this summer. It may, however, have helped Australia play a little better, draw a little closer, enjoy it a little more. Does David Warner carry on like a bit of tit? Almost certainly. But on your own side, such a tit can be perversely endearing.

As to the morality of sledging, there remains a debate to be had. The pity is that these arguments so frequently slip into clichés, non sequiturs, and slippery slope fallacies, of 'W.G. Grace was a great sledger' on the one hand, and 'You never heard Donald Bradman sledge' on the other.

Cricket is not all of a piece. It has many forms and many levels, and thus many differing degrees of intensity and licences for aggression. What you perceive as appropriate for cricket at its highest levels will necessarily differ from that allowable elsewhere. Indeed, the lower the level of the game, the stronger would seem the argument for sledging's restriction. At club, junior and school levels, where the range of abilities, temperaments and tolerances are naturally more diverse, cricket should not be primarily about arousal levels, individual zones of optimal functioning, catastrophe zones of anxiety, or any of the other jargon phrases of sports psychology. It should be about enjoyment, a mutual respect and a welcoming environment.

At a public gathering in Perth during the last Test, a school principal asked me how he was to instill in his charges ideas of sportsmanship and etiquette when Test cricketers seemed to pay them so little heed. I asked how it was that his charges were incapable of distinguishing between the importance of a school match and a Test match. If they could not work out that the behaviour in one might not be suitable for another, if they were simply slavish imitators of what they saw on television, then it was arguable that their coaches, teachers and parents had let them down.

Then there's the issue of the proper scope for aggression, as it differs between cultures. With the Indian team due here this time next season, that could be a very interesting discussion indeed. Staying on India's right side is these days about rather more than good manners – it is also good financial sense, for organisations *and* for individuals. David Warner might think he 'doesn't play cricket to make friends'. But some friends he might have more need of than others.

THIRD TEST W.A.C.A. Ground, Perth 13–17 December 2013
Toss Australia   **Australia won by 150 runs**

AUSTRALIA	1st Innings			2nd Innings		
CJL Rogers	run out		11	c Carberry	b Bresnan	54
DA Warner	c Carberry	b Swann	60	c Stokes	b Swann	112
SR Watson	c Swann	b Broad	18	run out		103
MJ Clarke*	c Cook	b Swann	24		b Stokes	23
SPD Smith	c Prior	b Anderson	111	c sub (JM Bairstow)	b Stokes	15
GJ Bailey	c Pietersen	b Broad	7	not out		39
BJ Haddin†	c Anderson	b Stokes	55	c Swann	b Bresnan	5
MG Johnson	c Prior	b Broad	39	not out		0
PM Siddle	c Prior	b Bresnan	21			
RJ Harris	c Root	b Anderson	12			
NM Lyon	not out		17			
EXTRAS	(lb 6, w 3, nb 1)		10	(b 8, lb 5, w 5)		18
TOTAL	(103.3 overs; 469 mins)		385	(6 wkts dec; 87 overs; 347 mins)		369

ENGLAND	1st Innings			2nd Innings		
AN Cook*	c Warner	b Lyon	72		b Harris	0
MA Carberry		b Harris	43	lbw	b Watson	31
JE Root	c Haddin	b Watson	4	c Haddin	b Johnson	19
KP Pietersen	c Johnson	b Siddle	19	c Harris	b Lyon	45
IR Bell	lbw	b Harris	15	c Haddin	b Siddle	60
BA Stokes	c Haddin	b Johnson	18	c Haddin	b Lyon	120
MJ Prior†	c Haddin	b Siddle	8	c Haddin	b Johnson	26
TT Bresnan	c Haddin	b Harris	21	c Rogers	b Johnson	12
SCJ Broad	lbw	b Johnson	5	not out		2
GP Swann	not out		19	c Smith	b Lyon	4
JM Anderson	c Bailey	b Siddle	2	c Bailey	b Johnson	2
EXTRAS	(b 11, lb 7, w 5, nb 2)		25	(b 13, lb 13, w 6)		32
TOTAL	(88 overs; 394 mins)		251	(103.2 overs; 452 mins)		353

ENGLAND 1st Innings	O	M	R	W	2nd Innings	O	M	R	W
JM Anderson	23	5	60	2		19	5	105	0
SCJ Broad	22	2	100	3					
TT Bresnan	23.3	4	81	1		14	3	53	2
BA Stokes	17	3	63	1		18	1	82	2
GP Swann	17	0	71	2		27	8	92	1
JE Root	1	0	4	0		9	1	24	0

AUSTRALIA 1st Innings	O	M	R	W	2nd Innings	O	M	R	W
RJ Harris	22	10	48	3		19	2	73	1
MG Johnson	22	7	62	2		25.2	6	78	4
SR Watson	12	3	48	1		11	1	39	1
PM Siddle	16	5	36	3		26	11	67	1
NM Lyon	16	6	39	1		22	5	70	3

FALL OF WICKETS Wicket	Aus - 1st	Eng - 1st	Aus - 2nd	Eng - 2nd
1st	13	85	157	0
2nd	52	90	183	62
3rd	106	136	223	76
4th	129	146	301	121
5th	143	190	331	220
6th	267	198	340	296
7th	326	207	–	336
8th	338	229	–	347
9th	354	233	–	349
10th	385	251	–	353

Umpires: BF Bowden (New Zealand) and M Erasmus (South Africa)
Referee: JJ Crowe (New Zealand)

THE FOURTH TEST: Melbourne

BOXING CLEVER?

Boxing Day: in cricket there is nothing quite like it, a day of national sporting thanksgiving held where Test matches all began, at the Melbourne Cricket Ground, almost 137 years ago.

You can be guaranteed the biggest crowd of summer. You can expect a vast recumbent audience of home viewers, still in a post-prandial stupor, looking forward this year to further lashings of roast pom. No, nothing much wrong with this scene. It's elsewhere that's not so rosy. Because Boxing Day in Australia, and the Ashes more generally, has become Test cricket's Potemkin village, hiding the decay of the format behind the veneer of its own continuity.

This summer, Boxing Day forms part of a tradition significantly overextended: the ninth Ashes Test of the year, in a series already decided, with a final leg of this money-minting decathlomarathon to go in Sydney. Yet that is not nearly so problematical as the dwindling away of the rest of the five-day game. Later the same Boxing Day in Durban, the world's number one, South Africa, will host India, the world's number two, in the second of two hugger-mugger matches between these nations.

The first of these, at Johannesburg, was a cracker, with every result possible going into the final over after five days of absorbing cricket, and the eventual draw being perhaps the fairest result. By Monday, however, M.S. Dhoni's team will be done with South Africa, and readying for a further truncated tour, this time of New Zealand, everything being squeezed together for the sake of the World T20 and the one-day Asia Cup. Make sense of this if you can: a game in which numbers one and two play off in two Tests in less than a fortnight, while numbers three and five play off in ten Tests over six months. In effect, the Ashes has gone from setting a sort of standard to existing as an outlier, its regulation five-Test length now being twice as long as the average non-Ashes series since 2000.

While South Africa's coach, Gary Kirsten, among others, has opined that a three-Test series is 'the minimum you need to test the skills and depth of the two teams', cricket administrators are little interested in the cultivation of skills, the ascertaining of depth, and the global good of the game; their agendas are narrowly national, their objectives essentially financial, their horizons mainly short-term.

As we know, too, South Africa were lucky to be allocated the little they have. For reasons it remains beyond the wit of any official involved to explain, India decided at first to ignore their undertakings to South Africa under the International Cricket Council's Future Tours Programme and drop in a couple of home Tests against the West Indies, providing the forum for a Sachin Tendulkar love-in.

As recently as six weeks ago, South Africa's cricket public had no idea whether they would be hosting India at all. The rest of the cricket world, Cricket Australia and the England Cricket Board included, sat cravenly by. CA and the ECB, in fact, were just about to meet with the Board of Control for Cricket in India to discuss a new carving of the spoils of ICC revenues for their substantial benefit. And while Cricket South Africa's team might be the best in the world, its administrators are now well and truly onlookers. Quite what the new dispensation will look like remains to be seen, but it is likely to involve this big three of India, England and Australia further pulling up the ladder after themselves, leaving the other seven Test nations looking at a closing trapdoor above their heads.

Funnily enough, everyone saw this coming. As far back as sixteen years ago, the ICC's full members discussed the divide opening between richer and poorer members, and how the reluctance of the former to visit was impeding the latter's development. Back then, there was still some conception of a common weal, and the membership went along with the idea, put by New Zealand Cricket's Chris Doig, of the FTP: a fixture matrix designed to guarantee that each full member played the other at home and away over a five-year period, thereby providing smaller boards with some financial certainty.

The first ten-year FTP was succeeded by a second, running, fittingly, to 2020. Because Twenty20, modern cricket's gaudiest format, has become a complicating factor. Into time once available for international tours must now be squeezed not just a superfluity of T20 internationals, but a World T20, and, above all, the Indian Premier League and the Champions League. This has meant more and more tours of the stipulated minimum duration – two Tests, three one-day internationals – like the visit India has grudgingly granted South Africa, and the one Australia granted South Africa two years ago. At the time, Dale Steyn commented ruefully: 'I go on holiday for longer than that series is going to last.' This current visit from India will make his holidays look like a lengthy sabbatical.

Nor can mammon alone be blamed. What used to be the Ashes' Asian counterpart, India v. Pakistan, has withered on a geopolitical vine: they have not played a Test match for more than six years. And in its thirteen years as a full member of the ICC, Bangladesh has never been invited to play a Test in India.

What of the future? 'It is no exaggeration to suggest that the calendar outlined by the second FTP has trapped Test cricket in a downward spiral,' observes Mike Jakeman of the Economist Intelligence Unit in his pithy new analysis, *Saving the Test*. 'It is not inconceivable – indeed some would say it is more than likely – that the fifth and sixth FTP will schedule only a few one-off Test matches. These would be sepia-tinged affairs, played as a concession to the sport's few remaining traditionalists, a mild diversion before cricketers and fans get back to the real business of T20. There is no doubt that the first step in the decline is already happening.'

Jakeman can be faulted only for being too optimistic, in envisioning a process that will take as long as five or six FTPs. The grounds for believing that the second will run its course are scarcely rock-solid. Nor should the World Test Championship finals scheduled for June–July 2017 in England be regarded as a sure thing. Test cricket is already sharing Boxing Day, a Big Bash League game being scheduled for the evening in Perth. Boxing Day 2023? Nothing is guaranteed.

Summary
CONDITIONAL SURRENDER

For once at the colosseum, it was the lions who were eaten. The second day of the Fourth Test was England's best of the Australian Ashes leg. Unfortunately for them, it was immediately followed by their two worst days – not as spectacularly bad as days at Brisbane and Adelaide, perhaps, but somehow the more abject because the visitors gave away a position of strength to Australians who could barely believe their luck, then went through the feeblest of motions as the hosts drew away from them. It was 2006–07 all over again but worse, because Michael Clarke had no McGrath, Warne, Hayden, Langer, Gilchrist bent on redemption as Ricky Ponting did; mind you, he did have Mitchell Johnson, who England's lower-middle order again tackled with all the morale and motivation of death row prisoners. Johnson accepted his second individual award of the series, and extended his record to 31 wickets at 14.3, almost twice as many for half as few as anyone else this summer.

To begin with, England were a thing of rags and patches, without their abrupt retiree Graeme Swann, succeeded by Monty Panesar, or their diminished vice-captain Matt Prior, replaced experimentally by Jonny Bairstow. Sensing their vulnerability, Clarke departed convention by inserting England amid encircling gloom, on a drop-in pitch where the ball would nibble about throughout. In fact, the surface was on the slow side, and good batsmen could adjust: Kevin Pietersen gave Australia a glimpse of his wicket when he hooked down fine leg's throat, only for the ball to by carried over the rope by the momentum of the throat's owner, substitute Nathan Coulter-Nile. But Pietersen soon settled to seeing off his nemesis Siddle and the yeoman Harris while resisting temptation against Lyon. It was a cool and judicious innings.

That still left Johnson, who propelled the second new ball at great speed at a flinching quarry, Stokes, Bairstow, Bresnan and Broad being simply waved aside, inducing Pietersen to his first *outré* stroke, through which he was predictably bowled early on the second morning. The rest of the day, however, was England's, thanks mainly to James Anderson, who returned to something like his crafty best against batsmen struggling to assimilate the drop-in pitch's inconsistencies after the highly specific conditions of Perth. Broad, Bresnan and Stokes bowled useful containing spells as well, and only Chris Rogers was up for what Herbert Sutcliffe used to call a 'dogfight'. In his swiftest spell since the Gabba, Broad hit the opener's tin lid and drew blood, but Rogers calmly ordered another, and pressed on with calm strokes, ordered defence, and a butterfly stitch in his cheek. Australia's other redeemer was, as ever, its other 36-year-old, Brad Haddin, who played with greater freedom than any batsman on either side during the match: cuts, pulls, his trademark lofted drive, a peachy glance. At one stage, Australia's deficit had looked likely to be three figures; Haddin, with help from Nathan Lyon, halved it. His run tally for the series reached an Ashes record for keepers of 390 and an irreverent thought briefly occurred: Was Gilchrist really *so* much better than this fellow?

In the hour and ten minutes to lunch, Cook played his best cricket of the summer, perhaps of 2013: off drives, leg glides, cuts square and late, as fluent as Carberry was subdued. Australia appeared short of a gallop, Clarke momentarily short of ideas. But what did Raymond

Chandler say about such quandries in writing? 'When in doubt, have a man come through a door with a gun in his hand.' Clarke deployed his equivalent, Johnson, to immediate effect. He hit Cook's front pad with a delivery of almost unplayable speed and appreciable reverse swing, then adjourned to mid-off where he ran out Joe Root, who was in an act of attempting a pointless single, and caught Ian Bell who was in the act of giving catching practice. In between times, Carberry's four and a half hours for 50 runs had been ended by Siddle, leaving England suddenly adrift at four for 87 with two scoreless batsmen. You'd have called it a car crash in slow motion except that it was almost faster than a car crash.

Pietersen was now the hope of his side, and played responsibly again, as well as annoyingly, exasperating Johnson with his eagle eye for disturbance behind the arm. As the wind stiffened the flags in the afternoon, little willy-willies of garbage swirled in the outfield; at one stage a toddler emerged in the vicinity of the sight screen then was snatched away by his father, leaving Pietersen and Johnson at cross purposes, with emphasis on the 'cross'. Funnily enough, it added to the accumulating intrigue of initiative versus delay, especially when it became obvious that Pietersen had decided he would bear Johnson's brunt rather than leave his cowed colleagues to it. Not that, in the end, this tactic bore fruit, because Stokes, Bresnan and Broad found the off spin of Lyon too much to cope with. The only exception was Bairstow, who hit Lyon for a couple of sixes, but to despatch whom Johnson needed only four deliveries. Feeling abandoned, Pietersen hit out, got out and walked out, tossing his gloves into his donned helmet with a look something like disgust. Clarke's Australians hugged themselves and each other with glee, rejoicing especially in the popular Lyon's successes, which included his hundredth Test wicket. Having looked at lunch like they would bat the day out, England afforded Australia eight overs before the close, during which Rogers and Warner made a sprightly start on their fourth-innings target of 231 by adding 30 without loss.

It should have been a harder task than it proved. No team had made so many batting last at the MCG since the advent of the drop-in. But after Cook dropped each of Rogers and Warner in the first six overs of the fourth morning, Australia's fourth victory was somehow never in doubt. The first miss could be blamed on Bairstow, who froze as a nick neared him, leaving his captain to make a despairing dive, and the second did not prove costly. Yet Cook's deflation, and England's, was palpable. Anderson alone bowled with discipline, Broad was apathetic, Bresnan and Panesar ineffectual, the fielding was slipshod when it wasn't ridiculous. A Test match that had inched along at 2.6 an over suddenly turned into one tootling along at 4.5 an over. Rogers applied himself diligently, then took some liberties as he felt the resistance giving way; Watson helped himself to some tasty second-innings runs again, their partnership of 136 in 167 deliveries more than twice the size of the match's next largest.

Watson struck Panesar for the winning runs at 2.27 pm on the anniversary of Shane Warne's hat trick, and all of a sudden it felt like Australian cricket's palmy 1990s all over again, with vast crowds to experience it: the official attendance on the first day of 91092 broke the ground's own 53-year-old world record, and the match total of 271865 was the fourth-highest for Ashes Tests at the MCG. They left well satisfied. Just enough opposition to make it interesting – and then the crushing verdict.

Day One
THURSDAY 26 DECEMBER

Close of play: England 1st innings 226/6
(KP Pietersen 67*, TT Bresnan 1*, 89 overs)

The boundary rope at the Melbourne Cricket Ground is not simply for the demarcation of the playing area, it is a further opportunity for corporate signage, bearing the web address of a global betting agency.

How suitable, then, that it should have played a part in one of the
worst wagers and luckiest breaks in Kevin Pietersen's career.

The odds were never really in his favour. Ryan Harris. Two men
back. A big boundary. Three for 115. Pietersen had at that stage eked
three scoring shots out of 45 deliveries, defending with the self-denial
that has this season appeared maybe just a little too showy, too man-
nered. Pietersen strung four singles together in his first 43 balls in the
Perth Test, only to swat indolently at the worst possible moment. He
can be like a well-meaning dieter still a slave to his cravings, convinced
somehow that maybe the calories won't count if he eats that Mars Bar
quickly while doing something else.

Harris's set-play bouncer steepled, and at fine leg the substitute
fieldsman Nathan Coulter-Nile could hardly have been better placed,
not far from where Allan Lamb caught Greg Chappell from his first
ball off Norman Cowans here thirty-one years ago, except that then
the fence was the perimeter, and a step too far risked impalement on
the old iron railings.

This isn't a pretext for deployment of the cliché about cricket being
a game of inches, because here there were feet at issue – specifically the
fielder's. Coulter-Nile had to move back and to his left but appeared in
complete control of the catch until his peripheral vision detected the
rope, whereupon a jogging step became a startled hop, and he let the
ball go in the hope of darting back into the playing field to accept it
at the second attempt. When the ball came to rest, however, it lay on
the grass between the rope and the fence, where the television cameras
had a nice view of the name of the betting agency, so someone else
gained by the transaction too.

How close it all was – how close to another day of media speculation about whose cranium was up whose sphincter in the view of
Graeme Swann, for this was the sort of shot to imply aptitude as a
contortionist with a show-stopping rectal speciality. But then with one
bound, or one stumble, Pietersen was free – and again when on 41 he
flailed Harris off the back foot to the left of short mid-wicket, where

the ball forced its way through Bailey's hands. In the end this was an honest, conscientious and at times immensely restrained innings. When Pietersen reached his half-century, the sightscreen flashed up another corporate message, this time referencing a beer, referring to 'a hard-earned 50', and just for once there was truth in advertising.

Pietersen is, of course, the proverbial big-occasion player, and at least at the turnstile there have been no bigger occasions, the nominal deadness of the Test making no difference to the live audience. In the lead-up to this Test, Pietersen had expressed the view that he was batting 'as well as ever' and had actually felt 'really, really good' on virtually every occasion he had batted this summer. If that's so, perhaps there had lain his trouble – a sense of invulnerability shading into illusions of impunity. Reminded here how easily hard work is squandered, he played within bounds, within reason. Siddle, his summer scourge, bowled him 69 balls; Pietersen scored from six of them. Invited to hook after tea, he stayed right on top of the ball to avoid top edges; invited to work to leg, he played late to avoid leading edges; invited to let the ball go, he obliged. Pietersen drove his last delivery of the day through mid-off, expressing his latent powers. He then risked Aleem Dar's displeasure with a bit of time-wasting to ensure the next over was the day's last, earning Tim Bresnan's gratitude.

Having finally been gifted an opportunity to bat first, England did not otherwise make best use of it. Cook started as fluently as at any stage this summer, back cutting and cover driving to the boundary, before chasing one he might have ignored. Root shrugged off having his front shoulder tattooed by Johnson, but fenced indeterminately at Siddle twice in the next over, and hung on till after lunch without ever suggesting permanence. Carberry got started for the fifth time in the series, only to peter out again, and there is a point at which a player making solid beginnings without going on to big scores goes from suffering bad luck to being guilty of bad management. He fell victim, let it be said, to some skilful bowling from Shane Watson, wide of the crease from round the wicket, and veering into off stump as though magnetised – but it was the fourth time he has fallen to bowling from that angle this summer.

On a pitch that actually gave less encouragement than Clarke would have wished after an act of insertion, his attack made their captain look prescient. Harris, Johnson and Siddle bowled hungrily, almost greedily, and pretty expeditiously, given the variety of interruptions during the day: Pietersen at one stage seemed to swallow a fly and required a drink, probably a flaxseed smoothie. Harris is one of the few bowlers I have ever seen who actually pulls himself up in his follow-through rather than naturally decelerating – having bowled, he cannot wait to bowl again. And unlike Watson, who returns to his mark head down as though scanning the ground for change, Harris seems to have his over ready in advance, and a personal deadline to complete it by, the hurry being part of the worry. Batsmen scored off only sixteen of the 120 deliveries Harris bowled as he toyed with another rope: the one around England's neck.

Day Two
FRIDAY 27 DECEMBER

Close of play: Australia 1st innings 164/9
(BJ Haddin 43*, 73.3 overs)

The whimsical Australian leg spinner Arthur Mailey once said that maidens connoted a 'lack of imagination': he took his fabled four for 362 here, as Victoria piled up their record 1107 eighty-seven years ago, without a single scoreless over. Maybe he was right. Some days the building of 'dot-ball pressure' seems like a strategy you have when you're not having a strategy. Often enough, however, the maiden demonstrates a genuine efficacy against the modern, boundary-addicted, strike-rate-conscious batsmen.

Both teams have striven for economy in this Ashes cycle. By and large, Australia have been better at it, accumulating another twenty-four maidens in England's first innings of 100 overs; today, however, England relearned the habit, and have already outdone their rivals, James Anderson, Stuart Broad, Tim Bresnan, Monty Panesar and Ben Stokes seeing through a total of 21 in 73 overs. A grim Test on day one has now turned downright bleak.

Another recurrent feature of the Ashes on both sides of the world has been the disproportionate value of runs on the board, the frailties of both teams being revealed by the demands of batting second and with regard to a target. When Michael Clarke chanced his arm here by inviting England to bat, he must have had this half in mind, acknowledging it also as a deficiency needing to be confronted.

On a pitch with the characteristic tennis-ball bounce of the drop-in, and against a little extra seam movement than they have been used to lately, the kind of pectoral-flexing batsmanship Australia have practised this summer has not come naturally. Neither David Warner nor Shane Watson, who dominated at Perth with the straightforward objective of quick runs to build on a healthy lead, looked likely to do so again here. Warner sawed at the air with his square cut, then tried manufacturing a pull shot, which went as high as some of his strokes at the WACA but up and down in the same place; Watson drove loosely, intent on self-assertion at a stage, on the eve of lunch, when self-preservation might have been wiser.

Confusion continued afterwards when Clarke left when he might have driven and Smith drove when he might have left. The most palpable victim of attrition was George Bailey, who in Perth, of course, plundered 28 from six balls of James Anderson's, but could make nothing of eighteen deliveries here, and in his frustration slashed fatally at the nineteenth. Australia's tail then struggled to come to terms with the pitch's two paces, which are unlikelier to become easier to distinguish.

There were vivid notes in the otherwise austere day. The irresistible force of Mitchell Johnson met the movable object of England's tail with results little less spectacular for their predictability. Stuart Broad then bowled swiftly, as menacingly as at any stage since the Gabba, with a liberal ration of short balls, one of them leaving an indelible impression on Chris Rogers as he ducked into it. The impact made a louder sound than any connection between bat and ball during the day – an ugly crunch like the crushing of an aluminium can.

Blood isn't often seen on the cricket field; it is a game of concussions and contusions rather than of cuts and abrasions. For that reason, and also because of the brilliance of red against the purity of white, it tends to come as a shock, like the intrusion on cricket of another game, equivalent to a spear tackle in soccer, or a matador wandering into the middle of a horse race. So when Rogers removed his helmet to expose an unsightly cut, there was an audible collective gasp. We'd seen Ricky Ponting and Allan Border bleed for their countries; longer memories went back to Graeme Watson in the Rest of the World XI game here forty-one years ago, unintentionally but horridly beamed by Tony Greig. But in this sanitised, bowdlerised, and amply protected high-performance age, direct reminders of cricket's corporeal reality are few. The physical is narrated to us mainly by reports of injury, spare and technical.

Of all the players on each side, however, Rogers seems the one least likely to be disturbed by such an incident. Opening batsmen accept body blows as carpenters accept banged thumbs, as occupational hazards, and Rogers is as seasoned as they come. He let team doctor Peter Brukner come, the next two deliveries go, and resumed a stoic resistance which he extended by a further three hours. Never quite free, he never quite let it vex him, until he miscued just after tea.

As ever, the most fluent Australian batting came from Brad Haddin, who picked his lengths to attack and did so with conviction, the three fours he took from Anderson's seventeenth over, with a cut, a lofted drive and a leg glance, providing a little tour de force. England were prepared to gift him singles, and for once the tactic bore fruit.

This was the closest England have come on this tour to exercising the kind of close control they did at home, and it is no fluke that

David Sandurski's pitch has been the slowest and also least consistent. Nor is it a fluke, I suspect, that the MCG has also been the venue where the Barmy Army have been the most voluble, reinforced, no doubt, by reserve battalions arriving for what they had imagined would be the summer's biggest Tests, but which are now the deadest.

Where the Australians turned to the Army towards the end of Thursday and made a show of shushing them, Alastair Cook's Englishmen gestured to them gratefully as stumps were pulled this evening. A Test unfolding at 2.4 runs an over turns out to have been the best entertainment that the visitors and their fans have had all summer.

Day Three
SATURDAY 28 DECEMBER

Close of play: Australia 2nd innings 30/0
(CJL Rogers 18*, DA Warner 12*, 8 overs)

So long has this Ashes cycle run that it is nearly encompassing entire cricket lifetimes. For Nathan Lyon, it has involved birth, growth, maturity and death – with, unusually, the death coming first.

Lyon began the series in England as the man out of possession, cropped from the XI at Trent Bridge in favour of a glamour teenager – an immensely tough and discouraging call for a bowler who had just achieved his best Test figures, albeit on a raging turner in Delhi. Today capped Lyon's steady, six-month comeback, his best figures since that Delhi Test and possibly his biggest impact yet: a bag of five in an Ashes Test at the MCG in his 29th Test, and at a respectable expense, in days when the odds are stacked against orthodox finger spin. Judging from the back-patting, hair-mussing glee of the teammates who celebrated his 100th Test wicket with him, it has been a popular rehabilitation.

Off spin in Australia can be a hardship posting, requiring degrees of resilience to cope with the inevitable punishment, and art in the flight to make up for the shortage of available sidespin: a remodelling of his action to get him more side-on at release, introducing a little chorus-line kick to his front leg, has enhanced the shape of Lyon's stock ball in the last year. Only twenty-six, he was not even a first-class cricketer when England were last here, and has had to pack in a lot of living in a short time.

But experience is not everything. It was a very experienced England team who faced him this afternoon, and made a ghastly hash of it, losing three for 1 in 6 balls after lunch, then five for 6 in 39 balls after tea – collapses that may not mean they lose this Fourth Test, but from which can be inferred that they barely deserve to win it.

Until England's first pratfall, Australia had actually rather laboured in the field. Ryan Harris was moving gingerly, flexing his knee, and retreated to gully. Steve Smith took a blow at short leg, wrung his hand, and retired to the dressing room. Shane Watson at mid-wicket turned a steady single into a three with a constipated jog alongside the ball. Alastair Cook had looked meditative and impregnable until Johnson thundered one into his front pad, swerving at high speed. Joe Root then stood rooted to the spot after being adjudged caught at the wicket by Aleem Dar, walked towards his partner Michael Carberry with a disbelieving shake of the head, then stood in mid-pitch limbo for two and a half minutes while the videodrome worked its way towards his exoneration. But half an hour on, and England could count themselves well ahead: 137 runs to the good, with nine wickets in reserve.

Then chaos, portended by the fact that while a front-line check was made on Carberry's lbw dismissal there were briefly three batsmen on the ground, Pietersen having walked halfway to the centre while his predecessor dallied near the boundary. It was an omen. Root promptly drove to mid-off where Mitchell Johnson's proximity and powerful left arm made a folly of his call for a single. Bell then drove in the air in the same direction, watching the shot's arc in mute horror as Johnson executed a far simpler piece of fielding with far greater deliberation, standing stock-still as the ball approached and clasping it solemnly. As teammates ran from all directions, Johnson held up both hands almost ecclesiastically, as though requesting a prayer of thanksgiving. Bell looked down, pained and penitent, before moving off.

Quite right too. There was the faint sense that Australia knew simply to bide their time while England battled with themselves, not sure what to make of an ascendancy after a summer with barely the sniff of one. Just before tea, Ben Stokes pushed into the off side, and had Siddle's aim been true would have caused Pietersen to be run out by a third of the length of the pitch. Just after, he wasted 70 minutes of discretion with a headstrong stroke down the ground to gift Lyon a second wicket.

A further game within the game was then in progress between Siddle and Pietersen, Siddle with the now-familiar personal entourage of Warner and Bailey at short mid-wicket, Pietersen with his determination both to take care and not to be bothered. Clarke pulled Bailey out, and Pietersen picked the gap for three. Clarke put Bailey back, and Pietersen clipped a full toss into the same airspace, where the fielder got a finger to a quarter-chance. Pietersen was drawn forward and edged short of slip to the boundary. Pietersen inclined to hook a short ball, then pirouetted out of the stroke as ornately as Derek Zoolander executing a left turn. With a pull shot and a cover drive to the rope, he at last broke free but only briefly.

The rapid expiration of the innings at the other end put paid to his further hopes. Bairstow hit two sixes off Lyon with the wind, but was quickly expunged by Johnson, and when Lyon changed ends he induced paralysis: Bresnan and Broad played him like they had never seen an off spinner before. And hitting into an even stronger gale than at Perth, Pietersen threw another hand away.

In seven Ashes Tests since his recall at Old Trafford, Lyon has taken twenty-four wickets. They have usually been timely and valuable interdictions too, including Pietersen four times, Bell and Root thrice each, Cook, Prior and Stokes twice each, Bairstow and Trott once each. Into the bargain he has proven harder and harder to remove with the bat, being unbeaten in his last five innings, and thrown himself around in the field, in contrast to an opposite number here who allowed a risible all-run four in the day's last few minutes. How accomplished Lyon is proving in his role as Australia's songmaster is only for an intimate circle to know, of course, but he is getting some practice – by this time tomorrow afternoon he will probably be getting more.

Day Four
SUNDAY 29 DECEMBER

Close of play: Australia 2nd innings 231/2
(51.5 overs) – end of match

The Ashes is cricket's original and definitive tradition, the one by which others are measured. But just today, as Australia cruised to victory at the MCG, it started to feel like an overlong reality-television series with a cast of characters grown cloyingly familiar.

This was always a risk when Cricket Australia and the England Cricket Board cooked up this back-to-back, home-and-away, urn-o-max wheeze between them, ostensibly to decouple the Ashes from the World Cup cycle but principally for their respective exchequers; the cricket has done well to sustain the drama and tension it has.

But the truth is that both teams have looked jaded in this game, thanks to the unavoidable frailties of flesh, blood and spirit. Ten Tests, eight of them in back-to-back couples: no matter how often you say it, your mind still boggles. And no fewer than four of them – 40 per cent of the cricket – will end up having no bearing on the holder of the Ashes.

Australia came through here by the continuation of winning habits established at Brisbane, Adelaide and Perth, with Mitchell Johnson on hand to provide a few helpful adrenalin shots. England's failures have also been of the habitual kind, like an unfortunate weakness one cannot kick, although batting collapses are hardly as much fun as fast women and slow horses. Even the crowd was subdued today, their attention wavering, their Mexican waves desultory. When the Barmy Army struck up a song after lunch, largely for nostalgia, locals could barely summon a 'Broad is a wanker' chant in reply.

England carried themselves wearily from the beginning, conscious that they had forfeited the game the day before, going through their activities now like clockwork toys winding down. Kevin Pietersen, Stuart Broad, James Anderson and Michael Carberry all perpetrated ham-handed misfields; Monty Panesar misfielded simply because that is what he does. From the outfield, throws came in high, wide and none too handsome. Then there were the inevitable drops. Off Broad, Rogers (19) gave a regulation keeper's catch to one who is not a regulation keeper, Alastair Cook making a last-minute dive when it became clear that Bairstow was auditioning for Madame Tussauds. Cook was more culpable when Warner (22) nicked Stokes, although the error proved less costly. A team that fields badly will always find themselves under the cosh, but a team under the cosh will also tend to field badly, because of the pressure their performance places on individual efforts, each chance arriving with a greater portent and obligation. Can't drop this, can't drop this, ugh, dropped it . . .

Australia, meanwhile, did what they had to do. There was a canny innings from Chris Rogers, as calmly dutiful as a well-trained husband accompanying his wife Christmas shopping. He summed the wicket up perfectly, playing fluidly behind point, creeping forward to make half-volleys, outscoring Shane Watson in a run-a-minute 100-stand, booking himself a tour to South Africa that had never really been in doubt anyway.

After his early reprieve, the sum of Rogers' alarms were an inside scrape to fine leg to go to 49, and an outside nick that eluded Bairstow's late-flung left gauntlet when he was 81. He reached his century with the best shot he played, a cover drive to the boundary from Anderson, and celebrated it with the cheekiest, a square drive to the boundary on the walk off the listless, lacklustre Bresnan. His record is now very nearly unique. This was his first Test hundred in Australia but his sixth first-class hundred at the MCG – he is not so much a late bloomer as a long one. Not since Lindsay Hassett has an Australian opener made an Ashes hundred when as old as thirty-six.

Man of the match Johnson looked on, with extra time for personal grooming. His work was done, both in terms of his eight wickets for 88, and the perplexity he spread elsewhere, the bash-and-block extremities to which Kevin Pietersen was driven in each innings owing everything to the infirmities of England's lower-middle order. The promise Bairstow showed with the bat at Lord's now seems a distant memory indeed.

But then, so does so much else. On Saturday night, Pietersen gave a surprisingly candid interview to Sky Sports in which he confided that England had struggled mentally with the business of defending the Ashes so soon after retaining them – that they had been, as he put it, 'a bit fragile' mentally coming into the series at the prospect of such 'a tough gig'. Not that he would have experienced or even expected much sympathy, for our tendency is to ridicule such comments: how dare these well-paid, superfood-scarfing prima donnas complain of human frailty! And at 0–4, everything sounds like an excuse. Yet nobody should neglect that England came to Australia with everything to lose, and Australia hosted them with everything to gain. For if that feeling has not played a part in the respective trajectories of these two teams then they truly are sporting automata.

Pietersen was mistaken in thinking that he and his teammates had undertaken something that had 'never been done before': ten Ashes Tests in a row occurred in 1901–02, when touring was a private adhocracy, and in 1920–21, when fans were ravening for cricket after a nine-year hiatus prolonged by World War I. But life was simpler then: there were only three Test nations and South Africa barely counted. (There were ten off the reel in 1974–75, too, but interrupted by the 1975 World Cup).

So if the Ashes have reached an otiose stage for onlookers, imagine how it feels to have been directly involved. I suspect, in fact, that some of the bad temper evident during this Australian half of the cycle is to do with the players being sick of the sight of each other. Make no mistake: the Ashes of 2013–14 have given onlookers in both countries much pleasure. But their structure should, quite simply, never be repeated.

2013 in Review

GOODBYE TO ALL THEM

Cricket has grown accustomed in recent times to a kind of permanent present, but this year a backward glance or two has been unavoidable. The farewells of 2013 began with Mike Hussey, ended with Jacques Kallis and Graeme Swann, and peaked, inevitably, with Sachin Tendulkar and his mother of all goodbyes. Throw in Sri Lanka's Tillakaratne Dilshan, England's Matthew Hoggard, that good and faithful servant of New Zealand cricket Chris Martin, and it's no wonder that even Kerry O'Keeffe is now thinking autumnal thoughts.

You would call 2013 the year of farewells, but for the fact that 2012 was pretty much the same. Its big seven included Ricky Ponting, Brett Lee, Rahul Dravid, V.V.S. Laxman, Andrew Strauss, Mark Boucher and Mohammad Yousuf, who basically had his card marked by Pakistan for the last time. And that for cricket raises some interesting issues.

The inclination at times like these is to contemplate the game's sublime cyclicality, its constant mingling of ends and beginnings. Yet the passing from international cricket of the aforementioned is surely quite a twilight of the idols: add together their records and they represent around 200000 runs, 2600 wickets, and 3500 catches/stumpings. Because exactly how well equipped is cricket to replace them? Who has emerged globally in that same span who strikes you as a natural inheritor of the mantles forgone?

Virat Kohli and Cheteshwar Pujara look like handy players in the making; likewise, in a lower key, Faf du Plessis, Kane Williamson and Asad Shafiq. But David Warner and Steve Smith apart, who themselves have taken time to become overnight sensations, Australia's Ashes triumph this season has been a triumph of old sweats. Having burst with promise at first, Joe Root, Shikhar Dhawan and Darren Bravo are finding the going tougher, while Ben Stokes's one swallow has hardly made a summer. The derisory quantities of international cricket played by Sri Lanka, Bangladesh and Zimbabwe, meanwhile, make their younger talents difficult to assess.

Look around the world at who is leading attacks at present and the names are decidedly familiar. South Africa still depend on Dale Steyn, England on James Anderson, West Indies on Kemar Roach; India and Pakistan have just recalled Zaheer Khan and Umar Gul respectively. There are Trent Boult and Vernon Philander, of course. But high speed is exceedingly scarce, with the world's most precocious bowling talent, Mohammad Amir, languishing in a purdah of his own making. And quality slow bowling is scarcer still, the cause being carried forward now by Saeed Ajmal. Sri Lanka have never replaced Muttiah Muralitharan. The West Indies have, for that matter, never replaced Curtly Ambrose and Courtney Walsh.

With the spread of supranational T20, there is more money and encouragement available for discovery and development of young cricketers than ever before. The Indian Premier League actually preens itself on its showcasing of youth and vitality, its trophy bearing the Sanskrit inscription *Yatra pratibha avsara prapnotithi*: 'where talent meets opportunity'. And it can point to Ravindra Jadeja and Ravi Ashwin as examples of players whose progress to international cricket has been accelerated.

But it's arguable that supranational T20 has been much less good at bringing new players to the fore than in harnessing the readymade. Its outstanding exponents remain cricketers whose careers were well underway before it began: M.S. Dhoni, Chris Gayle, Shane Watson,

Mahela Jayawardene, Brendon McCullum, Lasith Malinga, Brad Hodge, et al. The IPL auction, shortly to be held again, remains a law unto itself, settling windfall gains on flavours of the moment, from J.P. Duminy and Dan Christian to Glenn Maxwell and Sunil Narine, even if its greatest beneficiaries have tended to be peripheral Indian talents, lavished with rewards because of the restrictions on overseas players and of their local recognisability. None of Suresh Raina, Yusuf and Irfan Pathan, Vinay Kumar, Dinesh Kartik, Piyush Chawla, Amit Mishra or Robin Uthappa threaten to be other than good ordinary cricketers: Raina, the IPL's highest scorer, is a short-ball pushover in every other form of the game. But they are far better rewarded than vastly superior players from other countries and other times.

There is also a more general question about how we apprehend greatness. At least by our traditional usage of the word, 'great' is not a word that applies readily to T20. That's not a criticism, by the way; it's simply a function of scale. T20's key words are 'exciting', 'fun' and 'loud'. But 'great'? 'Great', in respect of cricket, still implies epic deeds and enormous endurances, the steady mounting of resistances and sudden shattering of deadlocks, none of which are part of the quotidian reality of the shortest form of the game.

You can be proficient in scoring the maximum runs off 60 balls and conceding the minimum runs from a four-over spell; you can even be 'brilliant' and 'spectacular', especially in executing a single individual feat, like hitting a timely six, delivering a crucial slower ball, or scoring a telling direct hit. But, at present, the appellation 'great' in the context of T20 makes no more sense than it would if applied to a burger, a music video or Piers Morgan. 'Greatness' is a quality that T20 must still truck in from elsewhere, and will remain so, at least until we reinterpret, liberalise or dilute the concept.

In this sense, then, the further erosion of Test cricket, which I discussed last week, places the game in greater danger than is readily comprehended. Greatness matters. Greatness stirs. Greatness, to use a word administrators actually *do* understand, sells. So the retirements of the last two years represent a significant depreciation of the game's elite capital. That will need rebuilding. In the process we will learn whether cricket has an ongoing capacity to make, rather than merely to pimp.

FOURTH TEST Melbourne Cricket Ground 26–29 December 2013

Toss Australia   **Australia won by 8 wickets**

ENGLAND	1st Innings			2nd Innings		
AN Cook*	c Clarke	b Siddle	27	lbw	b Johnson	51
MA Carberry		b Watson	38	lbw	b Siddle	12
JE Root	c Haddin	b Harris	24	run out		15
KP Pietersen		b Johnson	71	c Harris	b Lyon	49
IR Bell	c Haddin	b Harris	27	c Johnson	b Lyon	0
BA Stokes	c Watson	b Johnson	14	c Smith	b Lyon	19
JM Bairstow†		b Johnson	10	c Haddin	b Johnson	21
TT Bresnan	c Bailey	b Johnson	1		b Lyon	0
SCJ Broad	lbw	b Johnson	11	c Clarke	b Lyon	0
JM Anderson	not out		11	not out		1
MS Panesar		b Lyon	2	lbw	b Johnson	0
EXTRAS	(b 10, lb 7, w 1, nb 1)		19	(b 5, lb 6)		11
TOTAL	(100 overs; 435 mins)		255	(61 overs; 284 mins)		179

AUSTRALIA	1st Innings			2nd Innings		
CJL Rogers	c Pietersen	b Bresnan	61	c Bairstow	b Panesar	116
DA Warner	c Bairstow	b Anderson	9	c Bairstow	b Stokes	25
SR Watson	c Bairstow	b Stokes	10	not out		83
MJ Clarke*		b Anderson	10	not out		6
SPD Smith	c Bell	b Broad	19			
GJ Bailey	c Bairstow	b Anderson	0			
BJ Haddin†	c Bairstow	b Anderson	65			
MG Johnson	c Anderson	b Bresnan	2			
RJ Harris	c Root	b Broad	6			
PM Siddle	c Bresnan	b Broad	0			
NM Lyon	not out		18			
EXTRAS	(lb 4)		4	(nb 1)		1
TOTAL	(82.2 overs; 360 mins)		204	(2 wkts; 51.5 overs; 232 mins)		231

AUSTRALIA 1st Innings	O	M	R	W	2nd Innings	O	M	R	W
RJ Harris	24	8	47	2		10	1	34	0
MG Johnson	24	4	63	5		15	5	25	3
PM Siddle	23	7	50	1		15	6	46	1
NM Lyon	22.2	3	67	1		17	3	50	5
SR Watson	6.4	2	11	1		4	2	13	0

ENGLAND 1st Innings	O	M	R	W	2nd Innings	O	M	R	W
JM Anderson	20.2	4	67	4		11	2	26	0
SCJ Broad	20	6	45	3		10	0	58	0
BA Stokes	15	4	46	1		12	0	50	1
TT Bresnan	18	6	24	2		7	1	48	0
MS Panesar	9	2	18	0		7.5	0	41	1
JE Root						4	1	8	0

FALL OF WICKETS Wicket	Eng - 1st	Aus - 1st	Eng - 2nd	Aus - 2nd
1st	48	19	65	64
2nd	96	36	86	200
3rd	106	62	86	–
4th	173	110	87	–
5th	202	112	131	–
6th	216	122	173	–
7th	230	151	174	–
8th	231	162	174	–
9th	242	164	179	–
10th	255	204	179	–

Umpires: Aleem Dar (Pakistan) and HDPK Dharmasena (Sri Lanka)
Referee: RS Madugalle (Sri Lanka)

THE FIFTH TEST: Sydney

TWO OLD LAGS

For those of us who've been there from the start of this Ashes cycle, it's surely time to strike a commemorative T-shirt. 'I Saw All Ten – and Survived.' 'From the River Trent to Sydney Harbour.' 'Ashes 2013–14: Can Someone Tell Me What Happened? I Was Too Busy Filing for the Web.'

That will go for the hard core of us in the media centre for the Fifth Test in Sydney anyway. As far as the players are concerned, the ever-presents will probably constitute a round dozen, split evenly between the two teams: England's Alastair Cook, Ian Bell, Kevin Pietersen, James Anderson, Stuart Broad and Joe Root (assuming he's selected) and Australia's Michael Clarke, Peter Siddle, Steve Smith, Brad Haddin, Chris Rogers and Shane Watson (assuming his fitness, but, well, that qualification will never quite disappear).

In some respects, it's surprising there are so many: both captains, for example, have long-term back complaints. The unsung heroes of this Ashes cycle, then, have been the medical and physiotherapeutic corps on both teams, with an honourable mention for the MedX machine in Beecroft that keeps Clarke's vertebrae viable.

More than half the players concerned are thirtysomethings, with perhaps the most noteworthy being the two Australians who turned thirty-six along the way, Rogers in August, Haddin in October – for it also happens that across both series they have arguably been the most consistent contributors. A year before the Trent Bridge Test, probably neither would have expected to make it. Haddin had forgone his Test place for well-publicised personal reasons; unsure whether he would be offered a Victorian contract, Rogers was speculating that his career might wind down in county cricket.

A year ago in Sydney, Haddin's successor Matthew Wade scored a dashing century, and appeared on the brink of a long tenure as keeper; David Warner and Ed Cowan had opened in fourteen consecutive Tests, and were bound for India as the incumbent pair.

It was the retirements in short order of Ricky Ponting and Mike Hussey that created the vacuum of experience selectors abhor. With crisis in India came a mandate for change, and don't forget that Mickey Arthur was part of the selection panel that restored Haddin and recognised Rogers for the Ashes tour – not every positive development in Australian cricket in the last year can be sheeted home to Darren Lehmann.

Haddin has now taken forty-seven catches across nine Tests, and had no more than two or three days where his glovework has not been of the very highest standard. He leads a fielding effort of intimidating excellence and elasticity, and appeals that sound like veritable eisteddfords. His batting in Australia has, of course, gone from strength to strength, freeing those above and below him. He has been Australia's Mr Fix-It, comparable to Hussey, as well as to the abiding benchmark of Gilchrist.

More than that, Haddin is a busy, engaged, talkative presence, jogging from end to end between overs, often detouring to fine leg to catch up with a bowler and administer a bolstering bum pat. Watch Haddin and Clarke in the slip cordon for any sort of period. Their chitchat is more or less constant, their rapport deriving from parallel histories: Clarke's maiden first-class match was Haddin's fourth, more than fourteen years ago. The relationship also benefits from the simple reality that Haddin is not really a rival candidate for the Australian captaincy. This shouldn't matter in cricket, yet somehow does. Few positions are so ambivalent as that of the ambitious vice-captain in an unsuccessful team; in England, none cracked heartier than Haddin.

Rogers, meanwhile, has totted up 700 runs across the nine Tests, and failed to contribute significantly in only two, at Lord's and at the Gabba. He has had phases in both series of lesser fluency, when that crooked back leg and backlift towards fine leg have made him look ungainly. Every so often as he withdraws to the on side to recuperate between deliveries you sense a churning within, a perfectionism driving him on, a severity to his inner analyses. But as you'd expect of a player with his experience, he has 'found a way' to relocate run-making habits. Lately England has helped, or at least the retirement of Graeme Swann has, he being Rogers' conqueror seven times in their eight Tests as opponents.

After his maiden hundred at Riverside, Rogers gave a press conference that stood out for the emotion evident. 'I set myself high standards,' he said. Then he said it again. And again. Actually, I'm confident Rogers repeated it at least four times, and it stuck in my mind. This was not merely the deployment of a stock phrase, like 'good areas' or 'execute our skills': it struck me as a creed by which Rogers lived, a refusal to measure himself simply by a general standard, but always to demand from himself the better yet. Through Rogers' long first-class career, there must have been periods where the near-enough would have sufficed. Here spoke an acute self-knowledge.

As cricketers, then, both Haddin and Rogers have things to teach us. Older players are often characterised negatively – the old lags hanging around, the dead wood clogging up the system, the blokes who can't let go, who need the money, who fear the future. Yet there's another idea that also applies to them: the notion, somehow freeing, somehow rejuvenating, of 'raging against the dying of the light', of living as though there is 'no tomorrow'. For Haddin and Rogers this is almost certainly true. The next hiatus in their careers is bound to be the last. Perhaps it is as a result that they are playing the best cricket of their lives

Haddin and Rogers have points to prove, too, about the times they waited, looked on, were not thought good enough, were later written off. They are assuredly strangers to the entitlement mentality nourished by the outsized squad of contracted players belatedly scaled down by the last memorandum of understanding between Cricket Australia and the Australian Cricketers' Association. So they find themselves inductees in that special brotherhood of the ten, and none will cherish the achievement more. They probably deserve a bit more than a T-shirt, actually.

Summary
THE WHITEWASH BLUES

Dr Johnson said that while everyone admired *Paradise Lost*, none wished it any longer. Something similar might be said of the Ashes of 2013–14. Although the pursuit of a whitewash provided Michael Clarke's team with additional pre-match motivation and post-match satisfaction, the Fifth Test proved an almost needless confirmation of Australian superiority. England took all twenty Australian wickets for the first time in the series, but in other respects plumbed new depths.

It was not hard to pick the differences even before the game. Player after player from the Australian team emerged to entreat the selectors to stick with their unit, and thereby afford them the satisfaction of remaining unchanged in the series. England were proving to be the team that, not playing together, was not staying together. By including three debutants, pace bowler Boyd Rankin, batsman Gary Ballance and leg spinner Scott Borthwick (added from outside the squad), then inserting Australia on winning the toss, it was almost as though the visitors were squeezing their innovation quotient for the summer into a single Test.

Taking four for 94 by lunch, England could feel satisfied with their morning's work, and the half-hour afterwards, with Anderson and Broad scenting wickets, recalled the tension of the first day at the Gabba. Again it was Haddin who rallied the counteroffensive, pulling, cutting and driving sumptuously on the up as Ben Stokes dropped short and Boyd Rankin dropped out, twice leaving the field with a mysterious hamstring pain. Coming in off an amble and a hop, Borthwick tossed the ball up gamely, but with little shape or threat, giving up 21 in three exploratory overs, then 28 in a further four. The worst of it was that Panesar, on the evidence of Melbourne, could hardly have done better.

When Haddin nicked off for 75 after a partnership of 128, Steve Smith took the initiative in the same fashion as at the Oval and the WACA, with choice shots through the covers, including ten boundaries in his first 50, and hard running between wickets. When he went to his 142-ball century with a six and a four from Borthwick, it was like he was choosing from a degustation menu. He and Harris added a cheerful 50 in 42 deliveries to close off one final English opportunity, although three wickets in an over from Stokes had the perverse effect of leaving England with six overs to negotiate before the close. Johnson immediately bowled the day's four fastest deliveries; his eighth grazed Carberry's bat but elicited no appeal; his ninth drew a compulsive glance from Carberry and a quicksilver leg-slip catch by Lyon.

The first hour of the second day was then the series in miniature, Harris and Johnson then Siddle rampaging through England's petrified top order. Cook, Pietersen, Bell and the nightwatchman Anderson: these were victims of post-traumatic stress as much as pace, seam or swing. Joe Root would have looked on at the ordeal of his replacement Ballance with sympathy but maybe also relief. Johnson hit the newcomer's helmet so hard he almost knocked one of the lions off, and a ten-minute panel-beating delay ensued, long enough for Ballance to recover his sangfroid. He actually played as well as anyone, delaying Australian an hour and a half before defending loosely to Lyon.

Paradoxically, this was the best performance by England's bottom half for the series, albeit from a low base. Stokes played with maturity and discrimination, Bairstow tried to, Broad threw the bat, Rankin held it still. A hundred and thirty-two runs were added from England's nadir. England then yanked out Australia's first four wickets for 91, and it took the calm and collected Rogers to keep them from further harm. But that first hour had done for the visitors. Whatever residual fight existed was gone. Anderson and Broad walked back to their marks as numbly as soldiers on a long route march. Anderson did not even react when the fielders managed to turn a legitimate nick to third man into a seven, with the help of four overthrows from the ersatz keeper Bairstow on collecting a return from Bell, and the help of some good backing-up from absolutely nobody. For Borthwick, Ballance and Rankin, it must have been like a visit to an ancestral mausoleum.

Cook walked out for the warm-ups on the last morning on his own, and very, very slowly. He stopped in the middle to shape up briefly in his imagination, cutting a lonely figure, although it also occurred to you that he must have had very little time on his own in the preceding six months, such is England's propensity for management by committee. Then he waited in front of the O'Reilly Stand until his team joined him for a last sequence of running, jumping and not playing: they brought to mind Adam Gilchrist's likeness of Alec Stewart's Englishmen of fifteen years earlier to 'office workers turning up for a dreary day behind the desk'. The run-throughs were listless, the fielding was lethargic to the point of coma, Bairstow struggled through his keeping routines, Flower talked through the team's challenge in terms and tones that must have been familiar. The crowd members and commentators cavorting in pink for the McGrath Foundation's festivities largely ignored them, and they left to the sound of their own feet.

Having done so on scores of occasions in first-class cricket, Rogers scented a hundred and pursued it as keenly as a dog searching for a bone, before becoming one of Borthwick's three late victims. The work Australia has still to do on its batting was embodied by Bailey not quite reaching 200 runs for the series and Haddin leaving 3000 Test runs in his wake.

Australia were all out by five overs after lunch, England two down by drinks, Cook and Bell waving defeatedly outside the off stump; Bailey took his ninth catch of the series by diving backwards to accept a bat-pad chance from Pietersen, and later added a tenth. Less passive than usual, Carberry perished to an overactive cut from the second ball after tea, and the tail went down in a blaze of six sixes from Broad and Stokes, Harris bowling them both, then having Rankin caught high at slip by Clarke. At Lyon's instigation, the Australians came from all points to perform their victory song on the square itself. The All Blacks can hardly have performed a haka more ebullient.

Harris's figures were his best of the series, England's last innings their shortest, as though they could not wait to be done with it all. If it was any consolation to them, the Australian players at the presentation ceremony looked almost as exhausted. Not that the Englishmen seemed to be looking at anything in particular – theirs was just the thousand-yard stare of the defeated and depleted.

Day One
FRIDAY 3 JANUARY

Close of play: England 1st innings 8/1
(AN Cook 7*, JM Anderson 1*, 6 overs)

An old chestnut of military strategy is the injunction not to fight the next war with the weapons of the last. Looking back on this Ashes tour, history might render a similar verdict on England.

In the last few years, one of the most sought-after attributes among pace bowlers has been height. At the likes of South Africa's Morne Morkel (198 cm) and Pakistan's Mohammad Irfan (216 cm), batsmen have been looking up more than ever, and going under more often too, ducking and diving amid the chin traffic. For Australia, James Pattinson, Mitchell Starc, Trent Copeland, Ben Cutting and Pat Cummins have all peered down from more than 190 cm.

Picking their touring party for Australia this summer, however,

England's selectors took height into nosebleed territory, with four bowlers in need of extra-long beds and additional leg room on planes: 201-cm Chris Tremlett, 204-cm Boyd Rankin, and 200-cm Steve Finn, not to mention 195-cm Stuart Broad.

We're not talking about Garner, Croft, Ambrose and Walsh, of course. Only Broad was a certainty to play. But three years ago, Tremlett had been a matchwinner, brought to the antipodes on the strong urging of England's bowling coach, David Saker, who had spied him bowling in the nets at the Oval. What worked once was bound to work again, wasn't it?

The short answer to this question turned out to be no, and so, today, did the long answer, as Rankin, on his Test debut, broke down not once but twice in an afternoon. In seven weeks in Australia, he has not bowled a hundred overs; neither have Tremlett, not seen since the Brisbane Test, nor Finn, not seen on a Test field at all, and for all intents and purposes a rumour of a presence.

Rankin, a farmer's strapping son from county Tyrone, looks like he could be attached to a hoe and used to plough fields. But as he dragged his cramped left hamstring from the SCG for a second time at 4.15 pm, he was on his way to see England's medical staff for the third time in the day, having also been off the field for treatment during the warm-ups, thus missing the presentation of a cap he may now have little opportunity to wear. Curious.

So why has a tactic so successful three years ago worked nonstart this time? For one, it has lost such shock value as it had. The Australians have come prepared, unwilling merely to sway and swivel, ready to play their cross-bat shots. Morkel took fourteen wickets in three Tests in Australia last summer, but cost 3.7 runs an over.

What has gone for England all tour, too, applied again today: their bowlers' default lengths have been consistently metres short. Although they finally obtained their first lbw of the series, they bowled only a small proportion of balls that would have hit the stumps, fewer still full enough to swing.

This has not been height-specific: Ben Stokes never seems to tire of dropping the ball halfway down the pitch, even when he has mid-off, mid-on and extra cover set for the drive. Today he set Haddin in motion with two shoddy overs after lunch, and a second-change bowler in international cricket really has no business giving up a hundred runs on the first day of a Test, even for six wickets – five of which were gained, not coincidentally, by deliveries of fuller length.

The real problem for England, however, is that the tall bowlers they brought are just not very good – far from as good, one can't help thinking, as Graham Onions, left behind despite his outstanding first-class seasons for Durham in 2012 and 2013. England have invested not in a threat, but a theory.

Height seems to have come into vogue chiefly for two reasons: economy is a cardinal virtue; the ability to obtain consistent sideways movement and attain genuine pace is rare. But size does not matter, at least on its own: you still need craft, skill and variation. Indeed, it looks a different game when you see fast bowling of the classical mode, as practised today by Anderson just after noon, and Johnson just before stumps.

Anderson has had an indifferent series, but remains a delight to watch. He is of average height, like Larwood and Lindwall, and lithe build, like Holding and Donald, gliding over the ground, barely scuffing the creases. In seven overs either side of the break, he set to wobbling the seam around, varying the pace at which it came onto the bat, occasionally obtaining sharp movement into the bat, snarling at off stump. He trapped Watson with a nip-backer, almost did the same to Smith twice, unsuccessfully sought a review for caught behind against Haddin, and beat inside and outside edges. If he has not bowled brilliantly in Australia, he has seldom bowled badly.

Johnson had only eighteen deliveries to bowl to England in the gloaming, and took precisely four to rev his way to 150 kmh, confirmation of which on the big screen was greeted by a cheer like that for a familiar catchphrase. Pounded and pinioned for eight balls, Carberry could not control a leg-side tuck from his ninth.

Nightwatchman Anderson, still wearing the pants in which he'd fielded for seventy-six overs, had to negotiate the day's final rites, and the last war loomed again: this was a challenge he famously rather funked against Johnson in Perth three years ago, costing England the wicket of Paul Collingwood off a day's last ball – something of which the Australian cordon may have made some fuckin' mention.

Atonement was at hand. To protect his captain, Anderson declined a long single from Johnson's penultimate delivery, and played the day's last ball down in front of gully: a minuscule improvement in a summer involving so many, many declines.

Day Two
SATURDAY 4 JANUARY

Close of play: Australia 2nd innings 140/4
(CJL Rogers 73*, GJ Bailey 20*, 30 overs)

After the Perth Test, Mitchell Johnson, Peter Siddle and Ryan Harris posed for a photograph in the dressing rooms at the WACA, arms round each other's shoulders, faces lit with great beamish smiles, still in shirts stained with the sweat of their day's endeavours, now flecked also with victors' beer.

In years to come, the instant the photograph was taken will probably be forgotten, but you can imagine copies adorning the subjects' walls and mantelpieces, bringing forth memories of an unrepeatable summer when every morning dawned with promise and every evening closed with satisfaction.

At New Year, there was some talk of the hardworking Harris taking a break, and complaints that back-to-back Tests represented cruel and unnatural treatment for pace bowlers. Yet the message from the Australian camp, which the selectors heeded, was that the aches and pains were sweetness themselves. 'Jeez it hurts, but I love it,' as

Rod Marsh used to say of keeping wickets to Dennis Lillee and Jeff Thomson.

And who could not forbear a little strain and discomfort for the joy of bowling in an hour like the first of the second day of the Fifth Test? This was the stuff of ecstatic reminiscence in the making. The SCG pitch was lively, to be sure, hard beneath, and still shaded green despite a day's sunbaking. Allan Border's theory is that the cessation of the custom of cross-rolling under the present curator has resulted in less even surfaces, which are more prone to unexpected bounce and lateral movement, especially in the first hour of play each day. But there had been life the day before, and England had used it only spasmodically, even a little wantonly, despite first opportunity to try it out. Harris, Johnson and Siddle showed how to explore all its possibilities, at paces greater, lengths fuller and lines tighter – the crowd reaction as Johnson clocks 150 kmh now acts as a kind of delayed sonic boom.

To watch the first hour felt a bit like stopping to gape at a car accident in the hope of a bit of gore – almost a little tasteless. Alastair Cook's abstaining from a stroke to Harris's second ball set the tone of English paralysis, whether from caution, exhaustion, confusion, or even fear. Ian Bell's first-ball nick to Watson at first slip went begging, but commenced an hour in which a batsman with nearly a hundred caps and 6700 Test runs was capable of scoring from only a single delivery, might have been dismissed half a dozen times, and whose eventual fall constituted almost a kind of deliverance. Two other wickets fell, Anderson after a desperate vigil, Pietersen after a frantic cameo, losing his grip on the bat handle as well as on the situation.

Otherwise, England did as England does and England has this season, which is stick to what they know. Despite consistency having long since blurred into rigidity and predictability, nobody thought to adjust their guard, or bat out of their crease, or risk anything other than a leave or a defensive block, presenting as ever larger fish in an ever smaller barrel. A total of fifteen runs accrued, and it was difficult afterwards to recall a single purposeful stroke, as opposed to involuntary acts of personal self-protection. The best shot, an off drive by Stokes off Harris, was superbly intercepted by Rogers, whose spectacles and long sleeves bely his agility.

Stokes stayed to extend England's innings into the afternoon with some pleasing initiative and sound defence, but emulated his captain in unwisely offering no stroke, politely admitting Siddle to the top of his off stump. When a naturally positive cricketer who hits the ball as cleanly as Stokes is getting out without offering, you have to question the company he is keeping, if not the advice he is receiving.

On debut, Gary Ballance did enough to suggest that the spell check on one's laptop that automatically corrects his name to 'Balance' is not ironic. Johnson hit him on the helmet, but he got in squarely behind the next few. Not so secure against slow bowling, he played down the line to Lyon, and Haddin made an awkward catch look easy. Less than 15 per cent of Haddin's dismissals have been standing up at the stumps, but it has been from want of opportunity, not technique.

The tail twitched sufficiently to save the McGrath Foundation from an empty ground for its scheduled corporate functions tomorrow, a droll cheer greeting England's avoidance of the follow-on. And so the visiting bowlers found themselves at work after fewer than sixty overs off. With twenty overs to go, bowler Broad and mid-on Anderson bent their heads together for a long consultation, on which it was tempting to eavesdrop. 'You jammy bastard, Jimmy, you get to go home next week.' 'Sorry Broady, there's still some Aussies who haven't booed you yet.' 'Right, I'm going to complain about the footholds again to waste more time.' Which he did – Broad's sensitive soles could detect undulations in a dance floor.

The pitch actually continued offering encouragement to the bowlers, four Australians falling within fourteen overs, but it was of a backhanded kind, for England is set to bat last, chasing a total that already looks beyond them, with no batsmen of the resilience and enterprise that Rogers combined in the day's last two hours. Meanwhile, in the home dressing room, Johnson, Harris and Siddle were surveying the vertical and horizontal deviations with interest, resting up ahead of further photo opportunities.

Day Three
SUNDAY 5 JANUARY

Close of play: England 2nd innings 166
(31.4 overs) – end of match

So 5–0 it is, the Ashes Tests of 2013–14 having veritably hurtled to their variously emphatic conclusions: 381 runs, 218 runs, 150 runs, eight wickets, and today 281 runs. The gap in quality was repeated and irreducible.

That seems the way of it in these times. Trent Bridge last year has been the only Test since 2005 in which Australia and England have finished within sight of one another. For whatever reason – the explosive brittleness of modern batting, the vogue for back-to-back Tests, the lack of first-class matches between them – Ashes series are becoming virtual immolations.

In the vernacular of cricket, England today 'chased' 448. But it was a 'chase' like one of those undertaken by Buster Keaton or the Keystone Cops – the visitors even did their own stunts, with Michael Carberry's bat at one stage folding up at the splice like a comic prop. At issue was merely the finish time: would the match outlast the weekend? The beancounters were urging England on, but there was a sense of, as they say, déjà vu all over again. All summer, England have come into Tests with what has resembled a good team on paper, only for the paper to prove pure tissue. Alastair Cook, Ian Bell and Kevin Pietersen, batsmen with nearly 35 000 international runs between them, here contributed 41 in 110 balls, six of which dismissed them. Seven of this bedraggled touring party board an airliner for home this week, and they will probably already have packed – assuming they do their own packing, as the squad's swollen ranks probably include specialist luggage interface managers.

Yet there was something fitting about the day for Australia in its domination by two players who have been the acme of consistency over the last six months: Ryan Harris and Chris Rogers. Player of the match Harris performed his task with characteristic gruff efficiency, accumulating his first five-wicket haul of the southern series as the English strokeplay grew ever more blasé. It brought his record in both hemispheres to 46 wickets in nine Tests at 19.45, a manful achievement given that the green thatch on this SCG pitch has been really the first he has seen in that time.

Mitchell Johnson added the accolade of player of the series to his groaning trophy cabinet, but he's been blessed throughout by the control Harris has exerted at the other end in partnership with Peter Siddle and Nathan Lyon. For in addition to being a batsman's nightmare, the 34-year-old Harris is a captain's dream. Every time Clarke has thrown him the ball these last six months, Harris has provided a spell of blue-chip quality, bristling endeavour and unvarying economy, the kind around which plans can be laid and variations permutated. He is now paying less for his Test wickets than even Glenn McGrath; but for Alan Davidson, you must peer back through the mists to the nineteenth century for an Australian bowler claiming scalps more cheaply.

Before these Ashes, Chris Rogers had played a single lonely, trivia-question of a Test, in Perth in 2008. With 830 runs at 43.68 across these ten matches home and away, he was comfortably the highest scorer on either side: outstripping, for purposes of comparison, Bell (797 at 44.27), Pietersen (682 at 34.1), Clarke (744 at 43.7), Watson (763 at 40.15), Smith (672 at 39.52), Brad Haddin (699 at 41), and, of course, his pyrotechnic opening partner David Warner (661 at 44).

Like married couples, and owners and their pets, opening batsmen who partner up for a while can begin exhibiting one another's characteristics. That does not seem to have happened with Warner and Rogers. Warner bustles in to bat, all whirling arms and unconcealed objectives; Rogers walks to the middle with brisk, short steps, carrying his bat like a businessman carries a briefcase. Warner celebrates his hundreds with *jetés* of *joie de vivre*, Rogers with little fist pumps, and simple upraisings of the arms towards the dressing room. If anything, Rogers is batting in Test cricket ever more like himself at first-class level, playing the role of the calm, methodical, well-organised pro. In this, there must lie a powerful sense of vindication. Yes, he was ready for Test cricket, maybe all along. Those reassurances he must have uttered to himself from time to time were true.

Others have provided the vivid flashes and flourishes in these Ashes: Rogers' batting has been the wallpaper, a restrained and tasteful backdrop, appreciated only gradually. This time last year, Australia was bidding adieu to Mike Hussey, only twenty months older, at the end of a storied career – and *he* had been regarded as a late starter. Rogers is so far outside the ordinary as a Test cricketer he deserves to be judged by his own standards alone.

It is seven years, meanwhile, since the sun set across the SCG after another 5–0 rout, which ushered out a gilded generation of Australian cricketers. It marked the final Tests of Glenn McGrath, Shane Warne and Justin Langer; Damien Martyn had already gone, Adam Gilchrist and Matthew Hayden had less time than was thought.

There have been rumours of Australian retirements during this game, most audibly of Haddin, but they have lacked credibility, for this series has, despite the age of some of the protagonists, felt more like a beginning than an end. There has been a joyful quality to the Australia team's cricket, embodied in their public performance of the team song on the pitch within minutes of the fall of the final wicket: they are clearly loving the game and revelling in each other's company. Five-0? They'd have wished it could have gone on forever.

Review

CLEOPATRA'S NOSE

Little can be said to be lucky about the scoreline 5–0. It isn't a fluke or a stroke of fortune. Here lies a huge merit of five–Test series. They lead to judgements that brook no argument.

Nonetheless, the Australians' campaign to regain the Ashes has been full of things that went right and also did not go wrong – a reverse of their experience in England, where the fates and the elements seemed to conspire against them (and the Decision Review System against cricket more generally).

Their luckiest break this summer was, of course, playing at all. Had the Ashes held to its traditional timetable, this series would have been in 2014–15. It was brought forward because of occult reasons of scheduling, and because administrators refuse to believe in the possibility of too much of a good thing.

The back-to-back Ashes played hugely to Australia's advantage. They could treat the series in England as preparation, rather as Rocky Marciano used to shadowbox for five solid rounds before every fight. Which is not the same as saying that they strove less hard in the northern summer – merely that there was always for them the consoling thought that a further reckoning Down Under awaited.

For England the reverse was true – no matter what they achieved at home, it could be set at nought within months. Finger-pointing English fans currently trying to work out whether they would sack Andy Flower, Alastair Cook or both might want to look a little further up the management diagram, and wonder about the accountability of administrators.

Then there was cricket's system of official luck, the toss. The Sydney Test was the first in this Ashes cycle where ascendancy did not follow the fall of the coin. Australia's batsmen did not always seize their opportunities to dictate terms with both hands, but as long as one hand was Brad Haddin's this mattered less than it might have.

Injury, too, became a force to be subtly reckoned with, short-term and long-term. Watching Ryan Harris and Mitchell Johnson ascend the steps of the presentation stage at the SCG, as proud but unsteady as veterans at an Anzac Day march, was to be reminded of the physical toll of five-day cricket, and the debt Australia owed the acumen of physiotherapist Alex Kontouris and team doctor Peter Brukner.

England's infirmities lay deeper in the tissues. Australia knew that if James Anderson and Stuart Broad could be outlasted, England's support bowling would fall away. Graeme Swann's elbow was failing him. Tim Bresnan had barely recovered from a back injury, Chris Tremlett had never really recovered from his. England's order of battle under Flower has depended on keeping the game tight as the ball softens and perhaps reverses between overs 40 and 80, but here they lacked the personnel to implement it.

The contrast in Sydney was black and white. When Harris and Johnson took a breather, Clarke could fall back on the vegetarian iron man Peter Siddle and wiry, wily Nathan Lyon, with Shane Watson's variations in further reserve. For England, Boyd Rankin twice wandered off with undiagnosable injuries, leaving Ben Stokes and Scott Borthwick to give up almost a run a ball, much as Chris Woakes and Simon Kerrigan had at the Oval. That placed additional stress on Anderson and Broad, thereby further eroding their effectiveness. Looking at the depth of their bowling ranks over the last six months, in fact, England might be lucky to hold onto their new fifth ranking on the ICC ladder.

The indisposition that probably counted most, however, may or may not be reckoned an injury. This was the 'stress-related' complaint that mysteriously beset Jonathan Trott during the Gabba Test. Much sympathy was extended him – rightly so. But it left a legacy of stress behind, in terms of fellow feeling and also homeward thoughts. Would Swann have opted out of the tour had Trott not already done so? Would Root have fallen away so badly, having come to Australia as an opener, been demoted to number six, then promoted to number three, then finally dumped altogether? Would Cook by the end have looked so burdened that you just wanted to give him a hug?

As unavoidable as Trott's departure may have been, it heartened Australia at a critical juncture too. David Warner's comment about 'scared eyes' at the Gabba may have been tactless, and may not at that stage even have been altogether justified. But it put into words a growing Australian confidence that began reinforcing itself: there can be something about hearing your own thoughts, especially repeated, amplified and distorted by the media, that invests them with additional credibility. The Australians next seized on the intelligence that the England squad had received a shipment of additional protective gear before the next Test at Adelaide, and from there the swagger grew with each passing day.

Lastly, you can look back on a certain degree of luck in Australian selection. Had Matthew Wade shown merely an atom of improvement in India, Brad Haddin might have been an onlooker this series. Had Mitchell Starc or James Pattinson stayed fit, Mitchell Johnson may not have been a certainty – although I sensed that his became the inside running with the ODI series in England.

For that matter, had Darren Lehmann not been with Australia A in England around the time David Warner took a swing at Joe Root, just missed, and ended up effectively laying out his coach Mickey Arthur, would the Australians be under their present successful management?

Think of it had that punch actually landed. Root takes one for the team, cricket exile Warner segues into a cage-fighting career as the Matraville Mauler, Michael Clarke resigns in disgrace as captain as well as selector with Ashton Agar elected his successor by viewer poll . . . etc. It's a game of inches, all right.

To repeat, though: 5-0 remains above all a tale of skill. Because luck in the main apportions itself randomly, and what matters above all is the capacity, which Clarke's Australia exhibited on a daily basis, to seize and make use of it.

Review
GOOD, OR GOOD ENOUGH?

How good a cricket team are Michael Clarke's Australians? For the green and gold gathering at the Opera House today, the answer was . . . well, absolutely ace. Those resisting the urge to get carried away have tended to more circumspect judgements, such as good enough, good but not great, good but yet to be tested.

One answer on which all can agree is: better than was thought six months back. But not perhaps utterly transformed. It seems long ago, but Australia played some excellent cricket last summer, and would have been still more formidable had they enjoyed the services of a fit Ryan Harris and Shane Watson.

In order to assess Australian success fully, then, you need to fathom the nature of their unsuccess – how and why they lost six consecutive Tests in India and England, five of them by colossal margins, from March to July. The vague and self-serving explanations heard so far will solidify over time into the stuff of vague and self-serving autobiographies. Perhaps one day we'll have a fuller picture; but perhaps we also won't, because further and better particulars don't really serve anyone's interest.

Australia's most obvious advance is in the fusion of Harris and Peter Siddle with the misunderestimated Mitchell Johnson and the misoverscrutinised Nathan Lyon. Less obvious, perhaps, but little less fundamental has been the uniform excellence of Australia's outcricket. How poorly English batsmen have rotated strike this summer, seldom truly challenging the ring with aggressive calling or daring an arm in the deep with an extra run. But that is partly a function of the Australians, notably David Warner, being nearly as intimidating in the field as with the ball.

In manpower terms, Australia's balance is also improved. A year ago at the SCG, Australia fielded five batsmen, five bowlers, and a batsman-keeper in Matthew Wade; this time round it had six batsmen, four bowlers, and a keeper-batsman in Brad Haddin in the form of his life, with Watson and also Steve Smith available to bowl. And if Watson still calls to mind Norman Mailer's description of jungle-rumbling George Foreman – 'as slow as a man walking up a hill of pillows' – he has contributed usefully as Australia's most economical bowler, giving away just 2.26 runs an over. In Australia's next destination, South Africa, where in November 2011 he took five for 17 in Cape Town, he could be more useful still.

Amazing to say, even after ten consecutive Tests on both sides of the world, the Watson enigma persists, as lengthy and seemingly unresolvable as *Lost*. Sage judges now hold that he would be better off supplanting George Bailey at number six, handing on his number three spot to Alex Doolan.

This, however, may not be the time. Doolan has all the hallmarks of a fine player except perhaps for the first-class record, which is no better or worse than his state captain Bailey's: six hundreds and an average of 38 in 53 games, versus fourteen hundreds and an average of 38 in 103 games. Doolan would also be being asked to start a top-order Test career against a razor-keen attack without a first-class innings in two months.

With an average of 26, Bailey has hardly made every post of his first series a winner. But his best innings, in Adelaide, was cut short by a fine catch on a day England otherwise dropped everything, and had a rough DRS not gone against him in Melbourne and had Clarke delayed his declaration until lunch on the fourth day in Perth, he might now be deemed a qualified success. Critics and commentators will always wish for change – a cycle of new faces and climate of experimentation suit us. Decisions for selectors are less clear-cut, and must factor in time, place and chemistry.

Further argument for the status quo is also a matter of balance – the balance of personality. Duncan Fletcher once referred to what he called a team's 'critical mass', a sustainable ratio of 'steady men' to 'free spirits'. Fletcher put the ideal at 8:3, with a marked tailing off of results after 6:5. The exact arithmetic is less important than the sentiment, whose inference is that in changing a cricket team's personnel you also tamper with its humours. An unconscious sense of this has informed critiques of the rotation policy, and Australia's Ashes accomplishments have provided further evidence.

It has been success, of course, that has allowed Australia to play an unchanged XI this summer; but from what players were saying publicly before the Fifth Test, an unchanged XI has contributed to success. As a shrewd judge of the game summed it up for me in Perth, this side contains 'a lot of sensible cricketers'. Bailey is one of them: to exclude him now would amount to writing off the investment of a whole series, which seems wasteful.

This debate invites another question: how reflective is the Australian cricket team of the overall strength of Australian cricket? A golden summer does not make a golden era: in Haddin, Harris and Chris Rogers especially, the team is continuing to draw on its inheritance. Nor do there seem a host of players outside the XI clamouring for attention. James Pattinson and Jackson Bird have barely resumed cricket, Mitchell Starc and Pat Cummins are still to do so. How gratifying it would be right now were there a young batsman ripping up records in the Sheffield Shield; instead they are busy stonking balls out of various Big Bash League parks. Slow-bowling talent hardly abounds and the next best keeper is unclear. Cracks are being mortared, but remain some way from repaired.

Looking around the world, to be fair, such cracking is hardly uncommon. South Africa will represent a salutary challenge. But the standard of international cricket is at the moment far from healthy. How good a cricket team Clarke leads, then, might depend on whether the question is absolute or relative.

FIFTH TEST Sydney Cricket Ground 3–5 January 2014
Toss England   **Australia won by 281 runs**

AUSTRALIA	1st Innings			2nd Innings		
CJL Rogers		b Stokes	11	c and	b Borthwick	119
DA Warner		b Broad	16	lbw	b Anderson	16
SR Watson	lbw	b Anderson	43	c Bairstow	b Anderson	9
MJ Clarke*	c Bell	b Stokes	10	c Bairstow	b Broad	6
SPD Smith	c sub (JE Root)	b Stokes	115	c Cook	b Stokes	7
GJ Bailey	c Cook	b Broad	1	c Borthwick	b Broad	46
BJ Haddin†	c Cook	b Stokes	75		b Borthwick	28
MG Johnson	c sub (JE Root)	b Borthwick	12		b Stokes	4
RJ Harris	c Anderson	b Stokes	22	c Carberry	b Borthwick	13
PM Siddle	c Bairstow	b Stokes	0	c Bairstow	b Rankin	4
NM Lyon	not out		1	not out		6
EXTRAS	(b 10, lb 2, w 2, nb 6)		20	(lb 14, w 2, nb 2)		18
TOTAL	(76 overs)		326	(61.3 overs)		276

ENGLAND	1st Innings			2nd Innings		
AN Cook*	lbw	b Harris	7	c Haddin	b Johnson	7
MA Carberry	c Lyon	b Johnson	0	c Haddin	b Johnson	43
JM Anderson	c Clarke	b Johnson	7	not out		1
IR Bell	c Haddin	b Siddle	2	c Warner	b Harris	16
KP Pietersen	c Watson	b Harris	3	c Bailey	b Harris	6
GS Ballance	c Haddin	b Lyon	18	lbw	b Johnson	7
BA Stokes		b Siddle	47		b Harris	32
JM Bairstow†	c Bailey	b Siddle	18	c Bailey	b Lyon	0
SG Borthwick	c Smith	b Harris	1	c Clarke	b Lyon	4
SCJ Broad	not out		30		b Harris	42
WB Rankin		b Johnson	13	c Clarke	b Harris	0
EXTRAS	(lb 1, w 5, nb 3)		9	(b 5, lb 2, nb 1)		8
TOTAL	(58.5 overs)		155	(31.4 overs)		166

ENGLAND

1st Innings	O	M	R	W	2nd Innings	O	M	R	W
JM Anderson	21	3	67	1		15	6	46	2
SCJ Broad	19.5	5	65	2		14	1	57	2
BA Stokes	19.5	1	99	6		10	0	62	2
WB Rankin	8.2	0	34	0		12.3	0	47	1
SG Borthwick	7	0	49	1		6	0	33	3
KP Pietersen						4	1	17	0

AUSTRALIA

1st Innings	O	M	R	W	2nd Innings	O	M	R	W
RJ Harris	14	5	36	3		9.4	4	25	5
MG Johnson	13.5	3	33	3		9	1	40	3
PM Siddle	13	4	23	3		4	1	24	0
SR Watson	3	1	5	0					
NM Lyon	15	3	57	1		9	0	70	2

FALL OF WICKETS

Wicket	Aus - 1st	Eng - 1st	Aus - 2nd	Eng - 2nd
1st	22	6	27	7
2nd	51	8	47	37
3rd	78	14	72	57
4th	94	17	91	87
5th	97	23	200	90
6th	225	62	239	91
7th	269	111	244	95
8th	325	112	255	139
9th	325	125	266	166
10th	326	155	276	166

Umpires: Aleem Dar (Pakistan) and M Erasmus (South Africa)
Referee: RS Madugalle (Sri Lanka)

TESTS PLAYED IN AUSTRALIA November 2013–January 2014

AUSTRALIA - Batting and Fielding

	M	I	NO	HS	Runs	Avge	100	50	Ct/St
BJ Haddin	5	8	-	118	493	61.62	1	5	22
DA Warner	5	10	1	124	523	58.11	2	2	4
CJL Rogers	5	10	-	119	463	46.30	2	3	4
SPD Smith	5	9	1	115	327	40.87	2	-	7
MJ Clarke	5	10	1	148	363	40.33	2	-	8
SR Watson	5	10	1	103	345	38.33	1	2	3
MG Johnson	5	8	2	64	165	27.50	-	1	4
GJ Bailey	5	8	1	53	183	26.14	-	1	10
RJ Harris	5	6	1	55	117	23.40	-	1	4
PM Siddle	5	7	1	21	38	6.33	-	-	-
NM Lyon	5	6	6	18	60	-	-	-	5

AUSTRALIA - Bowling

	O	M	R	W	Avge	Best	5wI	10wM
MG Johnson	188.4	51	517	37	13.97	7-40	3	-
RJ Harris	166.2	50	425	22	19.31	5-25	1	-
PM Siddle	156.4	48	386	16	24.12	4-57	-	-
NM Lyon	176.2	42	558	19	29.36	5-50	1	-

Also bowled: **SPD Smith 11-1-58-1; SR Watson 47.4-17-122-4**

ENGLAND - Batting and Fielding

	M	I	NO	HS	Runs	Avge	100	50	Ct/St
BA Stokes	4	8	-	120	279	34.87	1	-	1
KP Pietersen	5	10	-	71	294	29.40	-	2	3
MA Carberry	5	10	-	60	281	28.10	-	1	6
JE Root	4	8	1	87	192	27.42	-	1	2
IR Bell	5	10	1	72	235	26.11	-	2	4
AN Cook	5	10	-	72	246	24.60	-	3	7
SCJ Broad	5	10	2	42	155	19.37	-	-	2
MJ Prior	3	6	-	69	107	17.83	-	1	10
JM Bairstow	2	4	-	21	49	12.25	-	-	10
TT Bresnan	2	4	-	21	34	8.50	-	-	1
JM Anderson	5	10	5	13	41	8.20	-	-	6
GP Swann	3	6	1	19	36	7.20	-	-	4
MS Panesar	2	4	-	2	4	1.00	-	-	-

Also batted (one Test each): GS Ballance 18, 7; SG Borthwick 1, 4 (2 ct);
WB Rankin 13, 0; CT Tremlett 8, 7; IJL Trott 10, 9

ENGLAND - Bowling

	O	M	R	W	Avge	Best	5wl	10wM
SCJ Broad	161.5	24	578	21	27.52	6-81	1	-
BA Stokes	116.5	14	492	15	32.80	6-99	1	-
TT Bresnan	62.3	14	206	5	41.20	2-24	-	-
JM Anderson	190.3	43	615	14	43.92	4-67	-	-
GP Swann	142	21	560	7	80.00	2-71	-	-

Also bowled: SG Borthwick 13-0-82-4; MS Panesar 70.5-9-257-3;
KP Pietersen 4-1-17-0; WB Rankin 20.5-0-81-1; JE Root 32-5-98-0;
CT Tremlett 36-5-120-4